Presentation
PATTERNS

Presentation
PATTERNS

Techniques for Crafting Better Presentations

NEAL **FORD** | MATTHEW **MCCULLOUGH** | NATHANIEL **SCHUTTA**

✦✦ Addison-Wesley

Upper Saddle River, NJ • Boston • Indianapolis • San Francisco
New York • Toronto • Montreal • London • Munich • Paris • Madrid
Capetown • Sydney • Tokyo • Singapore • Mexico City

Many of the designations used by manufacturers and sellers to distinguish their products are claimed as trademarks. Where those designations appear in this book, and the publisher was aware of a trademark claim, the designations have been printed with initial capital letters or in all capitals.

The symbols that appear on the front cover and in the text are all from The Noun Project collection (www.thenounproject.com) and are either in the Public Domain or are covered by a Creative Common License. Please see pages 244 through 246, which constitute a continuation of this copyright page.

The authors and publisher have taken care in the preparation of this book, but make no expressed or implied warranty of any kind and assume no responsibility for errors or omissions. No liability is assumed for incidental or consequential damages in connection with or arising out of the use of the information or programs contained herein.

The publisher offers excellent discounts on this book when ordered in quantity for bulk purchases or special sales, which may include electronic versions and/or custom covers and content particular to your business, training goals, marketing focus, and branding interests. For more information, please contact:

U.S. Corporate and Government Sales
(800) 382-3419
corpsales@pearsontechgroup.com

For sales outside the United States, please contact:

International Sales
international@pearson.com

Visit us on the Web: informit.com/aw

Library of Congress Cataloging-in-Publication Data
Ford, Neal.
   Presentation patterns : techniques for crafting better presentations / Neal Ford, Matthew McCullough, Nathaniel Schutta.
        p.   cm.
   Includes bibliographical references and index.
   ISBN 978-0-321-82080-8 (pbk. : alk. paper) 1. Presentation graphics software—Handbooks, manuals, etc. I. McCullough, Matthew (Matthew J.) II. Schutta, Nathaniel T. III. Title.
   P93.52.F67 2012
   005.5'8—dc23   2012018963

ISBN-13: 978-0-321-82080-8
ISBN-10:   0-321-82080-0

Text printed in the United States on recycled paper at RR Donnelley in Crawfordsville, Indiana.
First printing, August 2012

Editor-in-Chief
Mark Taub

Acquisitions Editor
Greg Doench

Development Editor
Eileen Cohen

Managing Editor
John Fuller

Full-Service Production Manager
Julie B. Nahil

Project Editor
Scribe Inc.

Copy Editor
Scribe Inc.

Indexer
Scribe Inc.

Proofreader
Scribe Inc.

Interior Designer
Scribe Inc.

Cover Designer
Chuti Prasertsith

Compositor
Scribe Inc.

CONTENTS

List of Figures ix

Introduction 1
    Origins 2
    Toward Patterns 3
    How This Book Is Organized 10
    How to Use This Book 11
    Summary 11

Part I Prepare **13**

Chapter 1 Presentation Prelude Patterns 15
    Pattern: Know Your Audience 16
    Pattern: Social Media Advertising 18
    Pattern: Required 20
    Pattern: The Big Why 22
    Pattern: Proposed 24
    Antipattern: Abstract Attorney 26

Chapter 2 Creativity Patterns 29
    Pattern: Narrative Arc 30
    Pattern: Fourthought 34
    Pattern: Crucible 38
    Pattern: Concurrent Creation 41
    Pattern: Triad 43
    Pattern: Expansion Joints 45
    Pattern: Talklet 46
    Pattern: Unifying Visual Theme 48
    Pattern: Brain Breaks 51
    Antipattern: Alienating Artifact 53
    Antipattern: Celery 56
    Pattern: Leet Grammars 58
    Pattern: Lightning Talk 59

Pattern: Takahashi   60
Pattern: Cave Painting   62

Part II Build   **65**

Chapter 3 Slide Construction Patterns   67

Antipattern: Cookie Cutter   68
Pattern: Coda   70
Antipattern: Injured Outlines   71
Pattern: Peer Review   72
Pattern: Foreshadowing   75
Antipattern: Bullet-Riddled Corpse   77
Pattern: Greek Chorus   80
Antipattern: Ant Fonts   81
Antipattern: Fontaholic   83
Antipattern: Floodmarks   86
Antipattern: Photomaniac   89
Pattern: Composite Animation   92
Pattern: Á la Carte Content   95
Pattern: Analog Noise   99
Pattern: Vacation Photos   104
Pattern: Defy Defaults   106
Antipattern: Borrowed Shoes   108

Chapter 4 Temporal Patterns   111

Antipattern: Slideuments   112
Pattern: Infodeck   114
Pattern: Gradual Consistency   116
Pattern: Charred Trail   120
Pattern: Exuberant Title Top   123
Pattern: Invisibility   127
Pattern: Context Keeper   131
Pattern: Breadcrumbs   133
Pattern: Bookends   135
Pattern: Soft Transitions   137
Pattern: Intermezzi   139
Pattern: Backtracking   141
Pattern: Preroll   142
Pattern: Crawling Credits   143

Chapter 5   Demonstrations versus Presentations   145
   Pattern: Live Demo   147
   Antipattern: Dead Demo   151
   Pattern: Lipsync   154
   Pattern: Traveling Highlights   157
   Pattern: Crawling Code   162
   Pattern: Emergence   164
   Pattern: Live on Tape   165

Part III Deliver   169

Chapter 6   Stage Prep   171
   Pattern: Preparation   172
   Pattern: Posse   174
   Pattern: Seeding Satisfaction   175
   Pattern: Display of High Value   177
   Antipattern: Shortchanged   181

Chapter 7   Performance Antipatterns   183
   Antipattern: Hiccup Words   184
   Antipattern: Disowning Your Topic   186
   Antipattern: Lipstick on a Pig   187
   Antipattern: Tower of Babble   188
   Antipattern: Bunker   190
   Antipattern: Hecklers   191
   Antipattern: Going Meta   193
   Antipattern: Backchannel   195
   Antipattern: Laser Weapons   197
   Antipattern: Negative Ignorance   199
   Antipattern: Dual-Headed Monster   200

Chapter 8   Performance Patterns   203
   Pattern: Carnegie Hall   204
   Pattern: Emotional State   207
   Pattern: Breathing Room   208
   Pattern: Shoeless   209
   Pattern: Mentor   210
   Pattern: Weatherman   211
   Pattern: Seeding the First Question   214
   Pattern: Make It Rain   215
   Pattern: Entertainment   216
   Pattern: The Stakeout   218

Pattern: Lightsaber   219
Pattern: Echo Chamber   221
Pattern: Red, Yellow, Green   222
Conclusion   225
Patterns Redux   225
Build Your Own . . .   226
Summary   228

Glossary of Patterns   229

Resources   241

Credits   243
Contributor Acknowledgments   243
Symbol Credits   244
Personal Acknowledgments   246
About the Authors   247
Contact   249

Notes   251

Index   255

LIST OF FIGURES

Figure 2.1	Narrative arc	30
Figure 2.2	Flowchart of the structure of a presentation	31
Figure 2.3	Overall structure of the *Test-Driven Design* talk	32
Figure 2.4	Representation of a mind map for Neal's *On the Lam from the Furniture Police* keynote	36
Figure 2.5	The gloomy end of the second act	44
Figure 2.6	Stock-photo series used for *Emergent Design* presentation	50
Figure 2.7	Representation of a Cave Painting demonstration showing a lengthy set of steps	63
Figure 2.8	Cave Painting implemented in Keynote	64
Figure 3.1	Two slides that contain one continued idea	69
Figure 3.2	Second slide, continuing the idea by retaining the title	69
Figure 3.3	Foreshadowing an upcoming case study	77
Figure 3.4	Greek Chorus character indicating that better examples will appear shortly	80
Figure 3.5	Representation of an Oracle status-update slide featuring Ant Fonts	83
Figure 3.6	A slide designed by a Fontaholic	84
Figure 3.7	Slide designed by an adept font user	85
Figure 3.8	Floodmarks eat a lot of space in this representation of a conference template.	86
Figure 3.9	Image compromised to fit within Floodmarks	87
Figure 3.10	Making the image big enough to see overlaps the Floodmarks in an unattractive way	88
Figure 3.11	Conceptual clash between subject and (very pretty) stock photo	90
Figure 3.12	Slide suffering from Photomaniac stock photos	91
Figure 3.13	Composite Animation in Keynote	93
Figure 3.14	Composite Animation in PowerPoint	94
Figure 3.15	The "home" slide from Neal's *Á la Carte Content Agile Engineering Practices* presentation	97

Figure 3.16   Setting a hyperlink in Keynote's inspector   97

Figure 3.17   Setting a hyperlink in PowerPoint   98

Figure 3.18   Subramaniam's Programming Language Puzzlers
game on the home screen   98

Figure 3.19   Subramaniam's Programming Language Puzzlers
game with a question opened   99

Figure 3.20   A noisy font nicely contrasts the refined line drawing   100

Figure 3.21   The added fringe focuses the picture around
the important part, fuzzing out the rest   101

Figure 3.22   The stroke property for lines in Keynote   101

Figure 3.23   Noise helping nonverbally convey the messiness
of learning over time   102

Figure 3.24   Purposeful use of noisy fonts and lines   102

Figure 3.25   Allowing the user to "pick up" the chalk   103

Figure 4.1   Merlin Mann giving his *Time and Attention* talk at Google   114

Figure 4.2   Gradual Consistency: Introducing the "Pattern" concept   117

Figure 4.3   Gradual Consistency: Changing only the first letter   117

Figure 4.4   Gradual Consistency: Adding "idiomatic" to further the definition 118

Figure 4.5   Gradual Consistency: Using Exuberant Title Top
to migrate the title to the top   118

Figure 4.6   Gradual Consistency: Adding two subcategories   118

Figure 4.7   Gradual Consistency: Adding subcategory examples   118

Figure 4.8   Gradual Consistency: Adding examples for the other subcategory   119

Figure 4.9   Gradual Consistency: Adding the last definition nuance   119

Figure 4.10   Gradual Consistency: The slide inspector in Keynote
highlighting the complex life of the "pattern" text box   119

Figure 4.11   Charred Trail slide in the designer   120

Figure 4.12   The same slide during presentation   120

Figure 4.13   *Effect options* dialog in PowerPoint   121

Figure 4.14   Slide inspector showing *by highlighted bullet*
approach for Charred Trail   122

Figure 4.15   Exuberant Title Top (beginning position)   123

Figure 4.16   Exuberant Title Top with body   123

Figure 4.17   Exuberant Title Top + Charred Trail   123

Figure 4.18   Exuberant Title Top slide in designer   125

Figure 4.19   Exuberant Title Top slide in designer   125

Figure 4.20   Exuberant Title Top slide in designer   125

Figure 4.21   Exuberant Title Top in the PowerPoint designer   126
Figure 4.22   Invisibility slide as presented   129
Figure 4.23   Invisibility slide in the Keynote designer   129
Figure 4.24   Ghost image of the invisible element   129
Figure 4.25   Inspector with 0 opacity setting   130
Figure 4.26   Using a hashtag + *magic move* as a Context Keeper   132
Figure 4.27   Fading recurring element to keep it from
               becoming a distraction   132
Figure 4.28   Representation of a mind map providing a
               good breadcrumb overview   134
Figure 4.29   Highlighting the breadcrumb to make your
               location unambiguous   134
Figure 4.30   An opening Bookend slide   137
Figure 4.31   A closing Bookend slide   137
Figure 4.32   Transition styles help define narrative flow   138
Figure 4.33   Using sprout pictures to separate major sections
               and create a Unifying Visual Theme   140
Figure 5.1   The Nikon D4 live demonstration   149
Figure 5.2   Traveling Highlights in source code   158
Figure 5.3   Information-dense status-report slide   159
Figure 5.4   Using boxes and lines as Traveling Highlights   159
Figure 5.5   Using zoom and opacity for Traveling Highlights   160
Figure 5.6   Keynote Inspector for size, motion, and opacity settings   161
Figure 5.7   Traveling Highlights in PowerPoint   162
Figure 5.8   Apple's page for Live on Tape videos   167
Figure 8.1   Representation of Neal's heads-up display in Keynote   212
Figure 9.1   Relationship between presentation tool
               features, patterns, and recipes   227

INTRODUCTION

As you can discern from its subtitle, this book is about crafting better presentations. But why should anyone write yet *another* tome on the subject? Although most existing material on creating better presentations and becoming an improved presenter is useful, it *doesn't go far enough*. It lacks the overarching principles that guide the way to successful presentations and—perhaps even more important—it's not sufficiently actionable. Maybe you've learned how slide shows are like a serene state of mind and how to find harmonic tones on color wheels. But how will that knowledge help you create an effective new presentation *next week*? Abstract knowledge lets you judge whether something is good or bad, but you need concrete advice to advance to the next level: creating something great.

Generally, instruction in crafting presentations involves the mechanics of how presentation tools work, not how to use them effectively. Unless you majored in speech, you must learn most of the skills required to deliver effective presentations on the job, frequently under duress. Public speaking is stressful, so thoughts on effective presentation techniques tend to wane as the dreaded due date creeps ever closer.

Most nascent presenters are lucky if they've been treated to a one-day class on how to use a presentation tool, absent any instruction or guidance on how to leverage it to craft *effective communication*. The default path is to use the wizards and other helpers built into the tools. Unfortunately, many of these wizards and helpers make your communication *less effective*. For example, the default slide type in many templates is the bulleted list. Although useful in isolated cases, it generally leads to what we've defined as the Bullet-Riddled Corpse antipattern. We advise against using default templates because they accidentally make *your* presentations look like everyone else's. We offer motivation toward putting a good audience experience foremost in your mind with the Defy Defaults pattern.

This book's authors have developed a unique perspective on presentations tied to our background in software development. This perspective helps us understand and discuss presentations at a deeper level. *Presentation Patterns* is the distillation of our knowledge and experience into practical techniques for crafting and delivering compelling presentations. Knowing

1

how we came to our distinctive view of presentations will help you understand how this book can give you an edge.

Origins

All three coauthors write software for a living, which classifies us as computer geeks. But we're an odd breed of geek: We *like* speaking about building software to sometimes large crowds of other geeks. As software developers, we crave concrete solutions to problems. All three of us specialize in *agile* software development, one of whose tenets is the concept of *improvement via feedback loops*. When you're programming something new, one strategy is to write the source code for a small portion of it, find out if it works properly, write a little more, and iterate, while checking the results all along the way. The key concept is that of establishing a feedback loop. This concept can apply to improving presentations as well as software. If you could organize a boot camp that uses feedback loops to teach better presentation skills, what would it look like? Each recruit would be required to create a variety of presentations covering many technical subjects, deliver the presentations to knowledgeable audiences of varying sizes, receive detailed feedback from the audience after each talk, and quickly revise the presentations to improve them before giving them again.

As it happens, this book's authors have been living in just such an environment for the past five years. The story of our experience in No Fluff, Just Stuff is this book's first *interlude* (a feature we'll explain in detail later in this introduction).

No Fluff, Just Stuff

Generally, if you are a computer geek who loves to talk about technology, you'll struggle with putting together a conference talk and, if you're lucky, you'll get to give it two or three times at most. Technology moves quickly, and there just aren't that many conferences or other speaking opportunities. Except for No Fluff, Just Stuff.

No Fluff, Just Stuff is a traveling technical conference series covering a wide variety of topics related to software development and management. It visits 25 to 35 cities a year throughout the United States and occasionally elsewhere. The "tour" has a core of 12 to 15 speakers—this book's authors included—who do virtually every show each year. We each have talks we've given more than 50 times and a few of them more than 100 times. After you've delivered the same technical content many times, it becomes quite polished. No Fluff,

Just Stuff also provides a unique laboratory for observing and testing presentation styles and techniques. Most speakers don't speak in every time slot, leaving them time to indulge their interest in other topics and speakers.

One of the outstanding features of the No Fluff, Just Stuff conference is a well-thought-out evaluation form. Each attendee is encouraged to complete it after every session and to include comments. That closes the feedback loop, enabling us to experiment and quickly discover what works. As a speaker, you have the opportunity to see what works, apply it, get feedback, and iterate.

No Fluff, Just Stuff is the secret ingredient in our presentation perspective. At a certain point we've covered a talk's technical material so many times that we have it down pat. That lets us expand our thinking into different ways to present difficult material, and an instant feedback loop lets us know if they work or not. Lather, rinse, and repeat, year after year.

Toward Patterns

Not surprisingly, presentations are a popular conversational topic among the regular No Fluff, Just Stuff speakers (sometimes lubricated with copious amounts of Scotch whisky). In the course of such conversations, Neal conceived the idea of applying a common concept from the software-engineering world—*patterns* and *antipatterns*—to presentation techniques.

The software world stole the idea of patterns and antipatterns from Christopher Alexander, an architect (the building kind, not the software kind) who wrote the 1977 book *A Pattern Language*.[1] Alexander described recurring architectural patterns he observed that spanned cultures, regions, and time, cataloging and categorizing them. Other architects viewed Alexander's book as an interesting new way of grouping and thinking about similar elements and styles but not as revolutionary. However, Alexander's book did inspire similar efforts in other fields.

The pattern concept was popularized in the software world by the seminal book *Design Patterns*,[2] called the "Gang of Four" (GoF) book after the collective nickname of its authors. Software engineers use the pattern concept to describe many common problems. The GoF book defined a format for patterns that became a loose standard throughout the software world.

Pattern Structures   Our book borrows some of the structure of patterns from the GoF book. That structure provides an efficient means of organization, offering a consistent way to present value statements, cautions, and processes for each described pattern. We give each pattern a name and a definition and include content sections that are appropriate to that pattern. Our pattern parts are shown in this table.

Section Name	Description
Name	The name of the pattern or antipattern designed to create memorable associations
Also Known As	Other names for the pattern or antipattern
Definition	The definition of the pattern (or antipattern)
Motivation	Why you want to use this pattern or avoid an antipattern
Applicability/Consequences	The types of presentations that a pattern works best for, and possible consequences (both good and bad) for a pattern or antipattern
Mechanics	The steps required to make this pattern work or ways to avoid an antipattern. This is the actionable part of each pattern, including step-by-step instructions for patterns or concrete avoidance advice for antipatterns.
Known Uses	Common examples of where this pattern has been used
Related Patterns	Other patterns or antipatterns that add nuance to, oppose, or enhance this pattern

Where we show concrete techniques, we illustrate them in both Keynote and PowerPoint. But patterns exist at a deeper level than tool features. We use presentation tools to implement our patterns, but our list of patterns isn't a mere laundry list of the features of Keynote and PowerPoint. The Mechanics sections frequently illustrate that a particular pattern can have very different implementations based on the tool features (for an example, see the Invisibility pattern).

Our categorization of patterns isn't perfect, and we deviate from it where it makes sense to do so. But *any* categorization scheme is better than none. One of the benefits the software world reaps from patterns is the format and nomenclature that all patterns share. No common language exists to talk about design and execution in the presentation world—until now.

To give you a preview of what a pattern looks like, we'll show you the simplified Infodeck pattern here, with annotations explaining each section:

The title of the pattern, a memorable name that captures the essence of what's good (or bad) about it.

Pattern: Infodeck

Other names for this pattern, either ours or ones we've heard in the wild.

Also Known As   Death by PowerPoint, "A Deck"

The *Definition* section offers our definition of the pattern (or antipattern).

Definition   An Infodeck is a document created with presentation tools that is intended to be distributed—and never presented before an audience—to convey information.

The *Motivation* section describes the reasons to use a pattern—or in the case of an antipattern, why some presenters fall prey to it.

Motivation   You can use spatial layout to help enrich your explanation beyond the traditionally monotonous paragraphs of text. Frequently, presentation tools have better drawing support than word processors, and slides evoke "canvas" more readily than a blank word-processor screen.

They discourage long prose that people don't read. If the bullet points convey all you want, leave it at that rather than write a lot of purple prose around your bullet points.

It's easy to include diagrams as primary elements in the communication or let the diagrams, rather than prose, lead the narrative.

Applicability refers to the situation where this pattern is most applicable. Patterns sometimes work better in certain circumstances, and sometimes patterns work in contexts you might not have thought of.

The *Consequences* aspect of this section discusses any possible side effects, both positive and negative, you might want to look out for when using this pattern or things like trade-offs between presentation flexibility and preparation time. For example, in this pattern, we discuss the negative consequences of trying to present an Infodeck.

Applicability/
Consequences   As long as you can avoid allowing an Infodeck to become Slideuments, presentation tools are effective ways to craft succinct communication. However, the desktop-publishing features of most word processors do

this job better, without some of the limitations of a tool used counter to its original purpose.

In many ways, this pattern itself is a litmus test. If you set out to create a presentation and end up with an Infodeck, something went wrong. The subtle advantage that presentations have over other communication media is the control that you as the presenter have over the rate of knowledge exposition. Don't surrender that control lightly.

Don't try to present an Infodeck: Because you have put no effort into transitions or animations, you'll present a series of textually dense slides, utilizing none of the features that make presentation tools effective.

> The *Mechanics* section shows how to implement the pattern or an alternative to the antipattern. For patterns that involve slides, we show examples in both Keynote and PowerPoint. This is frequently the most detailed and complex section—one you'll come back to often to implement the pattern.

Mechanics   None of the rules we've laid out in the book change when you create an Infodeck. Those in the Creativity Patterns chapter are especially apt.

Don't use transitions and animations for these types of slide decks. Rather, spend your time on concise and informative layout of information. Don't forget the Cookie Cutter antipattern, which specifically applies here.

> The *Known Uses* section indicates places where we know it's common (as in this pattern) or specific examples from our and other's presentations.

Known Uses   Every corporation that hasn't explicitly banned Infodeck presentations uses them.

> The *Related Patterns* section points to other patterns in the book related to this one and briefly explains how they are related.

Related Patterns   Slideuments are usually a failed attempt to create an Infodeck. Decide early if you need a presentation or an Infodeck; don't try to create both.

The Cookie Cutter antipattern applies especially in Infodeck presentations: Don't allow the *slide* to become the unit of thought.

Just because you are creating an Infodeck, you shouldn't ignore Creativity Patterns like Narrative Arc. Being allowed to avoid transitions is one benefit of this pattern, but it doesn't require you to throw other good techniques out the window.

Patterns, Not Recipes

First, patterns operate at a lower level than recipes. A recipe has steps, and the steps consist of instructions like "sauté" or "peel." Patterns resemble the lower-level steps found inside recipes; the techniques you must master to be considered a master chef or master presenter. You can use the patterns in this book to construct your own recipes for different contexts such as business meetings, technical demonstrations, and scientific expositions and keynotes, which we discuss in the concluding chapter. Second, there's no such thing as an "antirecipe." Recipes are by their nature positive because they are about building something. But many of the problems in the presentation world come from the decades-long presence of tools that encourage bad habits. One of the most useful parts of the patterns movement in software is the identification of *antipatterns*—common but not obvious mistakes to avoid. A significant portion of our advice is about how not to fall into common bad habits that tools and years of bad exemplars promote.

Presentation Patterns

Neal's original spark of an idea to apply patterns to presentations was mostly a lark, a side effect of being a geek who relentlessly applies software metaphors to the real world. But being geeks, all three authors instantly understood the utility of applying the patterns-and-antipatterns concept to presentations. In the software world, patterns enable you to label complex concepts using a single, universally accepted term, which lets people converse about them more efficiently.

To get a feel for a pattern, we borrow one from Alexander's original work about architecture, a pattern named Light on Two Sides of Every Room.[3] The pattern states,

> When they have a choice, people will always gravitate to those rooms which have light on two sides, and leave the rooms which are lit only from one side unused and empty.
> Therefore:
> Locate each room so that it has outdoor space outside it on at least two sides, and then place windows in these outdoor walls so that natural light falls into every room from more than one direction.
> —Christopher Alexander

The pattern goes on to discuss the experiments that lead them to this conclusion; the implications for other parts of the architecture; and some consequences, both good and bad, of choosing this pattern. Like our patterns, it encapsulates a *memorable name* along with *actionable advice*, including *positive and negative* consequences.

We started analyzing presentations together using patterns (and antipatterns) to encapsulate complex interactions and implications in concise terms. Over time, it also enabled us to *think* about presentation elements in new ways. Using a categorization scheme like patterns showed us commonalities we couldn't recognize before and let us abstract them to a higher level to enhance our understanding. For example, we identified several patterns that help you indicate to your audience how far along you are within the presentation. Those patterns include the Breadcrumbs and Bookends patterns. We realized, however, that both patterns manifest the more general Context Keeper pattern, enabling us to think of some general rules that apply to the different ways it is implemented. As we compiled our list of patterns and antipatterns, we started seeing them in our own presentations, which gave us an opportunity to clean up some antipatterns that had sneaked in there.

This book introduces that shorthand to you. We believe that establishing patterns is the next level in converting presentations from a vague "I know it when I see it" exercise into a way to think objectively about them. We're providing the terms and concepts to enable you to think and talk about presentations at a higher level than you have previously.

Converting an Infodeck into a Presentation

Many presenters use presentation tools to jot down basic ideas as quickly as possible, usually in the form of a bulleted list. During the presentation, they use the slides as reminders, reading each bullet point and then elaborating on it as the audience suffers alongside. We believe that sitting through one of these presentations is a form of torture. A presenter who uses this approach has made a useful pattern (the Infodeck) into an antipattern.

The Infodeck pattern describes a presentation, created in a tool like PowerPoint or Keynote, that is never intended to be projected onto a screen. Rather, it's passed around, typically via e-mail, as a coarse-grained summary of a subject. Infodecks are the standard language spoken in most corporations. Although we show some techniques to make them better, we focus more on crafting presentations destined for a screen or wall. One of the key differences between an Infodeck and a presentation is the rate at which information appears. In an Infodeck, the reader controls the pace. In presentations, the speaker controls the information flow—and that makes all the difference.

Presentations have two huge advantages over Infodecks: *richer channels* and *extra dimensions*. In his book *Presentation Zen*,[4] Garr Reynolds makes the perceptive observation that presentations have two information channels. One channel comes from your voice, body language, and tone. This channel primarily appeals to the logical parts of your brain—the parts that are accustomed to listening and analyzing. It's human nature to want to skip ahead, so showing a slide of bullet points guarantees that everyone will read the entire slide as soon as it appears. If you are following the standard corporate playbook for presentations, you'll slowly read each bullet point that everyone has already read, elaborating on each one. It's difficult to make this interesting, even if the audience is predisposed to be interested in what you say. If your slides mimic the words that you say, you have created a perfect storm of boredom.

The other communication channel is more holistic, pattern-matching, and emotional; it is more likely to use humor, fear, or surprise. Using visuals to access the nonanalytical part of your audience's brains adds significant punch to your presentation. Instead of overloading the analytical channel and starving the holistic one, you can hit both at once, making your message resonate more strongly. Although you can write prose that has the same effect, that's harder because part of what makes the secondary information channel effective is surprise.

This brings us to the second important difference between an Infodeck and presentation: the added dimension of *time*. When you pass around an Infodeck, the reader—not the author—controls the exposition rate. Nuanced information is easy to miss, making it more difficult for authors to make sure their prose is unambiguous. When presenting the same material, an experienced presenter will use slide transitions and animations to enhance the message. Many of the patterns we talk about are designed to leverage time to add punch to your message. The presenter also has luxury of seeing which concepts are difficult, leading to richer question-and-answer sessions. Presentations are often thought of as a flat medium—a mere set of pictures to be printed on paper or to PDF. However, when done well, presentations are one of the richest forms of communication, surpassed only by Hollywood films. Presentations allow the creative use of all four dimensions. We talk more about these techniques in patterns such as the Weatherman pattern and the chapter on Temporal Patterns.

Some of the techniques we discuss might seem elaborate for a one-off presentation to your coworkers or classmates. However, compelling messages tend to find audiences. How often have you created a presentation that communicated something useful and then been asked to deliver it several more times to different constituents? Although some of the pattern mechanics are elaborate, most can be automated using the facilities in modern presentation tools like PowerPoint and Keynote. For example, one of our most popular patterns is the Charred Trail pattern. It takes a bit of setup but can be implemented once via the slide template and then used repeatedly.

How This Book Is Organized

We cover the entire life cycle of presentations, from ideation through creation and delivery. The book has three parts.

Part I, Prepare

A presentation project starts with decisions about what you'll talk about, to whom, for how long, and where. This part includes patterns that relate to practical considerations about your intended audience, how to get the word out, and a variety of Creativity Patterns. These patterns help guide your burgeoning thoughts into coherent form, ready to present. We also cover some practical advice for collaborating on a presentation like the Concurrent Creation pattern and point out some things to avoid, like Alienating Artifacts.

Part II, Build

This part covers the mechanics of how you think about slides and the steps that take you from your ideas to producing slides; all its chapters cover ways to build presentations. In Slide Construction Patterns, we provide concrete advice for effective ways to deliver ideas, along with some common but avoidable traps. The Temporal Patterns chapter contains patterns that manipulate time during presentations, allowing you to greatly enhance the punch of your presentations. Finally, we cover how to distinguish between Demonstrations versus Presentations and strategies to make both better.

Part III, Deliver

Once you've built the killer presentation, *delivering* it is next. This part highlights techniques to make your actual "standing in front of the room" presentation better, starting with Stage Prep, things you must consider before the presentation, such as how to encourage your audience to like you via Seeding Satisfaction. Next, we divert from our normal topical intermingling of patterns and antipatterns and call out the Performance Antipatterns first, the things you should avoid during a presentation. Then we cover Performance Patterns, techniques guiding you toward a better presentation.

Interludes and Personas

The patterns in this book are generic. You can use them to create all manner of presentations, be it for the boardroom, classroom, or banquet hall. The patterns themselves are self-contained (although they frequently reference other patterns), and each is more applicable to some types of presentations than others. When discussing a pattern, we talk about it in its most "natural" setting—the context where it makes the most sense. That said, many patterns apply broadly—but it is sometimes difficult to see how a given pattern applies to a different domain. For example, we talk about structuring your talk using the Narrative Arc pattern, which clearly applies to keynotes but also to business presentations. One of the mechanisms this book uses to show alternate uses for patterns is the *interlude*.

Interludes are short vignettes that we insert between patterns. They highlight a problem that a pattern solves, provide additional context for understanding the pattern, show alternative uses for the pattern, or add some entertainment. By its nature a patterns book is choppy: The patterns cut it up into little chunks. Interludes add some narrative interest to the book, highlight alternate usages, and tell some fun stories. Each interlude features a persona, some of whom appear in other interludes. Some of the personas are real people and some are figments we've summoned to help us out. Each of the personas has a real problem to solve, though, and our patterns help them.

How to Use This Book

Patterns books are traditionally textbooks, meant to be suffered through in a classroom setting and used for reference after the fact. We hope and anticipate that this book will become an invaluable reference. However, we also want it to be readable as a "real" book, which is one of the purposes of the interludes. We hope that those stories—some of them true anecdotes about experiences that led to the development of a pattern or antipattern, others lighthearted fabrications that serve as object lessons—help to make the book an enjoyable read even the first time through.

Feel free to leverage the book's structure to cherry-pick your way through the patterns. We extensively cross-reference the patterns, always leading you to material that relates to whatever you started searching for.

If you're itching to get to the hardcore "building slides" part, skip to Part II, Build. But you might want to make a quick stop by the Creativity Patterns chapter first to make sure you're building the right thing.

If you've already built your slides and need to present them to their fullest potential, go to Part III, Deliver, which covers everything you need to know (and avoid) when presenting.

Summary

We've created a way of thinking about presentations that puts the tools in your hands to make your presentations better. Our advice is concrete, opinionated, and general, covering many types of presentations. The extra effort you invest in your presentations by following this book's advice will be well worth it, for at least four reasons. First, the techniques in this book will enable you to communicate and therefore influence people more effectively.

Second, if your presentation is compelling, you'll probably be asked to deliver it many times because you've captured a strategy, a useful way of explaining things, or the right mission statement. Third, given the ubiquity of portable cameras, it's increasingly likely that someone will film your presentation to show later. The longer it lives, the more it will be viewed—all the more reason for it to be your best work. And fourth, even a seemingly hidden quality can shine through. Steve Jobs was famous for making sure the *insides* of Apple computers were aesthetically pleasing. Pride of workmanship is evident throughout the product, even in parts that the consumer doesn't normally see. Audiences might not directly notice subtle quality embedded in your presentations, but when they compare your presentations to ones without those characteristics, it will be clear to them which are superior.

PART I
PREPARE

WHEN YOU START THINKING ABOUT PUTTING TOGETHER A presentation, the first ideas that come to mind are probably about the talk's content, the tool you'll use to construct the slides, and the visuals you'll show. However, those pieces rest on a foundation made of up decisions about *what* you'll talk about, *whom* you'll be talking to, *how long* you'll talk, and *where* you'll talk. Accordingly, this book begins with patterns that relate to getting a talk scheduled, the thought process behind constructing and delivering it, the constraints dictated by the venue and time slot, and the importance of calibrating the presentation to your specific audience. These foundational layers are every bit as important as the talk's content to the presentation's ultimate success.

Presentation Prelude Patterns cover a variety of concerns you must consider before launching your presentation tool. Creativity Patterns cover designing your talk, choosing and implementing the appropriate structure, and dealing with headaches such as shared creation.

CHAPTER 1

PRESENTATION PRELUDE PATTERNS

YOU NEED TO DEAL WITH A HOST OF CONSIDERATIONS before you start building a presentation. Long before you launch your presentation tool and start browsing around for cool templates—and whether you'll present at a business meeting, a refereed conference, a local special interest group, or any other setting—you must handle some common concerns first.

# Pattern: Know Your Audience

Also Known As   Due Diligence, A Little Birdie Told Me

Definition   Preparation is paramount to a successful talk, and the key to being prepared is knowing all you can about the event. Be an informed participant: Learn as much as you can about your audience.

Motivation   Perhaps the most important early determination you can make is the composition of your audience: its experience level, knowledge, attitude, and so on. Ultimately, you want to walk into your presentation room knowing as much as you can about your crowd. Who are they? How old are they? How technical are they? Is their skill set blended or are they on one end of the spectrum?

A brilliant presentation delivered to the incorrect audience is merely a bad presentation. Many a bad review is a result of mismatched expectations: Your audience thought it would get different content from what you delivered, or your talk was radically above or below the audience's skill level. Either scenario is a recipe for less-than-stellar results. Taking even just a few minutes to research the event pays off in spades.

Applicability/ Consequences   If you get this pattern wrong, it's virtually impossible to get anything else right.

Knowing about your audience enables you to mold your talk to the specifics of the crowd. You can craft your message to match the demographics of the audience, going deeper for a more technical group or highlighting stories that are more appropriate for a given crowd. Some events are *known* for a deeper dive, whereas others are higher-level; a talk that's warmly received at the former might be soundly rejected at the latter. If you know a crowd is looking for a deep technical dive, give it to them!

Never forget that a prepared speaker is a relaxed speaker. Knowing you've done everything you can do to put on a successful talk goes a long way to calm the inevitable nerves brought on by public speaking. Knowing your audience is one more way to put yourself into a position to succeed.

Mechanics   For presentations you give at your job, make sure you know who is on the invitation list and ensure that you get any updates. The detailed report with a Unifying Visual Theme of skiing might be awesome to the regional manager but less so to the corporate vice president who just decided to attend.

Among the many ways to gather information about a public event, the Internet is usually easiest. Spend some time on the event's website. What does it tell you about the show? Is it a small local event or a massive international conference? Registration fees will also tell you a great deal; people expect considerably more from of an event that charges high fees than from a free one. Pay special note to sponsors, especially those with the most prominent placement. A talk that is critical of a company that paid top dollar to the conference may not engender a return invitation.

While you're on the conference website, take note of the other speakers. Reach out to any you know and ask if they have spoken there before. Take a few minutes to look at the site for the previous year's event; again, contact anyone you know and get their input on the crowd, the talks, the venue—anything you're curious about.

After you've mined the conference website, it's time to turn to social networks like Twitter, Facebook, and blogs. Most conferences today use a hashtag to mark comments about the event; search them. Blogs are another great source of intelligence. Give your favorite search engine a workout and read what people wrote about last year's show. What do they say about the event, the talks, or the speakers? Did people expect deeper content than they received? Which talks rocked their world? Which were disappointing?

Many conferences post slides or even recordings of previous presentations. Familiarize yourself with them. What are the presentations like? What are presenters wearing? What topics were covered? Some presenters post their slides on their own websites or on sites like SlideShare, and speakers have been known to blog about events as well. If their contact information is on their sites, ask them about their experiences.

The event organizers are another key source of information. Odds are that they know quite a bit about their audience (or at least the audience they're aiming for). Ask them about previous years' events and the general level of the attendees. In addition to session evaluations, most conferences also do event evaluations. Don't be afraid to ask the organizers what they've changed in the basis of feedback. Which talks were the most or least popular? Some organizers even create artificial *personas*—personality profiles that describe common attendee characteristics—for their attendees.

Related Patterns Part of Knowing Your Audience is ascertaining its Emotional State when it comes time to deliver the presentation.

Seeding Satisfaction is an effort to bond with the audience shortly after you begin delivering your presentation.

Scratchy Scott and What Audiences Remember

Frequent presenter Scott Davis experienced a speaker's worst nightmare—he lost his voice during a conference where he was to present multiple talks. Despite his best efforts (avoid coffee and tea, stick to hot water with honey) he could manage little more than a whisper.

He spent the entire conference wrapped in a proverbial blanket, his raspy voice made audible by a handheld microphone. It was hard to miss Scott's lack of a voice and you'd think it would stick with his attendees.

Amazingly, it didn't. A year later, Scott ran into an audience member from that show. Scott apologized for his lack of a voice that weekend—something the attendee didn't remember at all. Scott's message still made it through and that's what his audience remembered.

Pattern: Social Media Advertising

Also Known As	Tweets, Blogs, Facebook, Spam
Definition	Exploit electronic channels such as Twitter, Facebook, wikis, blogs, websites, and mailing lists to advertise and promote your presentation.
Motivation	The easy breadth of reach that digital channels give you at low or no cost leaves you no excuse not to leverage them for promoting your upcoming presentation. A well-designed event web page, Facebook event entry, Meetup.com site, or retweeted Twitter announcement can, at a *conservative* estimate, boost an open-to-the-public talk's attendance by 50 percent.
Applicability/ Consequences	Public talks benefit the most from social media advertising. A close second are closed events that require a paid registration. We've heard from prominent event coordinators that tweets and blog posts about presenters and their topics increase paid attendance. Paid events are a collaboration in which high attendance is a win for both the presenters and the event organizers. The presenters benefit from a professional-recognition standpoint, and the event organizers benefit from a revenue standpoint. The organizers are far more likely to invite back speakers who've attracted high numbers of attendees in the past.
	Increasing the visibility of your upcoming talk also increases the stakes. Digital advertising leads to heightened awareness on the digital-communication channels. It increases the frequency with which people will use Twitter, Facebook, YouTube, e-mail, and blogs to report on the success or failure of your presentation via the Backchannel—in real time while you are still delivering it. However, with sufficient preparation, you can view this in a positive light: It's another opportunity for people to spread the good word about your incredible talk and their impassioned reaction to it.
Mechanics	Social Media Advertising may be one of the easiest patterns to implement. But it's also a challenging pattern to do *well*.

The longest form—a web page—should include all of the attractive topic details along with an easy means of signing up, getting there, finding the room, and knowing what to expect. A "web page" can mean anything from a complex dedicated website, to a page developed with the assistance of excellent services such as Meetup.com, all the way down to a simple entry on a public-facing wiki or blog.

The short-form digital advertisements on Twitter, Facebook, and instant-messaging services should use an attractive tagline or catchphrase plus a link to the web page that provides full details.

Known Uses Individual presenters, especially in the marketing and technology spaces, are using digital-channel advertisements in ever-increasing numbers. In addition to individual-presenter broadcasts, helpful services such as Lanyrd.com and Meetup.com are blossoming. These sites take advantage of your established social graph on Twitter or Facebook and cross-reference friend lists with conference attendance, "interest-matching" algorithms, topic-based conferences, and even one-off events listed in event directories, and then advertise the events in an unobtrusive or mildly obtrusive way to your friends.

Related Patterns The same Backchannel that discusses your talk after the fact should be leveraged to advertise it beforehand.

A great way of publicly Seeding Satisfaction is to use Social Media Advertising.

Doctor Dana Answers the Call for Papers

Doctor Dana loves what she does: seeing patients, curing ailments, and occasionally making some minor discoveries that could help others doctors with their patients. She has always yearned to share some of her discoveries with others, but no conference organizers have knocked down her door, and the chief physician at her facility hasn't made any strides to get her placed at any of the national medical congresses. If she's going to show her findings anywhere, only a purely self-motivated effort will make it happen.

By asking around, Dana learned that there are three common routes to becoming a presenter:

1. Required

    You have no choice but to give the talk, perhaps for as mundane a reason as the desire to keep your job.
2. Proposed

    You strive to present at a particular (type of) venue and want to use the opportunity to enhance your career.

3. *Invited*

You've earned enough recognition in your area of knowledge that an event's organizers unilaterally reach out to you to present at the event.

Obviously, the Proposed route is the one for Dana. She's discovered that most conference presentations in that category emerge from a submission and selection process that starts with a *call for papers*. The call for papers lays out the criteria for acceptance and provides guidelines on how to prepare and submit talk proposals or abstracts. Reviewers on the organizing end of the event examine the submitted proposals and share their feedback with one another to reach consensus on which proposals to accept.

The vast majority of speaking opportunities require you to use either a document template or a web-based submission system for your proposal. The more formal and well-established the conference, the more likely it is to use an Internet-managed workflow, complete with log-ins, photo uploads, and review-progress status indicators.

Invitations to speak at conferences are pretty rare, so we limit our discussion to Required and Proposed talks.

Pattern: Required

Also Known As	Do It or Else
Definition	You must do a presentation as part of your job or for some other nonoptional reason.
Motivation	Ms. Moreshares, an important figure in your firm, left you a voice mail today saying she needs you to give a talk on the latest product your division has released. "Wait!" you exclaim. "We have a sales team for this!" That's true, but Ms. Moreshares feels that only the engineers on this project are fully equipped to give a technical talk about your team's accomplishments over the last nine months. With a heavy sigh, you adopt the look of a condemned prisoner.

When you're required to give a presentation, the motivation can be the most elementary of all: the desire to keep your job. However, you can also look at this as a low-risk opportunity to gain positive notoriety. |
| Applicability/ Consequences | The Required pattern commonly appears in corporate boardrooms, in branded conventions, and in national association symposiums for which an organization has purchased a sponsored slot for a speaker. |

A Required presentation often puts a dampener on the excitement you'd more likely feel with a proposed or invited talk. The biggest hurdle is to "do it right" even though your motivation doesn't come from within. However, you can adopt a positive attitude for two reasons. First, this opportunity can raise your visibility at the company in a meaningful way. If you do an excellent job with the presentation, you may be invited to give higher-profile presentations. Additionally, if the talk gives you a chance to socialize with the next level of executives, that might help open your opportunities for career advancement.

Second, you can practice your presentation skills in the relatively friendlier environment of your employer. This will help you to give an even better presentation at other venues where you might deliver it at a later date. Think of this talk as a stepping stone rather than a millstone. Deliver it with confidence, and use it as a first step toward a Proposed talk that you'll submit to a conference you've always wanted to attend. If you have a hand in selecting the topic you'll be presenting on, consider what subject will provide the most reuse possibilities. Building a talk is time-consuming, and many speakers take the "foundation" of a great talk and redeliver it with minor customizations time and time again.

In short, at least you'll have practiced a presentation. You will likely have added several new concepts to your knowledge portfolio, added a few lolcats or humorous pictures to your image collection, and learned to refrain from ever using them in your slide decks (see the Photomaniac antipattern). Presentations change under the Crucible of performing them; pay attention each time you deliver yours and invest effort in harvesting feedback.

Mechanics   Because this is a required effort, you might have other colleagues at your disposal to facilitate use of the Concurrent Creation pattern. Recruit them mercilessly to help with the research effort. In the same vein, engage some representative of the final audience in the construction of your slides, or at least ask that individual the review the deck. This will get that person or persons "on your side" before the talk occurs. Specifically request that an ally sit in the dreaded first row (see the Posse pattern). You'll have a friendly face there—possibly even someone who will break the ice by laughing at your humorous anecdotes.

Related Patterns   The Proposed pattern is a sibling type, another way to find yourself in a position to prepare a presentation.

If you are Required to do a talk in a hostile environment, consider using the Posse pattern to bring reinforcements.

Venkat's Cross-Globe In-Flight Preparation

Our friend and colleague Venkat Subramaniam once had to give a talk in India, far from his home in Denver, Colorado, in the United States. The talk's subject was a new programming language that Subramaniam didn't know . . . yet. During the transpacific flight, he studied, wrote examples, and slept in two-hour cycles. He finished preparing his talk just as the plane landed. Subramaniam describes it as one of the most risky and intense efforts he's ever embarked upon.

The audience gave the talk an ecstatic reception. It covered many facets of a difficult topic, baked in the speaker's mind just hours earlier.

We never advocate waiting until the last minute to prepare for a talk, but this story illustrates that a last-minute talk is not a predetermined failure. In fact, it can be a roaring success. The secret to Subramaniam's success was his experience and his ability to learn at lightning speed. At the core of those traits is his *passion* for learning and for conveying knowledge.

 **Pattern: The Big Why**

Also Known As	Motivation, Keep on Keeping On, Deliver What You Agreed To
Definition	Before you submitted your conference proposal or accepted an invitation to present at an event, you should have asked yourself the core question, "Why am I really interested in presenting material?" Your answer should be a *great reason* that motivates you to follow through with your commitment to deliver the presentation.
Motivation	When you accept a speaking invitation or acknowledge the acceptance of your talk proposal, you're making a big and probably visible commitment. Event organizers often use speaker acceptance as a trigger to begin marketing the talent and talks they have lined up. After all, the right talks and the right speakers are the magnet that sells tickets to the event. In addition to all your reasons for wanting to give the presentation in the first place, one of your motivations for following through should be the public visibility of your commitment.
Applicability/ Consequences	However strong your initial desire to give your presentation, perhaps you've harbored the thought that you can always back out as the event date nears if you just can't do it. Don't. You know what it's like when a speaker cancels a talk you've been looking forward to. The disappointment (or worse) sticks with both the audience and organizers for quite

some time. Right or wrong, little allowance is given for cancellation, even in extenuating circumstances.

On the constructive side, help the event make the most of your participation. Market yourself just short of annoying your friends and colleagues. The more you talk about the presentation as a done deal, the more you'll invest in it. The more you talk it up, the more you are mentally committed to it. The more you market it, the more it will enhance your professional reputation if you deliver it well. Make the most of the effort that you put into constructing the talk, psych yourself up for the delivery, and enjoy the sense of achievement you'll get by following through.

Mechanics We cannot provide motivation for you, but we can present a catalog of ten common motivations on which you can overlay details relevant to your own field.

1. Care about the Technology
   a. A certain technology has made you more productive.
   b. The advancement of a tool has made a process more timely or cost-efficient.
   c. Regulations in the pipeline will require this technology; prepare early.
2. Care about the Audience
   a. You feel empathy with a group that needs encouragement.
   b. You want to teach a life skill.
3. Product Sales
   a. This is a chance to demo a product in the real world.
   b. You can gain more public relations attention for the product than a website or online demo can.
4. Philanthropic Effort / Open Source
   a. You want to do social good.
   b. You want to support a specific community.
5. Peer Recognition
   a. Presenting could lead to advancement on the corporate ladder.
   b. Presenting increases your visibility to management.
6. Professional Recognition
   a. Presenting can lead to consulting jobs.
   b. Presenting increases your visibility to potential clients.
   c. Presenting marks you as an expert on the product, service, or solution.
7. Concept Sales
   a. Your presentation prepares decision makers for later sales opportunities.
   b. Your presentation contributes to future marketing campaigns.
8. Convincing
   a. Your presentation lays groundwork for volunteers.

       b. Your presentation establishes new "baseline" for future boundary-stretching ideas.

9. Professional Growth
   a. Deadlines help reinforce already self-motivated learners by providing concrete goals. (A presentation is due!)
   b. You want to improve your marketable skills and your resume's technology list. Speaking about a topic is terrific credentialization.

10. Personal Fulfillment
    a. Personal fulfillment is perhaps the best of all reasons to give a talk.
    b. This motivation can encompass many of the others (care, recognition, growth).

Related Patterns You must have a strong motivation to apply practice patterns like Carnegie Hall and Crucible.

Pattern: Proposed

Also Known As And Then They Said Yes

Definition Following the route of the typical by-your-own-bootstraps presenter, submit abstracts or excerpts to relevant events that you find via Internet search engines, hear about from friends or colleagues, or trip over via advertisements. Days, weeks, or even months later, you may receive the e-mail message you've been anxiously awaiting: A talk you've proposed has been accepted!

Motivation The right reason to seek the opportunity to speak about something in public—whether at a conference, special interest group meeting, or any other venue—is to share information of importance with a particular community. A less altruistic but equally valid reason is to increase your professional visibility.

Applicability/ Consequences Proposed is the way to reach for the chance to present for an event whose organizers don't know you well enough to invite you or one at which you're not required to speak.

The style, voice, and supplementary materials you provide in your submission packet convey your personality as well as your talk's potential fit for the event. Prepare it with care.

Submission of your proposal should imply a commitment to give the talk. Many conference and special interest group organizers have confidentially told us that they frown upon accepting speakers who then decline because of a time conflict. Even though you could argue that you can't commit because you don't know in advance if you'll be accepted, organizers want signals that their event is special to you and that you intentionally chose it. Select the events you submit to carefully, identifying the aspects that make them appeal to you more than others with similar content and function. Treat the proposal as a commitment that you'll keep if it is accepted.

Mechanics First, make sure you've applied all the lessons in the Big Why pattern, leading you to choose an appropriate topic.

Next, you must understand the conference proposal system, which are almost universally web based and sometimes oddly quirky. Make sure you understand the fine print for the submission guidelines, including file formats, deadlines, review processes, and myriad logistical details. For many conferences, the only actual artifact you must produce at the proposal stage is an *abstract*, a short description of a topic. Check the guidelines; some conferences have strict rules on length, content, style, and so on. Some require details about what you expect your audience to learn, so you need to have applied the Know Your Audience pattern.

Once you understand what you must produce for the proposal, you must write the abstract. Apply the Peer Review pattern to your proposal text to create grammatically correct and to-the-point prose. Write in an active voice and keep the proposal within the guidelines. This text is your sole proxy with the people—sometimes volunteers—who will decide which proposals to accept. They will rely extensively on first impressions. You can give yourself a competitive edge by having a friend or colleague proofread your proposal and by running it through a spelling and grammar check in the word processor of your choice.

Lean toward describing any new information your talk will convey and the benefits that the audience will derive. Conference or special interest group organizers generally sell tickets on the basis of the usefulness of new information, announcements of new discoveries, or novel perspectives on existing concepts. Be sincere as you sell yourself and your talk; convince the readers why *you* should be the one presenting *this* topic. Highlight any related experience, past writing, and successful presentations. A globally known technology conference recently shared that the proposal-review team gives a significant preference to submitters who include a link to their videos or scores from past speaking events.

Known Uses By our informal tally, 90 percent of the more than 1,000 conferences at which we have collectively presented use a web-based call for papers (CFP) process. Events that use this process include such well-known technology and medical conferences as the following:

- No Fluff, Just Stuff[1]
- Jazoon[2]

- Devoxx[3]
- JavaOne[4]
- American Academy of Physician Assistants Annual Conference[5]
- American Academy of Orthopaedic Surgeons Annual Meeting[6]
- American Institute of Chemical Engineers Annual Meeting[7]

Related Patterns

The Required pattern is the sibling to this one—one of the other ways you find yourself preparing a presentation.

To make sure the prose for your proposal is adequate, look at the tips in the Peer Review pattern and Injured Outlines antipattern.

Antipattern: Abstract Attorney

Also Known As

Talk Title Terrorist

Definition

Someone attends your presentation with the apparent goal of unearthing minute deviations from your agenda or conference abstract. Instead of focusing on the learning the material you do present, an Abstract Attorney channels virtually all their energy into finding minor differences so they can catalog them in e-mail messages, expose them via Twitter, or complain about them on an evaluation form.

Motivation

Motivations for this antipattern are as varied as the personality quirks of those who exemplify it. Perhaps it's the satisfaction of "catching" the presenter in a perceived inaccuracy or perhaps a belief that that intentional subterfuge is the root cause. *Why* this antipattern manifests isn't nearly as important as how you, the presenter, can prevent it.

Applicability/ Consequences

This antipattern pops up any time you prepublicize what you're going to talk about, whether it's via an agenda e-mail, a conference brochure, or a web page announcing your appearance. Most conferences publish the agenda and abstracts so that attendees can plan which talks to attend. It's common for material to take on a life of its own and wander in (you hope) more interesting directions after you write the initial agenda or abstract. A mantra among experienced conference speakers is that you don't really know what a talk is about until the third or fourth time that you present it. Unfortunately, it's difficult to remember to revisit the abstract to reflect the talk's current content.

It's demoralizing to give a killer presentation and then receive negative feedback based not on the quality of what you presented but on the perceived lack of adherence to a talk description. Ideally, audience members simply ask, "Did I walk away with increased knowledge on the topic presented?" instead of looking for an opportunity to snitch on the slightest deviation from the talk's outline.

Mechanics   If you know the material well (e.g., last month's sales figures or a tutorial on a web framework that you've used on several projects), produce a comprehensive outline or abstract. In this case, writing a generic abstract is lazy; by doing it right the first time, you defang the potential Abstract Attorney. (But don't let the dread of an Abstract Attorney keep you from straying from the agenda during your talk if doing so makes the presentation better.)

Be vague if you can afford to. For example, don't spell out all the details in advance if you're presenting at a required meeting; everyone will learn them when they attend. Otherwise, you only empower an Abstract Attorney at no benefit to you or your audience. Vagueness can also serve a more positive purpose. For example, Neal's keynote addresses always have cryptic, mysterious names and an abstract optimized to pique curiosity rather than convey hard facts. At developer conferences, the keynote is typically the only talk offered in that time slot, so everyone at the conference tends to show up. Keynotes tend to be more conceptual than "normal" technical presentations, and an explicit description for a keynote doesn't help entice people; it just empowers the potential Abstract Attorney.

If vagueness is unwise and you are still in the conceptualization phase, write an abstract that includes only broad strokes, and remind yourself to revisit it (perhaps several times) as your ideas gel and you start building a real Narrative Arc. Given our emphasis on planning before you start using a presentation tool (see the Fourthought pattern), plan for the following milestones as opportunities to update your abstract:

1. Create a first draft during the ideation phase that includes only the three (or so) things you plan to talk about (see the Triad pattern).
2. Update it after you have a good outline and you're ready to start creating the presentation.
3. Refine it again when you finish the first draft of the slides.
4. Make a final set of tweaks after you've been through the talk a few times (see the Crucible and Carnegie Hall patterns).

If this is a talk that you'll end up presenting repeatedly (such as a conference talk), plan to update the abstract yet again after the fourth or fifth time. You'll be surprised at how much your talk has changed under the pressure of presentation. Consider putting a reminder on your calendar to revisit your abstracts a month or two in the future.

Even if your abstract has changed, you can disempower an Abstract Attorney by putting your abstract on your first slide so that the attendees can read it as they are settling in to their seats. We are fans of using the Preroll pattern to place a variety of housekeeping details on the first slide (your name, title, abstract, reminders about cell phones, etc.).

Known Uses   This antipattern occurs in nearly all technical conferences, amplified in direct relation to the level of scientific detail the talk offers and the abstract promised.

Related Patterns   Abstract Attorney is a specific Hecklers type—typically not as malicious as those who outright aim to embarrass or undermine the credibility of the presenter for their own perceived glorification.

CHAPTER 2
CREATIVITY PATTERNS

BEFORE YOU CAN GIVE A KILLER PRESENTATION, YOU HAVE to *build* it. Before you can build it, you need to come up with something interesting to say (although this clearly hasn't stopped some people from doing presentations in the past).

We're not going to help you find your muse or give you the crystal-clear explanation of your complex topic. We *will* show you patterns that can help you develop and refine your ideas.

This chapter contains patterns and antipatterns related to creating the content of your presentation. We discuss how to structure your presentation with the Narrative Arc pattern; how to use visuals effectively; techniques to credentialize yourself, such as Leet Grammars; and ways to destroy your credibility using the Alienating Artifact antipattern.

Pattern: Narrative Arc

Definition

A *narrative arc* is the sequence of events in a story from beginning to middle to end. A typical narrative arc describes the trials and tribulations of the story's characters as they move through the plot and how they are resolved. Much literature follows this basic structure—and much of presenting is actually storytelling.

Motivation

We start with a quote:

> Get your protagonist up a tree. Throw rocks at him. Then get him down.
>
> —Syd Fields

Presentations imply a strong storytelling context: You are in a group, set aside from the others, conveying information to them. People have heard stories their entire lives; we have an innate feel for how stories work. By leveraging an ability we all developed in childhood, you can create more-compelling presentations.

Narrative arc is a type of fictional plot structure, defined as a series of events that cause and heighten a conflict of forces, bringing them eventually to a climax and then to resolution. It is called an arc because of the shape of rising and falling tension when diagramed, as shown in Figure 2.1.

Applicability/
Consequences

This pattern won't work for all kinds of presentations, but don't automatically discount it if it doesn't obviously fit a certain presentation type. Even a product demo can use this structure: Set up differentiators for your

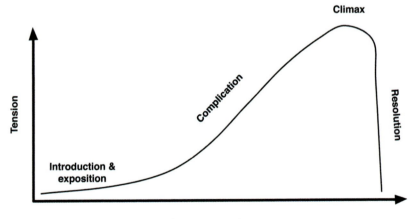

Figure 2.1 Narrative arc

product, show how other products in that space don't match up, and finish by showing how cool your product is.

The effectiveness of this pattern comes from people's ability to recognize familiar story types. For example, one of the compelling plot elements of superhero movies is the *origin* story, or how the superhero came to have special powers. This story arc is familiar all the way back to mythology. When presentation attendees recognize the narrative arc, it helps them understand your material because they understand the basic framework. The longer the arc, the bigger the potential payoff.

Mechanics   Discovering the narrative arc in your material is by far the hardest part of applying this pattern. Think about the reasons you are doing a presentation about your subject: There must be some story to tell or you wouldn't be standing at the front of the room. One way to help discover this structure is to think in threes (which we cover in the Triad pattern). If you can find three things that you want to get across, think about putting them into a three-act structure.

Frequently, presentations that follow the Narrative Arc pattern build on the implicit problem/solution structure of your material. If you have a hard time seeing your topic in that way, consider creating a flowchart-like view to help navigate your topic's structure. You must do this planning work before you start putting slides together; trying to ascertain structure

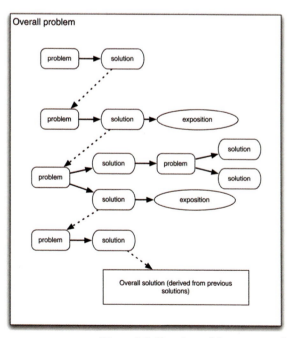

Figure 2.2 Flowchart of the structure of a presentation

while you are in the middle never works. Figure 2.2 shows an example of such a flowchart.

In Figure 2.2, the overall problem is posed, but the talk exposition immediately starts posing smaller problems with corresponding solutions, which in turn lead to other related problems, which have solutions, and so on. In some cases, the solution bifurcates because a problem has more than one solution, and each of those solutions in turn leads to more exposition and other problems and solutions. This pattern of setting the context for a problem, showing a solution, leading to the next problem, and so on is the Narrative Arc for the presentation. Ultimately, through this gradual illustration of common problems, solutions, and added nuance based on deeper understanding, the *story* of the talk comes out, providing value to the audience not merely by facts but by the shared context for how those facts came to be.

Narrative Arc is really a specialization of the Context Keeper pattern, using the narrative device as a way to provide consistent and repeating context.

Known Uses   One of Neal's popular technical talks for software developers is about test-driven development (TDD)—the impact of a certain kind of testing on the design of source code. This might not sound like a good candidate for a narrative arc. However, because Neal is trying to solve a problem that crops up in large software projects, he could portray a conflict that everyone in the audience would recognize. He wanted to set up many little epiphanies during the talk in which he posed little problems with immediate solutions. The overall structure of the talk is illustrated in Figure 2.3.

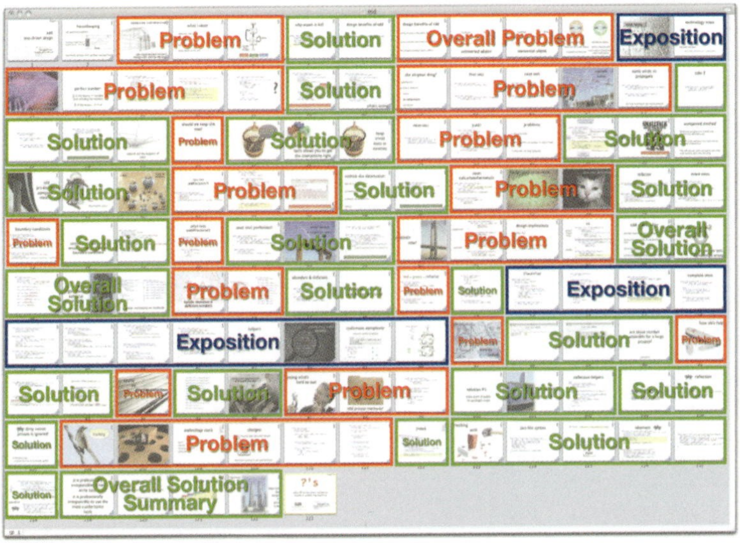

Figure 2.3 Overall structure of the *Test-Driven Design* talk

In the TDD talk, Neal poses an overall problem, then starts with small problem/solution arcs. Each solution smoothly transitions into the next problem, which creates a nice rhythm. The sections marked *exposition* introduce tools that the attendee might not be familiar with and presents some foundational material. However, as you can see, the bulk of the talk follows the problem/solution structure. Near the end of the talk, you can see a couple of places where Neal presents a problem that has multiple solutions delimited by separate "solution" boxes for a single problem.

When presented, this material flows naturally. Neal starts with an overall problem statement, then immediately jumps into incremental ways to solve that problem. Each partial solution solves one or more aspects of the original problem, but each solution introduces either a new problem or a nuance of the original problem. For attendees Neal has polled afterward, this talk seems much shorter than 90 minutes because it flows so naturally from one topic to the next.

After the attendee has seen a few of these problem/solution cycles, the overall structure becomes clear. Neal emphasizes the structure by placing Intermezzi at each of the important solution boundaries, which are distinguishable as slides with a single terse statement and related imagery. To complete the effect, the Unifying Visual Theme of the talk is "construction," so most of the incidental photos reinforce that theme.

Related Patterns   The Triad pattern suggests you put everything in three acts, which is a familiar and common Narrative Arc.

Frequently, your Bookends and Intermezzi relate to and reference your Narrative Arc; these natural placeholders provide a nice location to add to the backstory. Bookends that seem only marginally related but help metaphorically tie your overall message together are a great way to tease and reinforce your Narrative Arc.

Generally, your Narrative Arc and Unifying Visual Theme are closely related; you can sometimes use the Unifying Visual Theme to drive or reinforce the narrative.

Pattern: Fourthought

Definition

Don't spend all your preparation time using a presentation tool. Think and organize before you start building a presentation. The four stages of building a presentation are *ideate*, *capture*, *organize*, and *translate*.

Motivation

It might seem like a waste of time to play with Post-it notes, mind maps, and outlines before you get to the "real" work of building a presentation. You always think you can let the tool help you organize your thoughts. Trust us: You can't.

One of the unintuitive experiences that all three authors discovered independently is that you should *stay away* from the presentation tool as long as you can. You must have something worth talking about before you can present it; spending time first getting your thoughts organized pays off hugely when it comes time to put the talk together. For example, finding the proper Narrative Arc is harder when you cast your thoughts to slides prematurely.

Applicability/
Consequences

Trying to build a unified message while building your slides is difficult because the tool forces you to chop your concepts into slide-sized bites. Ideas almost never come out that size on their own. We capture this negative effect separately in the Cookie Cutter antipattern. Your presentation design needs to take into account much more than what the slides say. Using the presentation tool to guide the design puts undue organizational emphasis on that one aspect of the overall presentation.

We're not suggesting that you do all the design of the talk up front and dogmatically translate that into a presentation. Building the visual part of the presentation will and should change the way you think about presenting it. But we advise that you don't *start* the design process in the presentation tool.

Mechanics

Stuart Halloway, a well-known software deep thinker, hosts a popular blog. He says that it takes him three morning runs to compose a blog entry in his head and 15 minutes to write it. If building slides is the most time-consuming part of building your presentations, you are doing it wrong! Presentations go through four distinct creative phases:

- *Ideate*: Generate the idea(s) for the presentation. Even if it is a Required presentation, you must still think about how you are going to tell the story effectively. For example, if your job is to present quarterly results, you may still have ideas for a Unifying Visual Theme that includes pictures from the company picnic. The output from this phase consists of ideas that may or may not make it into the presentation but that you think have some connection to the topic, however tenuous.

- *Capture*: Capture your ideas in a way that doesn't preshape them. It's a mistake to try to add structure to your ideas too early, because it will hide interesting connections that don't fit into rigid hierarchies. All the authors are fans of *mind mapping* tools, which enable you to organize information in nontraditional hierarchies, but index cards work just as well. The worst place to put your ideas in this stage is in a presentation tool, because you are forced to mash your ideas into Cookie Cutter size. The second-worst place is an outlining tool, which imposes a strict hierarchy. In this stage, you want to find opportunistic connections between the elements of your presentation.
- *Organize*: Organize and linearize your ideas. After you have a good idea of the extent of your topic, move it from your unstructured storage into an outline. You can use either a stand-alone outlining tool or the outline facilities in the presentation tool. The goal in this stage is to take the ideas and organize them in time so that you have a compelling Narrative Arc. This is the point when you include the crosscutting subjects you identified in the *capture* phase as part of the overall presentation subject. Many of the topics you captured won't make this cut, but don't worry. Capturing ideas frequently generates lots of side topics that are interesting but don't contribute to the story you are telling now.
- *Design*: Use the presentation tool to translate your thoughts into slides, using the patterns in this book.

Entire books have been written about the use of both analog (paper, Post-it notes, etc.) and digital (mind maps, outlines, etc.) creativity tools, so we won't cover that subject here. However, we can provide you with an example workflow.

Neal's Creative Workflow

While I'm on the road speaking at conferences, I tend not to build a lot of presentations; instead, I'm thinking about next year's topics, the *ideate* phase. I brainstorm a list of topics I'm interested in pursuing, adding to it as I encounter interesting new things, and start thinking about which aspects of the topic to present. I constantly make notes: observations, insights, brain storms (or drizzles)—anything that applies to that topic, even if the connection seems transient or tentative at the time.

I am an enthusiastic user of mind maps for the *capture* phase. I take all the little bits and pieces I've gathered as notes and dump them into the mind-mapping tool, without much regard to structure. I prefer a mind map at this early stage because I'm trying to gather the disparate parts of the topic in one place that doesn't have a forced structure, unlike an outline or presentation tool. I use a mind map the way Dumbledore in the Harry

Potter books uses the Pensieve (a magical device that extracts thoughts from your brain so that you can organize them).

When the time arrives to build the presentation, I use the mind map to add structure to the thoughts. Generally, 50–75 percent of the thoughts I've had about the subject over the last six months make the cut. It's at this stage that I try to come up with the larger structure: the major themes, the topic order, Unifying Visual Theme, and so on. Most of my design work takes place in a mind map. You can see one of my mind maps in Figure 2.4.

Notice all the crisscrossing lines in the mind map in Figure 2.4, which illustrates one of the advantages of this type of tool over an outline. Mind maps enable you to create hierarchical layouts but also to identify these cross-cutting connections between items in the outline. Most of the time, those connections are the most interesting parts of the presentation because they show unconventional, nonlinear thinking about the subject.

After I get everything organized in the mind map, I move it to an outlining tool, which is the *organize* phase. The important task here is to linearize the emergent structure in the mind map into an outline. Presentations with slides are linear because time is linear; at some point you must decide the order of the points you want to make. When translating the mind map to the outline, pay special attention to any crosscutting connections you've identified. They might give you clues for the Unifying Visual Theme, and finding a surprising connection enables you to use the

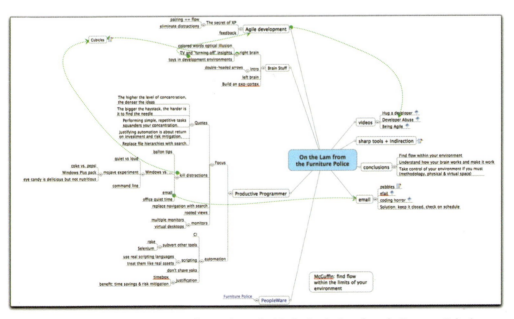

Figure 2.4 Representation of a mind map for Neal's *On the Lam from the Furniture Police* keynote

Backtracking pattern effectively. Although each presentation has a primary topic, you add depth and interest if you can also include ancillary insights without diminishing your primary message.

Only after the topic has a linear structure do I use the presentation tool to start creating slides from the outline—the *design* phase. Having a pre-defined basic structure enables you to concentrate more on the presentation's visual aspects and less on exposition.

Related Patterns | The ideas for your Unifying Visual Theme generally come during the *ideate* or *capture* phases.

The Backtracking pattern shows a powerful reinforcement technique; the subject for backtracks will come from the *capture* and *organize* phases in this pattern.

Work done when applying this pattern leads you to your Narrative Arc for the talk.

Constraining *Creativity and Constraint*

RailsConf, a big conference in North America for the Ruby on Rails developer community, is known for innovative presentations and out-of-the-box thinking about technology. In 2010, Neal was asked to present a keynote as a replacement for a speaker who had dropped out. Neal had about three months of preparation time for the talk, so he solicited ideas from friends and colleagues. David Bock, author of the foreword to Neal's latest book, suggested a study of the effect of constraint on creativity: The correct amount of constraint enables creativity more than total freedom does, but too much constraint places too many road-blocks in the way of creativity.

In accord with the talk's theme, Neal vowed (and succeeded) not to touch the presentation tool until 24 hours before the talk. That doesn't mean he didn't work on the presentation; quite the contrary. He worked on it in bits and pieces, using mind maps and outlines to structure the talk. During this process, the way Neal thought about the subject changed, and he came up with a fascinating tangent to the main theme he hadn't considered before. Although the *creativity and constraint* subject was good, he realized that the supporting elements for the subject also supported another, more radical idea. About four days before the keynote, Neal realized that he had transformed the talk's primary theme; it was now about the possibility of finding art in source code itself, as a written medium, rather than finding art in what code does when it's compiled and functional. This is still related to *creativity and constraint* because the artistic medium defines the constraints that artists must labor under, much as programming languages provide constraints. What if we approached the constraints of programming languages the way artists approach constraints in their media?

True to his word, Neal started working on the slides exactly 24 hours before the talk. Constructing the presentation itself was easy: All the hard parts had been resolved during the extensive design phase. He ended up with 108 slides for the 45-minute talk that fit together nicely and delivered the message he wanted.

By delaying the visual part of the talk, Neal was able to refine (and redefine) the talk's theme, divorced from concerns about transitions, animations, stock photos, and the like. He focused on honing the real message first, and then he did the mechanical work of translating ideas into slides.

Pattern: Crucible

Also Known As	Presentation Construction and Refinement
Definition	*Delivering* a presentation isn't the same as *constructing* it. But the presentation will change (sometimes drastically) under the pressure of giving it. Learn to embrace and leverage these potential improvements.
Motivation	The brilliant ideas you had about your presentation's narrative flow change when you actually perform it in front of people. None of the authors has ever had a talk that didn't change (sometimes substantially) after the first time he gave it, and some of the authors are relentless fiddlers—constantly tweaking talks every time they're done because one little piece didn't work correctly. The crucible of performance changes what you thought you knew about how to talk about the subject. This pattern describes ways to leverage that valuable experience.
Applicability/ Consequences	This pattern applies to all presentations regardless of type or context. Neal has some presentations that he's done more than 50 times that he still fiddles with when something isn't perfect. The number of performances is irrelevant: Over time, you know when something doesn't work as you give the talk, so try to iterate your way toward a clearer message.

The most desirable consequence is that your talk gets much better over time. For that to happen, though, you must keep an eagle eye on what works and doesn't work while you're presenting. This is hard because you are also thinking about the presentation itself (see Crucible: Mechanics for more details).

> Helpful people are annoying.
>
> —Robert Fripp

A critical part of practice is feedback. It's all fine and good if everyone compliments your great job, but that isn't helpful criticism. You need to find someone who will be brutally honest about the strengths and weaknesses of every aspect of your presentation. Make sure that person sees at least one iteration of your presentation. And do the same for him or her. Working with a good feedback partner gives you a huge advantage over other presenters.

The first time you present a talk, you must pour all your concentration into making it as good as possible then and there. During subsequent performances, you can think about how to make it better the next time.

This advice might seem to contradict the Fourthought pattern, which suggests that you spend significant time up front designing your content before starting to use a tool. However, these two patterns peacefully coexist and complement each another. The Fourthought pattern is about the *architecture* of your presentation—the important topics that justify the effort to create a presentation. These are the things that will be hard to change later because doing so would change the entire meaning of your presentation. The Crucible pattern is more about refining the ideas after you know what your presentation is about, using stepwise refinement to improve it gradually.

Mechanics   If you have the rare luxury of lots of time and a willing audience, you can use this pattern to make incremental refinements to your presentation. Start with the barest possible draft (one-quarter to one-half of the anticipated total), present it, make modifications based on feedback, and repeat. Iterate over your material this way several times, and you'll find you have a much clearer view of what you should be talking about.

Taking an iterative approach also helps if you suffer from writer's block. There's a saying that a crappy first draft is better than a perfect idea with no implementation. Even if you don't have the big picture, you can start with something you know must be present and iterate toward the ultimate goal.

> The best is the enemy of the good.
>
> —Voltaire

Trying to create a perfect talk is paralyzing, so don't try to make yours perfect right away. If you have the time and audience, start with imperfection and iterate toward perfection.

While you're presenting a talk, it is quite common to realize there's a subtle flaw in it. It might be something as minor as two main points that you felt were in the right order as you constructed the talk but realized in flight should be transposed. The problem is that after the talk, it is difficult to remember those exact problems. The next time you present the material, that same flaw manifests again, but you still can't remember it (and all the other subtle flaws). You're left with a vague feeling that you know there are some minor flaws but can't remember all of them.

The obvious solution is to annotate the problem spots as they happen, but no one wants to stop in midstream and make a note while being stared at by a roomful of people. Here are a couple of ways to subtly make notes.

You can keep a pen and paper sitting next to your computer, and when you find one of those little flaws, jot a little note or even just the slide number. It doesn't need to be highly descriptive (or even lucid to anyone else); it serves as a reminder to yourself of the flaw. Immediately after the talk, transcribe those notes and either fix the flaws or supply enough context to your future self to fix them.

A recording device is an even better way to capture little flaws. Neal uses an iPhone application that lets you record short voice memos. He turns the phone on just before the presentation, changes the settings so that it never goes to sleep, and leaves the recording application open. During the talk, when he finds a little flaw, he records about 15 seconds of the talk at that point. After the talk, he goes back through the recordings and makes a note of the fixable things. Neal finds that just that little bit of context is enough to jog his memory of what he didn't like.

Of course, you can videotape the entire presentation (which is a good idea), but it's tedious to watch it over and over to harvest little flaws. Recording just a little context is enough to jog your memory.

Try to notice these things when giving the talk so that you can incorporate them into subsequent versions of the presentation:

- Turns of phrase or jokes that solicit big responses from the audience. Pay attention to what works. Experienced presenters modify their wording and timing when presenting the same material over and over. Over time, you hone the presentation with proven material, much as stand-up comedians hone their material over time.
- Things you consistently highlight with a laser pointer. Turn those elements into Traveling Highlights. Also, avoid accidentally falling into the Laser Weapons antipattern.
- Dull parts. No matter how riveting you think a digression might be, watch the audience's reactions. If it's not really necessary, remove it. If it is necessary background material that you must cover before the exciting stuff, consider using the Brain Breaks pattern.

Experienced speaker consensus suggests that presentations undergo major refinement over the first three (or so) performances and the pace and scale of changes tends to diminish but never really stop.

Related Patterns   It is common to use the Brain Breaks pattern to add bits of humor and other harmless distractions to keep the audience engaged. Crucible suggests that you pay attention to the Brain Breaks that work the best and hone them each time you deliver the presentation.

Matthew's Joke Catalog

Because professional technical speakers and instructors present the same material over and over, they become sensitive to the nuances in the material that might affect one group differently than another. Matthew admits to having a joke *catalog* ready for certain parts of some presentations. At any given time, he can choose which joke to do, depending on the crowd.

Pay attention to which parts are most effective when you present. It will surprise you. The parts you think are lackluster may well be the most popular or entertaining parts. Finding verbal twists and turns that catch the audience's attention are worth keeping. Over time, your talk will consist of proven parts that work well.

Pattern: Concurrent Creation

Definition

Don't feel compelled to create your presentation materials in the same order as the presentation itself. When creating a presentation as a group, follow certain practices to retain sanity.

Motivation

If you are creating a presentation as an individual, all the materials you need are rarely available at exactly the correct time. It's not a bad idea to create the material in nonchronological order anyway. One common trap when you build a presentation at the last minute is a fever trance in which everything makes perfect sense at 4 a.m. but seems like a random collection of slides by the light of day. Creating materials out of order forces you to understand and verify your Narrative Arc.

If you are creating a presentation as a group because of a tight deadline (so often the case), you must assign someone as the *Slide Wrangler*, the person who owns the master slide deck—the one you'll present from.

Applicability/ Consequences

The pattern appears quite frequently in corporate settings when a group must collaborate in a rush to create a single presentation.

Trying to merge multiple slide decks together is a disaster because there are always subtle differences among templates, default settings, and other aspects of the presentation tool. It is wiser to have one person "own" the master deck.

Mechanics

Whether you are an individual working asynchronously on a presentation or as part of a collaborating group, be sure to add a slide to your template that has the ugliest color/font combination you can imagine to indicate a part requiring further attention. As you create the presentation, leave those slides in place for future material. Use your most diabolical creative skills to make them ugly. They must be hideous enough that they never, ever make it past even a light-table view of the presentation.

Modern presentation tools are terrible at enabling collaboration, so if you find yourself in that thankless situation, the best you can do is establish some rules:

- Make one person the Slide Wrangler. This is the only person who touches the official deck.
- Make sure everyone is using the same template or theme for the fragments they create.
- No one is allowed to change the template or theme without taking responsibility for making sure that every single person has an updated copy. This is designed to discourage you! Changing a slide in a template or theme will cause duplications and names that include "copy," none of which is useful.
- Each collaborator sends slides to the Slide Wrangler, who imports them into the presentation. This step is important because it will override any template changes made by other people, respecting the template in effect for the target presentation.
- Set a cut-off time when all contributions to the official deck must be in, preferably with enough time for the Slide Wrangler to do a good job.

Known Uses   Every corporation everywhere.

Related Patterns   The Talklet pattern works particularly well in conjunction with this pattern; each person builds a Talklet, and the Slide Wrangler applies a minimal Unifying Visual Theme.

⊂⊃⊂⊃⊂⊃ **Pattern: Triad**

Also Known As   Three-Act Structure

Definition   Build your presentation around three central ideas.

Motivation   Presentations have two purposes: inform and entertain. A presentation with too much information harms the audience's attention span and retention, regardless of the presentation's entertainment quotient. Limiting your topics to a small number ensures that you can cover them sufficiently without overloading your audience.

Applicability/ Consequences   This pattern applies to all types of presentation formats including the Infodeck. It works best in keynotes and other abstract presentation formats, where you're talking about big ideas and want to leave the audience with firm impressions. This pattern also works well in more-concrete presentations, because it is a well-known structure for information, closely related to the three-act play. If you find yourself with more than three major themes, you should reexamine your material. Although not unheard of, creating a presentation that enables your audience to retain huge amounts of information is difficult.

Don't try to fit an overly complex subject into artificial parts just to take advantage of this pattern. The benefits won't outweigh the damage you do to your subject!

Mechanics   Long before you start using a tool to start building a presentation, think about the information you want to convey, leveraging the Fourthought pattern. Don't have too many core themes; attendees will never remember all of them. We've found that three is a good number: It lets you easily use the familiar Narrative Arc of the three-act play: exposition, conflict, and resolution. This narrative flow is older than written language, and everyone in your audience has heard stories with that structure since early childhood. Why not leverage that innate structure to make your point come across more effectively?

This pattern works particularly well with the Talklet pattern: You create three talklets, each with a major theme, and build the longer presentation using talklets as acts by adding a little glue material.

Known Uses   In Neal's *Ancient Philosophers & Blowhard Jamborees* keynote, he uses a traditional three-act structure. The first part explains what the keynote is about, the second part talks about global challenges to the ways that we've traditionally written software, and the third part lists action items to help audience members avoid career danger. The other speakers on the conference circuit started calling it the "Angel of Death" keynote, because it becomes quite gloomy toward the end. Neal had structured the second section to get darker and darker in mood, piling depressing fact upon fact. It reaches a point with a dark, gloomy slide containing vocational-training advice, as shown in Figure 2.5.

Neal wanted a depressing and gloomy mood at that point in the presentation because the entire remainder dispenses advice on how to prevent all the bad news from the second act. He makes the audience members gloomy together and then makes them happy together at the end. That shared audience experience makes the presentation more memorable.

Related Patterns   This pattern doesn't obviate the need for a compelling Narrative Arc.

During the Fourthought stages of the presentation, see if the material aligns itself to work well with this pattern.

Figure 2.5 The gloomy end of the second act

Pattern: Expansion Joints

Also Known As

Goldilocks; Short, Medium, Long

Definition

Despite your best practice and planning, the guarding of your room and time slot, and other proactive measures, you'll always find that *time* is a challenging variable. Plan for uncertainty by including material in your talk that can expand or contract depending on environmental factors.

Motivation

Building presentations that precisely consume an allotted time is tough because of factors you can't control. If you are conducting a meeting, you must carefully control the amount of interaction to ensure that the agenda doesn't explode. For more-formal presentations, you generally *want* audience participation: It indicates interest, engagement, and feedback. But if you build time into your talk for audience interaction and end up, say, in the upper Midwest—where breathing is considered exuberance—you'll have far too little material.

Building either *implicit* or *explicit* Expansion Joints into your presentation helps you expand or contract the talk to fit the allotted time—and to tailor your presentation on the fly for every audience type you might encounter.

Applicability/ Consequences

This pattern works well when you have a fixed time slot to fill and are unsure how external time sinks, such as audience interaction or meal breaks, will affect the pace of your presentation.

This pattern also works well when you don't know the audience's appetite for detail in advance. Using Expansion Joints enables you to expose detail as the audience requests it.

This pattern is also applicable for presentations you give numerous times in a wide variety of environments and circumstances because the level of audience interaction will almost certainly vary too.

It takes extra work to add *explicit* Expansion Joints to your talk, so you need a strong justification to bother with this pattern.

For experienced speakers, the hazard is generally having too much material and talking too long. Martin Fowler, a well-known speaker and contributor of a few of our patterns, uses Expansion Joints as a safety net. He never has too little material but always fears that he might, so he always adds a few implicit Expansion Joints just in case.

Mechanics

You can implement either implicit or explicit Expansion Joints.

Implicit Expansion Joints

An *implicit* expansion joint is a topic that you know you can add at a critical juncture and improvise on for a variable length of time. It can be as simple as a slide that you keep at a strategic location where it makes sense to digress onto a side topic. Depending on circumstances, you can either show the slide and talk about it for a few minutes or skip over it as if it weren't there.

It's important to practice *skipping* slides gracefully. Don't show a slide, mutter that you don't have time for it, and move on (a good example of the Going Meta antipattern). Know where your Expansion Joints slides reside, and learn the keyboard shortcuts in your presentation tool for skipping over unwanted slides smoothly.

Explicit Expansion Joints

Explicit Expansion Joints are slides you keep within your presentation with their own Narrative Arc as a fully realized digression. To implement this pattern, keep a subset of slides that support a contextualized digression that fits into the overall Unifying Visual Theme of the main talk.

Explicit Expansion Joints work well when you must support several different (in length or detail) versions of the same presentation. For example, you could have a high-level overview presentation you give to management that includes detailed Expansion Joints that you only use when you give the same talk to the engineering team.

Related Patterns

The Talklet pattern works nicely with this pattern if you build one of the segments with Expansion Joints.

Make sure your Expansion Joints match your Narrative Arc; it's distracting to add a random digression merely to soak up time.

Pattern: Talklet

Contributed By

Martin Fowler, Chief Scientist, ThoughtWorks[1]

Definition

A Talklet is a small, self-contained presentation designed to be embedded within a larger presentation, which can consist of a series of talklets. In Martin's original definition, he focused on this concept as a Suite of Talks, each as a small, self-contained presentation; his focus was on the *combination* of small talks, while we've broadened it to discuss the Talklet itself.

Motivation

You want to create presentations with a good Narrative Arc, but what if you aren't sure how much time you have? Or you're sure that the presenter preceding you will run long. By building a larger talk consisting of small, self-contained units, you can still have a compelling story as a chunk rather than trying to edit a longer talk on the fly to make it shorter.

Neal's colleague Martin Fowler, a well-known figure in the technical-presentation world, created this pattern defensively to help ward off the following recurring situation. Neal and Martin frequently present to clients or customers, often in unusual circumstances. All too often, we hear, "The CTO only has 45 minutes, so can you do your 90-minute presentation in 45 minutes?" Presentations are not fractal; it's impossible to build a compelling 90-minute presentation that can be arbitrarily broken up and still retain its message.

Applicability/ Consequences

Psychological research shows that the average adult attention span is about 20 minutes. People can renew their interest with a little effort, which is why they can enjoy movies. Given this natural biological tendency, the Talklet pattern fits into that 20-minute time frame exactly, enabling you to renew audience members' attention with a new topic just as their concentration on the current topic naturally wanes.

This pattern works well when you have discrete, mostly orthogonal topics. If the topics relate only in peripheral ways, you can construct a larger talk consisting of talklets and build a unifying theme around their intersection points.

By using this pattern, a presenter with a highly variable schedule can set boundaries, creating a fighting chance for a good presentation. Fowler's preferred talklet length is 20 minutes, giving him 20-, 40-, and 60-minute options. It's a reasonable constraint to say, "No, I can't do the 90-minute presentation in 45 minutes, but what if I do two talklets in 40 minutes?"

This pattern works nicely when encapsulated within the Á la Carte Content pattern. Each of the options you present your audience with can be constructed as a Talklet.

Related Patterns

You lose some of your ability to construct a long-running narrative arc. You can (and should) still use the Narrative Arc pattern within each talklet, but its effectiveness is slightly diminished because you don't have as much time to build tension.

The Foreshadowing pattern can act as "glue" between the otherwise stand-alone Talklet pieces, especially when combined with Backtracking.

This pattern works extremely well with the Á la Carte Content pattern, with each Talklet offered as an option.

Pattern: Unifying Visual Theme

Definition

Use a common repeating visual element to tie the disparate parts of your presentation together.

Motivation

Using a visual theme that relates to your presentation content provides numerous benefits. First, you can create nonverbal associations between your topic and conceptually related topics—either positive or negative, depending on your goals. Second, it makes your presentation more visually interesting. Instead of showing boring bullets and text on slides, you provide a useful backdrop to accentuate what you are saying. Remember, delivering a presentation affords you two information channels: verbal and visual. Using compelling, *relevant* imagery helps you make connections with your audience that would be hard to make otherwise.

If you're stuck with a corporate slide template dripping with Floodmarks and other noxious antipatterns, implementing a good unifying visual theme takes some extra creativity. If the color scheme is unalterable, then use embedded visual elements. For example, if your talk is about building up your internal construction capacity, use pictures of tools in the slides' excess whitespace. Depending on your organization and the importance of the presentation, you might want to Defy Defaults and avoid using the worst parts of the supplied template. Corporate templates exist for a good reason—to give everyone consistent building blocks—but that constraint prevents you from building presentations that are even more compelling because they break the rules.

Applicability/ Consequences

Don't use the clip art and images that come with your presentation software. Because everyone picks from the same stock, it taints your presentation with a commodity feel, making it harder to distinguish it from other presentations.

You might create a problem that many TV and radio commercials have: Your catchy theme and metaphors are so memorable that no one remembers the important parts. Don't let the visual or metaphorical adornments get in the way of your main message.

It's also a bad idea to bend your message to match a visual theme that, although very cool, doesn't really match your talk. Don't push metaphors too far, because it harms the comparison to the real thing. Similarly, don't go out of your way to keep a theme going that doesn't really work. It's not worth muddying your main message just to get a cool theme to work.

Mechanics

Brainstorm as you think about your subject to help come up with visual themes. Frequently, you want to create a metaphorical rather than literal connection to your subject. For example, in Neal's presentation about the benefits of testing in software development, the imagery throughout consists of high-quality photos of large-scale construction projects, creating a metaphorical connection between construction projects and their analogs in software development. Neal never acknowledges the comparison verbally, but the consistent imagery creates a lasting connection in the attendees' minds.

Finding high-quality, appropriate stock photos is difficult. You can't just do a Google search for images and use whatever you find: Most of those images fall under copyright protection, and it may be illegal to use them. Be careful about using images from comics, movies, magazines, or public websites.

A good source of photos with fewer restrictions is Flickr. It has a special section for photos licensed under one of the Creative Commons licenses. One of the common variants of this license includes the *attribution* clause. This means that you are free to use the image as long as you provide attribution to the original creator. There is debate within the presenter community as to whether that credit should go alongside the photo or if it's acceptable to put all the photo credits on one slide at the end. We don't like the attribution appearing alongside (or on top of) the photo, no matter how tiny you make the font. It adds needless noise to the presentation. You're trying to get the audience to embrace your narrative, which is harder when orthogonal distractions keep showing up.

We're big fans of stock-photo websites. A few free stock-photo sites exist, such as Morguefile.com. Otherwise, you buy credits on the website, and each image is priced in credits, enabling the site to give volume discounts. The killer feature for a good stock-photo site is its *metadata*—the data the site maintains that enables you to find suitable images. Any photo site lets you to type in *cat* to get cat pictures. You need a site where you can use more abstract search terms, such as *pensive*, and get relevant results. Don't just look at the first page returned by the search; interesting nuanced versions of your query may appear later, giving you a new perspective or appropriate metaphor that you hadn't thought of previously.

The mere fact that a picture appears on the Internet doesn't give you the freedom to use it in your presentation, especially if you are showing it in public. For example, you don't have the rights to use a *Dilbert* strip in your presentation without following the official policy at the *Dilbert* website.[2] If it's an important presentation, spend $2 or $3 and acquire a thematically appropriate image.

An alternative approach for the artistically inclined is to draw your own adornments. A well-known presenter in the technical world draws little stick figures to fill empty places on his slides. The drawings are hardly high-quality, but they are consistent across his presentations, and he can make the drawings match the topic precisely.

This pattern is pervasive in the technical presentations and keynotes given by all three authors. The following are some examples:

1. In Matthew's presentation on the Sonar software-metrics tool, he uses submarines as the visual theme.

2. *Emergent Design* by Neal uses an image series discovered by accident on a stock-photo site. He was looking for a plant in the desert and stumbled upon a series showing a plant breaking through hard soil; the series is shown in Figure 2.6.

   The "sprout in the desert" theme turned out to be perfect for the talk, and Neal even found special thematic uses for the five stock photos that clearly originated from the same photographer.

3. For his *Evolving toward REST-Based Integration* technical presentation, Neal wanted something distinctive as Intermezzi. The gist of the talk was the observation that many organizations "solve" the integration problem in ways that make the problem worse, not better. To contextualize the problem, the presentation goes over how the thinking has evolved over time. Ultimately, the presentation was about using web

Figure 2.6 Stock-photo series used for *Emergent Design* presentation

technologies in a novel way. While searching around for a good metaphor, Neal found a study in which researchers gave spiders various drugs and then had them spin webs, the quality and design of which the researchers then analyzed. This was the perfect metaphor, because it enabled Neal to use the fascinating spider images as a nice break between major topics and also incorporate a little humor. Early in the talk, he makes a joke about how poorly integration within enterprises is typically handled, ending with a reference to "software architects on drugs"—a nice introduction to the "spiders on drugs" theme. When he reaches the ultimate goal of the talk—showing how to do integration in a more sane way—he shows a normal spider web, making the joke that "it's finally time to see what the spiders who aren't stoned do."

Using spiders on drugs as the unifying visual theme serves multiple purposes. First, the spiders gave Neal a chance to have a few interesting Brain Breaks during which he talks about spiders. The break isn't really related to the main theme, but it's interesting and takes up little time. Second, it relates metaphorically to the subject at hand (using web technologies). Third, and most important, the "spiders on drugs" theme enabled Neal to plant a meme with the audience and set up an expectation that "we're going to see lots of drug-influenced spider webs." Saving the *sober* web to introduce the main point of the talk reinforces the fact that this is the important part. Foreshadowing a surprise gives the surprise more impact when you finally spring it.

Related Patterns	A related antipattern is Photomaniac, which hurriedly grabs loosely related photos from the Internet to cover inadequate preparation.

It solidifies your presentation if you can relate the Brain Breaks to your Unifying Visual Theme.

Take the advice of the Defy Defaults pattern and avoid overly clichéd images or clip art.

Pattern: Brain Breaks

Also Known As	Diversions, Rest, Interludes
Definition	Plan a diversion at regular intervals to keep the audience engaged.
Motivation	Research suggests that the average adult attention span is about 20 minutes. Plan something that breaks the concentration coma: humor, a story, something titillating, and so on.

You should strive to make all your presentations entertaining. However, this pattern is particularly important for speaking engagements (such as keynotes) that favor entertainment over information density or for presentations for which attendance (or continued attendance) is optional. This pattern also works well with presentations with high information density, because having a few breaks helps people refocus when the material gets serious again.

Contextualized humor is best. When you address an audience consisting of members or a certain profession or organization, try to tell some jokes that only that specialized group can understand. Inside jokes add to your credibility because they mark *you* as an insider, similarly to the Leet Grammars pattern.

The things that grab people's attention most effectively address the more primitive parts of their psyches. Reliable attention-getters include humor, sex, and gossip. But you should tread very carefully if you plan to use primal triggers as way to maintain attention. It has a tendency to backfire, especially if you don't know the exact composition of the audience. When it does backfire, Brain Breaks become an Alienating Artifact.

Contextualized humor is pure gold because you get to use it for free, as it were. For other types of humor, you sometimes need to wander a bit off the narrative path to get to something funny. With contextualized humor, you don't need to leave the subject at all and can still get a laugh. If you give a presentation more than once, play close attention to where in the presentation you get laughs, be it at planned locations or during spontaneous remarks. Neal keeps the recorder application active on his iPhone so that he can click on it and capture about 20 seconds of the talk, which is enough context to remember what the audience reacted to. We discuss this technique further in the Crucible pattern.

As you build your presentation, be opportunistic about asides and peripherally related content that make good raw material for brain breaks. Sometimes they are unplanned but come up circumstantially as you do the talk. That's a good reason to adhere closely to the Carnegie Hall pattern: If you are well-practiced, you are more likely to notice and incorporate unexpected occurrences.

Brain Breaks have additional importance in more-abstract presentations such as keynotes. When Neal does a keynote at a software industry conference, he tries to find avenues for little inside jokes and word play when he creates the presentation. When the keynote is completed, he goes back and checks to see how regularly humor breaks occur, and sometimes he does some light reorganization to create a more even pace. He checks to make sure something reinvigorating happens at least every 15 minutes, priming the interest pump at regular intervals.

This pattern is best applied after you have finished structuring most of the presentation's narrative flow. It's too difficult to figure out effective pacing to convey your message and get exact intervals for humor and other breaks. Once you have the basic structure in place, opportunistically find places you can insert levity.

Related Patterns   Leet Grammars are ways of interrupting the comfortable flow of pedestrian prose with a word that is unexpected, technical, or uniquely suited to the concept under discussion.

Narrative Arc, like a well-assembled Hollywood movie, provides intentional resolutions, resting points, and crescendos in the storyline at which the audience can silently summarize their observations.

The Entertainment pattern features lots of useful Brain Breaks.

Developer Dave's Surefire Crowd Pleaser

Note: Most of our stories are at least partially fictional, but this one is, unfortunately, based on real-life incidents encapsulated here.

Developer Dave's dream just materialized in his inbox: the acceptance notification to speak at the Big Tech Conference! Dave knows that his technology is good (his topic was chosen, after all), but he really wants to make a splash with his presentation. Some parts of the presentation drag a bit, because he must discuss a lot of context to get to the really cool parts. But if he can't get the crowd to pay attention during the boring parts, they won't be attentive during the impressive portions.

One tried-and-true way to keep people's attention is to surprise them regularly with something shocking or edgy. Dave decides to create a visual theme for his talk using scantily clad women in seductive poses and call it something like "Programmer Pr0n."

His plan backfires. No one at the conference is talking about Dave's technology. All they are talking about is his shockingly bad taste.

Antipattern: Alienating Artifact

Also Known As   Cursing, Swearing, Offensive Pictures, Insensitive Jokes

Definition   An Alienating Artifact uses some device (pictures, sounds, even allusions) to refer to something risqué as an attention or laugh generator. However, many times those devices alienate some segment of the audience, negating any other perceived benefit.

Motivation   Creating interesting presentations is hard, especially if you have dull subject matter and an immediately-after-lunch presentation slot.

A time-tested way to get people's attention is to shock them with language or imagery inappropriate for the context. Some presenters feel that it conveys a sense of insouciance and rebellion and helps ingratiate them with a certain clique. However, by purposely seeking inclusion in one group, you hazard inadvertently excluding other groups, including such traditional targets of casual discrimination such as women and minorities.

Applicability/Consequences   This device can be deployed in particularly dry sections of the talk or in particular deliveries of the talk to stoic audiences. If used sparsely, it makes one part of a presentation stand out as particularly emphatic, important, or memorable—but beware the consequences!

Chances are very good that you will alienate a portion of your audience if you use this antipattern.

> Profanity and obscenity entitle people who don't want unpleasant information to close their ears and eyes to you.
>
> —Kurt Vonnegut, through the narrator of *Hocus Pocus*

Mechanics   If you want to implement this antipattern, drop a bad word in an unexpected place. Use an inappropriate or shocking image.

Even language can be tricky. If you are going to curse, know your audience well and know how it will be received. If you have any doubts, don't. Some outstanding speakers inadvertently alienate a portion of their audience through language and innuendo.

Presenters sometimes use alienating artifacts as a credentialing device and to ingratiate themselves to the crowd by displaying hipness. However, for everyone you attract using this technique, you alienate others. Balance this carefully; alienating someone for trivial reasons obviates the entire purpose of your talk, whereas using a less offensive alternative offends no one.

Err on the side of displaying professionalism, intelligence, and passion within a conservative estimate of the tolerance of your audience. The downside of using caution is an order of magnitude smaller than the risk of being reckless. Leave the audience remembering the talk's content and your sharp delivery, not some gaffe or offensive point. Be inspiring and reinviteable above all.

Known Uses   In the advertising space, United Colors of Benetton shocked the world[3] with its strange imagery in its 1980s campaign. It is generally recognized that the effort[4] got Benetton press, but not the kind that increases sales or respect for the brand.

The less homogenized the audience, the more likely the chance of offending someone. This came to light during a keynote speech at a large technology conference in Ohio, where the opening keynoter, a well-known technology pundit, shocked some in the crowd with his repeated profanity and irreverence. Those who knew the speaker's reputation thought it provided an eye-opening perspective, but many audience members were so offended by the incidental parts of the keynote, they could not pay attention to the actual message.

We'll allow Venkat Subramaniam, a well-known speaker in the technical world, to sum up our feelings:

> If you think you need to curse to warm up the crowd, then (a) you need to grow up and learn something about giving exceptional presentations and (b) you're assuming your audience is feeble.
>
> When you have an audience, pure strangers in front of you, you need to be aware of the diversity of the audience, in terms of gender, culture, etc. What some speakers often do is pull a "do they have that in your city?" but not realize it, or worse, feel completely comfortable saying it.
>
> Ask yourself, what can you say that is profound, something humorous that can draw them in, catch their attention. And don't confuse vulgarity with these. Now go become an exceptional presenter my friend.
>
> —Venkat Subramaniam

Related Patterns If you Know Your Audience and are in tune with their demographics, personalities, and career situation, you will be unlikely to implement an unintentional Alienating Artifact.

Shock and Awe

An accomplished speaker, Tom often gave keynote addresses at technical conferences. Once, watching the introduction to a conference, Tom sensed a sleepy crowd and decided to use a little shock and awe to wake them up. He dove into his presentation, layering in plenty of salty language and a few religious references for good measure.

From his point of view, Tom had done what was asked of him: He started the show off with a bang. However, he went too far. Some attendees walked out, and a few choice comments showed up on various social networks. Some called for a public apology by the organizers. Tom generated buzz all right, but at what cost? Is swearing ever acceptable in a talk?

Certain radio personalities are popular because they're not afraid to jolt their audience. Tawdry tales and language that would make a dead man blush may make for great ratings, but they can sink a talk. We aren't saying that you need to walk on eggshells or refrain from any cursing, but don't go overboard. Think about cooking: A little bit of spice makes a dish pop, but add too much and it's all you can taste. An occasional salty word can get attention, but people should leave your talk discussing your ideas, not your language.

This advice goes double for keynotes. It's one thing to drop an F-bomb in a breakout room with 25 people, but when all eyes are on you, tread lightly. Tom went overboard, and the lifeline was clearly behind him. He'll be remembered, but will he be invited back? Probably not, and it's possible he's damaged his reputation. Word gets around, and Tom might have difficulty getting his talks accepted in the future.

Similar advice holds for risqué imagery. We strongly urge restraint. A technical talk at a Bay Area conference became widely known not for its content but for the ill-considered choice of pictures and the use of sexual innuendo. You may think any press is good press, but that wasn't true in this case. The talk did ignite a conversation, but we doubt it was the one the speaker intended. The conference organizer issued an apology.

¶¶ Antipattern: Celery

Also Known As   All Fluff No Stuff

Definition   A celery presentation is one that—like the vegetable, allegedly—burns more calories in consumption than it provides in usable energy. A celery presentation takes more effort for the audience to attend than they get out of it.

Motivation   You don't generally set about to produce a celery presentation. *It just happens.*

Applicability/ Consequences   Many situations generate this antipattern, including the following:

1. A Required presentation. You've been assigned a presentation on a subject that either don't know well or is inherently boring. In this case, you have to *find* something worth talking about or rely heavily on enhancements like Narrative Arc and Brain Breaks.

2. Misjudged audience sophistication level. If you find yourself doing a presentation on basic suture technique to a convention of expert heart surgeons, it doesn't matter how accurate or entertaining you are: You are presenting a celery talk. The best defense against this situation is to Know Your Audience.

3. Due date. This happens a lot in business scenarios. The schedule shows that you are due to give a progress meeting or update, which implies that you have something interesting to say.

The result of a celery presentation is an audience consensus of "well, that's an hour of my life I'll never get back." As an audience member, you realize you've stumbled into a celery presentation when you can't seem to find a comfortable position in your chair, or you're pretty sure the clock has started moving backward.

Mechanics   A celery presentation typically doesn't have a compelling Narrative Arc or other niceties such as Brain Breaks. Without a compelling story, premise, or motivation, you'll put your effort into making the surface shiny and consistent, just like the eponymous vegetable. It will mostly be filled with tasteless water, but it won't be outright offensive.

The best defense against falling into this antipattern is to Know Your Audience. Ultimately, you must make sure that they derive value.

If a meeting is scheduled that includes a status presentation and nothing interesting has happened, you may find yourself contemplating a Celery presentation. In this case, replace the low quality to time ratio activity of recapping facts everyone already knows and shake up the meeting with a higher value activity or cancel the meeting entirely.

If you find yourself in giving a Celery presentation, don't "solve" the problem by speeding through your material as fast as possible, which is the Disowning Your Topic antipattern. You're still better off doing the presentation as planned and hoping that some members of the audience learn something. It is a certainty that you won't make the presentation more nutritional by speeding through it, and the few people who might have learned something cannot because of the artificial pace. Alternatively, if the audience expectation is too far askew, cancel the presentation.

Known Uses   Most marketing presentations can tip toward being an implementation of the celery antipattern, especially if they rehash information that's available elsewhere. They really don't contain much of use for the audience members, even if they are keenly interested in the product. This mismatch is a true shame, because if the audience is interested, the first element of a successful presentation is being handed to the presenter on a silver platter.

Technical presentations are also highly at risk for being celery-like. The more technical the topic, the more easily the presenter can cover lack of useful information with attitude, animation, and a general sheen and polish to the delivery. The researchers in the now-famous *Dr. Fox effect* noted that "Fox's nonverbal behaviors so completely masked a meaningless, jargon-filled, and confused presentation."

Related Patterns   One way to deliver a Celery presentation inadvertently is by falling prey to the Disowning Your Topic antipattern: You fear that the audience already knows the subject, so you give a halfhearted presentation.

Pattern: Leet Grammars

Also Known As   Slang, Jargon, Eleet, Leetspeak

Definition   A *leet grammar* is an alternative alphabet (and grammar) for the English language that started via text messages and online game forums and has expanded to encompass highly contextualized slang. Using a leet grammar in your presentation helps you control your audience's perception of you.

Motivation   Unless your presentation is believable, its message will fall on deaf ears. Some communities and groups distrust people whom they perceive as outsiders. Using *their* language correctly helps you gain their trust by letting them see you as a peer.

Applicability/ Consequences   This pattern is highly applicable any time you speak to a group or community with highly technical or stylized jargon. It can also be used to deflate the formality of a presentation. For example, Lawrence Lessig uses the Takahashi format combined with Leet Grammars to nuance his material.

Using an appropriate leet grammar enables you to convey information and nuance in a concise way. The converse is also true: Using a leet grammar incorrectly is the best way to lose your audience irrevocably. Even making improper cultural or literacy references in the wrong context can hurt your credibility. At a popular developers conference called Strange Loop, which attracts lots of advanced developers (stereotypical geeks), one of the keynote speakers incorrectly attributed the quote "With great power comes great responsibility" to Yoda from *Star Wars*, not to Spiderman's Uncle Ben. He hurt the effectiveness of his entire presentation because of a seemingly trivial mistake.

If you use this pattern for slang rather than for technical jargon, commit fully to it. For example, don't use *l8r* in some places and *later* in others. If you commit to something as stylized as this as a presentation theme, embrace it. Otherwise, it looks like you couldn't decide or weren't brave enough to go all the way.

Related Patterns   The Analog Noise pattern also adds flavor by ostensibly breaking rules, using rough, hand-drawn lines.

Pattern: Lightning Talk

Also Known As	Flash, Ignite, Pecha Kucha

Definition

A presentation category characterized by fixed time limits and/or fixed numbers of slides, generally very short in duration and frequently performed in a sporting event-like atmosphere.

Motivation

Breaking the normal conventions of presentations allows for innovative creativity. By creating specific constraints that everyone must adhere to, these styles attempt to elevate presentations to an art form.

Applicability/ Consequences

Only certain topics can reasonably be done in Lightning Talk style. To be implemented beautifully, it requires a cohesive Narrative Arc and a willingness on the speaker's part to do extensive preparation in both crafting and practicing the talk. Timing is critical to creating the desired effect, so you must memorize all the material and never look at the slides for reference.

Applying the Carnegie Hall pattern is critical; you have no time for mistakes in a fast format. However, these presentations are usually only five minutes in length, so you can practice it more conveniently.

Mechanics

Assembly of a Lightning Talk presentation requires two to four rounds of authoring, reviewing, revising, and practicing. When creating a Lightning Talk talk, continue to follow the guidelines laid out in the Fourthought pattern: *ideate*, *capture*, *organize*, and *design*. However, the organization step becomes more complex when you have strict limits on number of slides and time.

Don't be afraid to gently Defy Defaults in these formats. For example, perhaps you are preparing a presentation for which you are allowed only 20 slides, but you want to talk about one subject for several slides' worth. It isn't against the rules to leave the same image in place for multiple slides with no slide transition, which creates the appearance of a single slide for longer than the allowed time.

Known Uses

Ignite presentations[5] are a branded form of this pattern—a structure derived from Pecha Kucha, a flavor of Lightning Talk talks, branded by O'Reilly Media and given the slightly shorter timing of 20 slides at 15 seconds apiece.

Damian Conway, famous in programming circles for his contributions to the Perl language, delivered an Ignite presentation at OSCON 2011 set to music. He showed precisely 20 slides, thereby conforming to the required format. However, he presented more than 300 images on those 20 slides. As a footnote to his presentation, he showed the design mode of the presentation tool to confirm to the audience that he had followed the rules but broken the form to make the presentation more interesting—a great example of the Defy Defaults pattern.

Related Patterns   A Lightning Talk makes a good building block component of a Talklet presentation; you can use several 5-minute talks to assemble a 20-minute Talklet.

Takahashi, Lessig, and Saying More with Less

Masayoshi Takahashi developed a distinctive presentation style using a single Japanese ideogram per slide. This works particularly well in Japanese because each "word" character carries not only the word's meaning but also rich connotation, enabling the presenter to add nuance without adding more stuff. We've broadened this style into the Takahashi pattern.

Lawrence Lessig popularized the Takahashi presentation style in the West using English. Although the layering of meaning isn't quite as compelling in English, the style is still quite distinctive: Hundreds of slides, each with a single word or short phrase, are delivered at a shotgun pace (typically a slide every few seconds). One of the ways that Lessig frequently adds nuance is through the heavy use of Leet Grammars (such as *l8r* for *later* or *pwnage* to signify crushing defeat), which adds back some of the connotation missing from the symbolic English language. If your audience knows the grammar, it carries significant connotation with it, enabling you to add nuance to your message without adding more words. He also uses the Analog Noise pattern to give his presentations a less formal feel.

 # Pattern: Takahashi

Also Known As   Lessig

Definition   A stylized talk format originated by Masayoshi Takahashi (and popularized in the West by Laurence Lessig) that uses extremely minimal verbiage or imagery on each slide and transitions through them very quickly.

Motivation   The Takahashi style is quite distinctive, so it works well in environments where you want to deliver a nontraditional presentation. This style is often used for keynotes, where a machine-gun-like delivery adds palpable energy to the talk.

Applicability/
Consequences   The Takahashi style works with virtually any type of presentation. For presentations with deep technical content, this style will likely be relegated to

the slides in between intensely detailed slides, which has the added benefit of forcing a change of pace between sections, offering a form of Brain Breaks.

Mechanics   To build a Takahashi-style presentation, you just need lots of slides! For each slide, place one element: a word, a few words, a photograph, a line drawing, and so on. The goal of this style is to show each slide for only a few seconds; you are trying to reveal your thoughts in the smallest possible increments.

Known Uses   Presentations by Lawrence Lessig are the classic examples of this pattern.

Related Patterns   Switching paces during your presentation is a nice implementation of the Brain Breaks pattern; using the Takahashi for a portion of your presentation is a great pace change.

Nathaniel's Taken with Takahashi

Nathaniel here. If you've ever seen one of my presentations, you know I'm a fan of the Takahashi pattern. I didn't always use that style; in fact, the slides for my first few presentations heavily featured the Bullet-Riddled Corpse antipattern. But then I watched a recording of one of Lawrence Lessig's presentations and I was hooked; the delivery, the tone, and the vibe all resonated deeply. Over the years, I've adopted his style as my own.

Even if you think this method might fit you like a glove, know that its use has consequences. First, you will have *a lot* of slides; it isn't uncommon for me to have 350 for a 90-minute presentation. More than a handful of reviews have commented on my presentations' high slide volume, and many other speakers were skeptical that I could get through them all when I told them how many slides my typical deck contains. I've also been accused of hating trees, because when my decks are printed, they're considerably longer than a "normal" presentation handout. That's rarely an issue *during* a presentation, but attendees who read along will likely notice the slide count, especially if you include slide numbers.

The Takahashi pattern is visually distinctive. Although this helps your presentation stand out in a crowd of clip art, you'll be surprised at how discomforting it can be to people accustomed to bullet-point extravaganzas. More and more speakers are adopting aspects of the Takahashi approach, making it more common at conferences. But the corporate world continues to believe that every presentation is made better with more bullets. Ultimately, a business-oriented presentation will most often be an Infodeck. My slides do not make for a particularly useful take-away artifact. But given the choice, I'll optimize for the live presentation.

Several years and a couple of employers ago, I built a presentation to teach software developers about testing. My slide deck used the Takahashi pattern, and I put together a lengthy document to support people who couldn't attend in person or wanted to review the material later. I was pretty proud of what I'd written; it was clear and concise and told the story of the presentation *in prose*.

Before I left the company, I was asked to "modify" my presentation because one person said that no one else could present that deck. I agreed, but I pointed out that whoever would own that class after I left would modify the slides to suit their own style. But my 15-page document and the existing slides weren't enough; I was asked to create a more "traditional" slide deck that my successor could use. So I did. It was the last time I ever created a Bullet-Riddled Corpse.

Pattern: Cave Painting

Also Known As Prezi (a popular tool that implements this pattern)

Definition Cave Painting is a slide-layout and presentation technique that uses a huge sectioned canvas with your presentation laid out linearly. You zoom in and out on the constituent sections as you proceed through your presentation.

Motivation A long, boring sequence of slides doesn't cut it sometimes. Cave Painting adds visual and organizational interest.

Applicability/ Consequences This pattern works well for fractal subject matters: The overall visual layout of the subject makes sense, and each subtopic also makes sense as you zoom in and out. It also works particularly well for origin stories: how this product came to be, where this idea came from, and so on.

This technique is particularly good in conjunction with the Lipsync pattern and other demonstration techniques because it keeps the overall context and goals visible during transitions between steps.

Cave Painting is a specialized version of the Context Keeper pattern: By zooming in and out of subjects, it keeps the overall context in the audience's mind while zooming in on particulars.

Believe it or not, motion sickness is a legitimate concern with the pattern, particularly with some implementations. Some people react negatively to the rapid zooming visualization that some tools use. Make sure your subject layout doesn't encourage the tool to make lots of big moves and zooms or else you'll need to pass out motion-sickness bags with your talk.

Don't try to use this pattern solely to tame a big, unruly subject. This technique doesn't scale upward in information density very well; the visual metaphors break down, and you are left with a lot of distracting, visually noisy, seemingly random movement.

Mechanics   Several commercial tools heavily favor this pattern, and add-ons are available for Keynote and PowerPoint that give you some of the same effect. However, you can implement this pattern easily and effectively without a specialized tool.

Storytelling is the primary purpose of the Cave Painting style. To implement it, you treat slides as a canvas on which the story slowly unfolds. Soft Transitions work well here because you want to hide the boundary between slides, letting the unfolding story drive the narrative.

Figure 2.7 shows an example from one of Neal's technical talks. In it, he must explain a lengthy set of steps showing how a particular problem arose and was handled by two developers interacting through a tool named Git.

In Figure 2.7, you see all the animations and transitions for four slides. The slide boundaries appear as the colored boxes. Each slide builds on the last.

One way to implement this pattern is to use only one slide and layer all your content on it. Unfortunately, layering elements is difficult, so you are better off constructing it over a series of slides. To make the transitions seamless, use Soft Transitions, and construct each slide so that the starting point for each slide is identical to the preceding slide.

Specialized tools make this pattern look nice because they handle the transition between slides with nice animations and elements that extend across multiple slides. You can replicate some of this effect with Keynote's *magic move* transition, which smoothly animates moving elements from their position on the current slide to their position on the next slide. Using graphic elements that "hang off" one slide "onto" another,

Figure 2.7 Representation of a Cave Painting demonstration showing a lengthy set of steps

then using transitions that move in that direction, you can create the illusion of continuity between slides. Consider the example in Figure 2.8, which shows two slides laid out to look like they are part of a larger canvas.

For more on implementing this pattern using standard tools, refer to the Context Keeper pattern, which shows variations on this same exposition technique.

Related Patterns This pattern is really a specialized version of the Context Keeper pattern, using the narrative you're relating as the context-preserving device.

If you want to use pacing as a form of Brain Breaks, you can alternate Cave Painting with Takahashi, creating two vastly different paces.

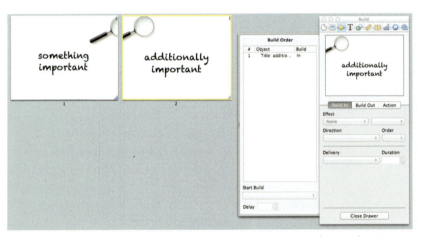

Figure 2.8 Cave Painting implemented in Keynote

PART II
BUILD

THIS PART OF *PRESENTATION PATTERNS AND ANTIPATTERNS* focuses on how to leverage slides to convey your presentation's content effectively. Modern presentation tools come with a multitude of templates and wizards, useful as jumping-off points. But what's easy is sometimes not what's best. When we create patterns, we focus on effectiveness first, then reverse-engineer ways to use tools to produce the desired effect.

Slide Construction Patterns cover a host of antipatterns to help you avoid traps laid out by modern presentation tools. It also discusses a number of patterns (including hands-on techniques) to help you build better slides.

Temporal Patterns cover the unique aspect that sets a presentation apart from an Infodeck: time. This chapter shows how to build presentations that work well when presented *and* printed, how to carry context across multiple slides, and a variety of other useful techniques.

The Demonstrations versus Presentations chapter explains the important distinction between a demonstration *of* something and a presentation *about* something, helps you decide which you should use, and offers a host of patterns and antipatterns to help you make either one more effective.

CHAPTER 3

SLIDE CONSTRUCTION PATTERNS

FOR ALL YOU PRESENTATION JUNKIES, THIS IS THE PART you've been waiting for! In this chapter, we delve into concrete techniques for building presentations. We discuss how to structure your presentation for maximum effect with patterns like Á la Carte Content and Foreshadowing, how to add visual punch for emphasis using patterns like Greek Chorus and Analog Noise, and how to avoid common traps like Ant Fonts and Injured Outlines.

The focus of this chapter is on *building slides*, so let's get started.

Antipattern: Cookie Cutter

Also Known As   One Size Fits All

Definition   The amount of information that will fit on a single slide is dictated by presentation tool vendors; it is not a reflection of the topic you're presenting. Trying to massage your content so that it will fit on single slide damages the narrative of your presentation.

Motivation   Copyeditors for magazines hate seeing blank space, so they are relentless in trying to find ways to fill it. This dislike of blankness has somehow migrated over to presentations. Lots of presentations cram too much related information on one slide, trying to make it fit by eliminating useful information while making up (generally insipid) content to flesh out slides that don't seem to have enough.

Applicability/ Consequences   The *slide* is the unit of creativity in presentation tools, making it seem natural that one idea should fit onto one slide. When you start *trying* to fill excess space on slides or eliminating information that you originally wanted to include because it won't fit on a slide, you're allowing the medium to alter the message. Don't fall for the feast-or-famine approach that is the path of least resistance in presentation tools. In fact, many of the tools include features that make this tendency worse. For example, PowerPoint has a feature that automatically shrinks the font size of the preceding bullets to make it easy to cram even more bullets on a slide. Slides don't cost any extra for as many as you want. Use them all.

Mechanics   The Cookie Cutter antipattern is an easy but avoidable trap. Get away from the idea that every slide must be complete. Paragraphs in written works have various lengths, suited to the subject matter. Think hard about the *idea* you want to convey and then think about the most concise way to convey that idea using a combination of your words and the visual presentation channel.

One way to avoid this antipattern is to "hide" the fact that you are transitioning slides. One common technique, covered in the Soft Transitions pattern, uses a slide transition such as *dissolve*, allowing the presenter—not the tool—to define the idea boundaries.

Here is an example of using Soft Transitions to carry an idea over multiple slides. Set the transition for each slide set to *dissolve*, and always put *entrance* animations on your slides. The overall effect is a seamless flow between ideas. Because everything fades in and out, viewers can't discern where slides begin and end.

Consider the slides in Figure 3.1 and Figure 3.2. The two slides together make an important point. All the slides in this presentation use the *dissolve* transition, so each slide seems to fade away before the first elements animate in on the subsequent slide. The audience becomes accustomed to this flow. However, to extend an idea over multiple slides, keep the slide transition (*dissolve*), but don't provide an *appearance* animation for the title on the second slide. As you can see in Figure 3.1, the title is set to animate in with a *dissolve* effect, and the slide is set to use a *dissolve* transition.

In Figure 3.2, the title has no *build in* animation, so it will already be on the slide when it appears.

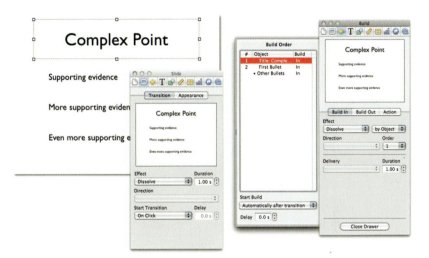

Figure 3.1 Two slides that contain one continued idea

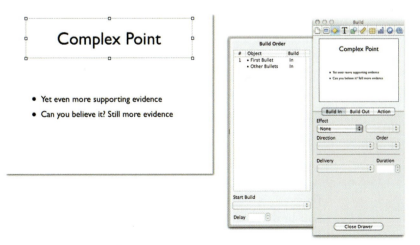

Figure 3.2 Second slide, continuing the idea by retaining the title

An effect of using both transitions and animations is that the first slide appears with its title and then, when the slide transition occurs, the title "stays" in place. It doesn't fade away like the rest of the slide body, helping you to continue making your point.

Related Patterns The Soft Transitions pattern is a good solution to the Cookie Cutter anti-pattern; it encourages you to build your ideas across many slides, hiding individual slide transitions from users.

♫ Pattern: Coda

Also Known As Reference, Citations, Further Reading, Epilogue, Outtro, Shed

Definition At the end of your slide deck (and without discussing them in your live delivery), provide a list of further reading or materials that were too lengthy to cover in the body of the talk.

Motivation When you want to give your audience a set of further reading materials, the Coda is the perfect place to store them. Less experienced presenters frequently place them within the core materials of the slide deck. But just as in a book, too many sidebars or copious inline details break the flow of the presentation's Narrative Arc. By leveraging the Coda pattern, you can give audience members a collated set of the materials you used to research the presentation but without the mental or visual distraction of embedding them in the presentation's core flow.

Applicability/ Consequences Almost any presentation that has significant research behind it, industry cross-references, or deeper-reading suggestions can benefit from a Coda. It is frequently a well-respected place to put more structured materials, even if your core presentation mostly consists of the Vacation Photos pattern. A Coda makes it easier for attendees to cross-check facts and ask detailed follow-up questions by e-mail if you give them the necessary links to perform such self-study.

The addition of a Coda can require more accuracy and preparation effort on your part.

Mechanics A Coda can take many forms. It often has a flavor somewhat different from the core presentation. Bullets are more acceptable in a Coda, and artistic flair in the Coda slides isn't expected. Generally, Codas take the form of a bibliography, though they need not be bound to any particular prescriptive citation style.

Known Uses   All three authors have a standard Coda slide template they place at the end of every talk. It's beneficial to include hints, references, and teasers in your presentation and help the audience to learn more about the subject you care so much about.

Related Patterns   An Infodeck often consists primarily of outlines and bulleted lists about a subject. Including a Coda with references for further reading allows the audience to dig deeper on subjects you gloss during the body of the slide deck.

Talks implementing the Vacation Photos pattern use stories atop themed photos. If the stories convey information that you want the audience to dig into more deeply, a Coda makes it easy for them.

Antipattern: Injured Outlines

Also Known As   Orphaned Outlines, Broken Outlines

Definition   Slides frequently show text as bulleted lists, which is formally an outline. Outlines have specific rules, which presentation creators usually abuse.

Motivation   When you consult a grammar text, you'll see that outlines should have the following characteristics:

- Subdivide topics by a system of numbers and letters, followed by a period.
- *Each heading and subheading must have at least two parts.*
- Be consistent. Use either whole sentences of brief phrases, but not both.

We've highlighted the second item because it's the one most abused in presentations. Presentation tools force you to mash your ideas into outlines (see the Cookie Cutter antipattern for more about that), so you should at least try to create *correct* outlines.

This isn't just grammatical nit-picking. The rules for outlines were developed for a reason. If you have a heading that has only one subheading, then the information in the subheading should just be the heading. Outlines (or slides) that don't follow these simple rules suggest that your thinking might need refinement.

Applicability/   This antipattern applies to any slide deck that shows outlines of informa-
Consequences   tion, including any presentation with bulleted lists or Infodeck.

Creating presentations that feature lots of broken outlines is common when you do too little prethought before moving to the presentation tool, as discussed in Thinking Is Not Designing. Unfortunately, in their quest to be helpful, both Keynote and PowerPoint make it trivially easy to create broken outlines. Many of the core content slides in their default templates automatically create bulleted lists for you.

When thinking about your topics, stay away from the presentation tool. You benefit more by using alternate tools to refine your thoughts, then moving to the presentation tool. Make sure that you know what information you are trying to convey, and plan your points accordingly. If you find yourself tempted into creating a slide with a title and a single bullet point, why not just make the title your main point and enlarge it in the center of the slide?

After you have completed your first draft, review it, concentrating on the clarity of the ideas. If you see orphaned outline items, either find a way to resolve them or consciously break the outline rule for effect.

Virtually every corporate slide deck in the world uses this antipattern.

The Cookie Cutter antipattern solution tries to lead you away from the Injured Outlines antipattern by discouraging you from using outlines at all.

The Fourthought pattern suggests that if you have fully considered your topic, you won't have incomplete outlines.

A Bullet-Riddled Corpse frequently features Injured Outlines; if your primary communication medium is bullets, you'll eventually create improper outlines with them as you mold them into more and more tortured narratives.

Pattern: Peer Review

Revisions, Copyediting, Drafts, Textual Healing, Passive Voice, Sentences on Slides

Text that seems great in the author's eyes can still benefit from a review by a literate colleague or a competent editor. A bit of review and editing can often eliminate or at least minimize spelling errors, grammatical mistakes, and unclear verbiage. Use a sparse, terse, clear, grammatically correct, suitably objective writing style when putting words on a slide.

Violating grammatical rules on presentation slides is clearly bad. But almost as bad are violations of seemingly nitpicky grammatical guidelines, such as avoiding use of passive voice. The wrong style of language can work against your goals in a presentation. For example, if you are trying to show your credibility and you have a serious, albeit common, grammatical error on a slide, can that possibly help your case?

All authors should strive for as clear a message as possible. Your message as a presenter directly depends on your choice of words. Investing in the accuracy and clarity of those words has a positive effect on the perceived value of your message and enhances its impact on your audience. Paying attention to this level of detail is what sets adequate and good presentations apart from great ones. Even if everyone doesn't notice every detail, the cumulative effect of your attention to detail will shine through. Someone will notice even the smallest detail.

Applicability/
Consequences

This pattern applies to every presentation, always. Poor grammar, inappropriate slang, and inconsistency will never enhance the perception of your presentation.

It's difficult to overestimate how much the words you use to frame your message can affect the perception of the company, product, technology, or process associated with your presentation. Every spelling mistake dents the credibility of the message, and every misused word communicates a front of "trying to impress" and lacking mastery of vocabulary. You reap extra benefits when you hone your words to be as sharp as possible because your audience appreciates the effort you've put into crafting a polished, clear message.

Mechanics

A common failing is placing complete sentences on slides. Unless it's a direct quote, the slide should summarize your thoughts. If you place complete sentences on your slides, you encourage the audience to read it rather than listen to you. Don't put complete sentences on your slides. It's an indicator that you're using the wrong communication medium. Perhaps you are creating an Infodeck when you should be creating a presentation.

Another common mistake is the use of *passive voice*. You're using passive voice when you make the object of an action into the subject of a sentence or phrase. This classic example converts the setup of a well-known joke to passive voice: *Why was the road crossed by the chicken?*

English teachers, grammar checkers, and copyeditors universally loathe passive voice—not only because it tends to sound awkward but also because passive construction often omits who or what is performing the action. That lack of precision makes the message weak at best and confusing at worst. For example, consider this comparison. First, the passive version:

Original files deleted

Now the active version:

Script deletes original files

The first version hides the fact that a script is doing the deleting. Without this information, the reader is left to conjecture (or to have to ask) who or what does the deleting. Passive voice makes you sound less sure of your expertise and of the presentation as a whole.

The one obvious time to use passive voice aggressively is when you *do* want to obscure the entity that's responsible for an action. Perhaps you can make use of this famous passive statement:

Mistakes were made.

You can employ several steps to polish your words. Each is progressively more expensive in time, and potentially in terms of hard cash. Proceed as far along this path as the situation calls for and the budget allows.

1. Use an authoring tool to spell-check and grammar-check your content. In this era of word processing and 100,000-word dictionaries, you have no excuse for misspellings. Experienced authors use a presentation-building checklist that reminds them to run spell-check manually after all authoring is complete. Add correctly spelled and cased technical terms, company names, acronyms, and other industry jargon to the authoring tool's or your operating system's custom dictionary.

2. Read what you've written *out loud*, even if it feels silly. Your brain sees what it wants to see, and this simple step catches those pesky typo-class mistakes. We guarantee you'll find some.

3. Have a friend or colleague who has a sharp eye for grammar and clear wording do a quick review of the presentation materials. A second set of eyes reading the materials for the first time often catches mistakes that your familiarity with your material prevents you from seeing. You generally shouldn't have complete sentences on a slide anyway, but you still must ensure basic rules like subject/verb agreement.

4. If your company has a documentation team or marketing department, both are usually quite willing, given sufficient advance notice, to review your materials to help put both your presentation and the company in the best possible light.

5. Hiring a professional copyeditor by the hour or by the project is not nearly as expensive or pretentious as it might sound. A first-rate copyeditor with whom you form a professional relationship over multiple projects can be your secret to rising above the fray at conferences, conventions, and other venues that have a wide range of presenter skills on display. A copyeditor will improve your choice of words, sentence arrangement, and ultimately the clarity of the entire message—but you will still sound like yourself. We've seen even inexperienced presenters receive hallway accolades for the clarity of their words—words that,

unbeknownst to the audience, were significantly improved by a technical editor who reviewed three drafts of the presentation narrative. The ease with which files can be shared over the Internet has flattened the global marketplace for copyediting skills. A friend's recommendation is usually best, but a simple web search will turn up service offerings fitting the most modest to the most flush of editing budgets.

Known Uses Behind almost every stirring presentation of great consequence is great copyediting. C-level executives have most of their public presentations reviewed and wordsmithed by a competent editor. A growing number of presenters are beginning to use copyeditors—either friends or a paid professionals. (Strategic presenters see this as a competitive advantage, so you might not hear it spoken of frequently in the break room or at the office.)

Related Patterns The Leet Grammars pattern suggests playing with grammar rules in a stylized way to help bond with your audience.

The Tower of Babble antipattern admonishes against too much opaque technical jargon.

Pattern: Foreshadowing

Also Known As Building toward a Final Effect

Definition Place little clues within your presentation that lead to a later revelation, either large or small.

Motivation Presentations are storytelling, and everyone likes surprises or hidden insights in the stories they read or hear. Foreshadowing is a literary device that places small, subtle clues in prose to suggest or highlight something that will happen later. It serves the same purpose in a presentation: You can add nuance and depth of meaning to your subject by leading your audience toward a shared epiphany.

Applicability/ Consequences This pattern works hand-in-hand with Narrative Arc because you can place clues about your overall story during the presentation. Other times, little foreshadowings appear to solidify your case, but not as the main thrust of the argument. Foreshadowing should be your goal for all presentations, although sometimes it's tough to find the right mechanism.

Mechanics The mechanics of this pattern have more to do with how you construct the presentation than with a particular tool. Find (sometimes peripherally) related items that amplify or nuance a point, and scatter them in subtle ways throughout. Ideally, you have either a major point you want to make or a subtle nuance to add to an existing point. Good foreshadowings "tickle" your audiences that something of importance is coming in a subtle way.

Foreshadowing can be explicit or implicit. Explicit foreshadowing places literal placeholders in your presentation to notify your audience that something interesting is coming later. (This is different from an agenda, which reflects the overall structure of the talk.) When you foreshadow something, you are in a context in which your audience understands that a related topic will appear but that now's not the right time in the general narrative arc to cover it.

Be careful: This technique is easy to overuse. Choose one or at most two anchor points for amplifying your message, and provide clues for them. Make sure that the clues have a strong metaphorical connection to the thing you're foreshadowing. Symbolism that confuses the audience has the opposite of the desired effect. Ideally, when you finally show the audience what you've been building toward, a sense of climax or epiphany occurs.

For example, in Neal's *Test-Driven Design* talk, he compares the metrics of two competing implementations of a solution, one of which, not surprisingly, comes out better. However, Neal knows that many attendees will immediately wonder, "OK, I can see your point for a tiny, trivial example, but can this scale to larger code bases?" Anticipating that question, he has a case study that illustrates that the technique he's discussing does scale nicely. But the case study also illustrates and summarizes a bunch of other things, some of which Neal hasn't covered yet. From a Narrative Arc standpoint, the case study belongs at the end. But Neal doesn't want to let the scalability question simmer for another 20 minutes until he presents the case study, so at the appropriate spot he shows the slide shown in Figure 3.3.

Known Uses   One of Neal's favorite techniques is to bring up an apparently irrelevant topic early in the presentation and then either ignore it or mention it again only in passing until the end of the presentation. Then that seemingly unrelated reference is suddenly revealed to be related in an unexpected way and provides deeper insight into the subject. The longer you can wait between foreshadowing something and revealing it, the bigger the impact because you give people longer to forget.

Rails in the Large, one of Neal's technical presentations, is a case study about a project he participated in for his employer, ThoughtWorks. One of the subtle messages he wants to convey in the presentation is that ThoughtWorks projects try as much as possible to infuse fun into the workplace. Throughout the presentation, he uses stock photos featuring a rock, paper, and scissors for his Intermezzi—with no explanation. The talk's very

> # are these numbers sustainable for a large project?
>
> **stay tuned!**

Figure 3.3 Foreshadowing an upcoming case study

last section is titled "Why all the RPS Stuff?" He goes on to talk about a particular unpleasant chore on the project and the fact that assignments are frequently made via a contest of Rock, Paper, Scissors (RPS). He goes on to say that all unimportant and some important issues at ThoughtWorks are handled by RPS, helping convey the overall message that ThoughtWorks doesn't take projects too seriously. The Foreshadowing created a little useful tension in the audience—they kept wondering how RPS was related to the overall subject because those slides kept appearing every ten minutes or so—and enabled Neal to make a strong case for one of the subtle points he wanted the presentation to convey.

Related Patterns It's easy to set up narrative effects like Foreshadowing if you have a strong Narrative Arc.

Antipattern: Bullet-Riddled Corpse

Also Known As Death by Bullet Points

Definition A Bullet-Riddled Corpse is a slide that prominently uses bullet points and more bullet points, sometimes in columns. In many cases, the slides are little more than speaker's notes. They're word-heavy and surprisingly comforting in their familiarity to both presenters and audiences only because of their pervasiveness.

Often the default slide style for many presentation templates, bullet points are de rigueur in most presentations. Inexperienced speakers rely on bullet points as presenter's notes. Less preparation may be required because you can simply read the slides to your audience. Those pressed for time often resort to a pseudo document "written" with bullet-point phrases instead of a well-written script with actual sentences and paragraphs.

This antipattern applies any time you want to bore an audience to death and simply don't have time to prepare or practice. When you prefer to have your audience read your slides rather than listen to you, this antipattern is your friend. Many audience members have come to expect this style of presentation in certain situations. Some corporate and educational cultures use presentation software in place of word processors, effectively replacing prose with an Infodeck.

Bullet-Riddled Corpse is a pattern for an Infodeck but an antipattern for a presentation. The primary purpose of an Infodeck in many cases is to outline some information in a more compact format than prose. Bullets work great in this context. However, they are a disaster for presentations.

When a slide full of bullet points appears during a presentation, *everyone in the audience reads every word.* It's just like rubber necking at an automobile accident: People can't help themselves. If the presenter keeps talking, the spoken and written word compete for the audience's attention. Some presenters defensively pause when revealing a new slide, which is a terrible solution to the problem!

Long lists of bullets violate many of our slide-design guidelines, discussed in the Cookie Cutter antipattern and Fourthought pattern, but they are barely tolerable if you at least use a simple *reveal* animation. Even better is a pattern like Charred Trail, which enables you to reveal information gradually but keeps the emphasis on the current point.

Bullet-heavy slide decks make for acceptable takeaways for audience members, but they're usually mediocre as both a presentation vehicle and a printed document.

Slide decks created in this fashion typically result in word-heavy slides with complete sentences rather than phrases. Presenters tend to jam more and more text onto a slide, creating something that is more like an eye-exam chart than a supporting document for a talk. In an effort to spice up the text-heavy deck, presenters often resort to liberal use of clip art. Still other presenters rely on different styles of bullet points (triangles, stars, squares, etc.) to try to mask the prevalence of bullets.

To implement this antipattern, following a classic outline format, simply type a phrase or complete sentence and hit enter. A new bullet point will be created. Rinse and repeat. When the text becomes too small to read comfortably, create a new slide.

Many presentation tools *try* to lure you into this antipattern. PowerPoint automatically resizes the text as you pile more bullets onto the slide, leading to the Ant Fonts antipattern.

You can avoid this antipattern by understanding the Cookie Cutter antipattern; just because the default slide style in the template you chose offers you a text box with bullets doesn't mean that it's the best option to convey your message.

We're obviously big fans of Fourthought, structured planning before your presentation, but we're also pragmatists and realize that preparation time is often a luxury. In case you fall into the trap of using the presentation tool as your design tool, use the outlining facilities in the presentation tool to construct a reasonable Narrative Arc. In most tools, this also generates slides with bullets that mirror your outline. Rather than use those slides directly, evaluate each slide and see if it makes more sense when presented to break some ideas apart. Remember, the differentiator between an Infodeck and a presentation is *time*; ideas that fit together in an outline may work better when introduced more slowly in a presentation.

Known Uses | The antipattern is heavily prevalent in the corporate or educational Infodeck—and in terrible presentations everywhere.

Related Patterns | The Cookie Cutter antipattern suggests that you shouldn't let slide size determine information density. The Frankensteinian creators of a Bullet-Riddled Corpse tend to use bullets to control the amount of information on slides, packing them onto information-rich slides.

When working with a Bullet-Riddled Corpse, presentation tools *encourage* you to add more and more bullets, automatically unleashing Ant Fonts.

The Fourthought pattern recommends you spend time building a real narrative for your presentation and rely less on bulleted lists to convey your ideas.

Neal's Craving for a Kibitzer

Neal does an introductory talk on the *Clojure* programming language, a dialect of *Lisp* whose syntax famously includes a multitude of parentheses. Another famous fixture in the Lisp world is a series of books starting with *The Little LISPer*,[1] which consists in its entirety of questions the authors pose and their increasingly illuminating answers.

In the spirit of *The Little LISPer*, Neal thought it would make a nice Narrative Arc for his talk to consist of a series of questions and answers in the Socratic style. Neal takes on the persona of someone learning the language alongside his audience, allowing the slides to drive the exposition. In a few places, though, an intermediate example is necessary to bridge from one concept to another. Neal wanted a way to "stay" at the abstraction of the current example but also indicate that a better technique exists—something that his student persona can't credibly do.

What Neal really needed was a knowledgeable commentator standing beside him who makes parenthetical observations—reminiscent of the Greek Chorus, a group of players in ancient Greek drama who comment collectively on the action.

 ## Pattern: Greek Chorus

Also Known As   "The Wørd" on *The Colbert Report*

Definition   Seed the audience with some partisans who interject comments, display enthusiasm, or help defend your case if you are outnumbered.

Motivation   It's nice having friends in the audience, especially if you are going to say something controversial. There is no shame in planting some people in the audience to help support your cause.

Applicability/ Consequences   This pattern is particularly applicable in presentation settings in which you are going against the status quo on some subject in front of a potentially skeptical audience. It's also crucial in business settings when you deliver news that disagrees with the world view of a portion of the room.

Greek Chorus doesn't even require extra people—just extra personas. For the talk referenced in the preceding interlude, Neal solved his dilemma by creating an alter ego to appear on slides to make ongoing comments. He wanted a simple graphical element that wouldn't be distracting, so— echoing the parentheses-heavy syntax of the language he was teaching—he created the character shown in the slides in Figure 3.4.

During the presentation, the head made of parentheses is the last element animated, sliding in from the right-hand side. It's there to indicate that although the current example is necessary for understanding, it isn't

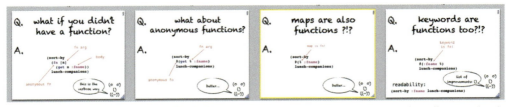

Figure 3.4 Greek Chorus character indicating that better examples will appear shortly

the proper way for experts to do it. By adding it as an ancillary character, Neal isn't required to make that point after every intermediate example; he has "someone else" to do it for him.

We are *not* suggesting some sort of stunt, such as a comedian or magician. Don't hide someone in the audience to ask a question at a particular time or to laugh at your jokes. If the audience or meeting senses you've done this, it will likely cause a backlash. With Greek Chorus, you're just trying to even the playing field.

Mechanics

Find a Posse of friends. Make them come to your talk. If you don't have any friends, make some line art on slides, or bring stuffed animals to your talk.

Related Patterns

The Posse pattern is the literal interpretation of this pattern; it advises you to bring real people to your talk to help bolster your case.

The Mentor pattern suggests an attitude you'd like to convey; a Greek Chorus might act in a side role from a different perspective.

Antipattern: Ant Fonts

Also Known As

Tiny Fonts, Microscope Not Included, "Can You Read This in the Back?"

Definition

To fit more content on a slide, simply reduce the font size. In fact, reduce it until it looks like a trail of ants marching across the projected image. You'll be able to fit literally reams of content on a single screen.

Motivation

When a presentation lacks a planned Narrative Arc, presenters have a natural tendency to compensate by putting as much as possible into the on-screen presentation materials. They think, "At worst, they can read what I was thinking about and all the facts that I gathered about this topic." This antipattern also is motivated by a desire to impress the audience with the volumes of research the presenter did for the talk—even the little facts that pertain only tangentially to the topic at hand.

Applicability/
Consequences

Ant Fonts are used in presentations that lack sufficient preparation time, a clear direction, or a creator who can "let go" of the less important things and present a compelling case via the highlights.

Audience focus is relegated to reading the projected text, which doesn't leave any comfortable space to be filled by the presenter's oration. When flooded with line after line of text, the audience gains no sense of which parts are most important to retain and which are ancillary facts that can be looked up later via reference material. And both the presentation and the printed slide text are a total loss for any audience member who is vision-impaired. As the working population ages, this will become problem for a growing number of attendees.[2]

Mechanics

To implement Ant Fonts, forcefully constrain each topic to a single slide. The bullets and paragraphs will not naturally fit, but by reducing the font from the typical 30-point default to 14-point or below, you will conquer the constraints and get that content to squeeze in.

To avoid Ant Fonts, make sure that the template you use for new presentations has nice big fonts for each of the defaults. And turn off the evil feature in PowerPoint that automatically shrinks your font sizes as you add more content to the slide. Like a cocaine dealer, it's encouraging you to do the wrong thing. This feature exists in Keynote, but it's well-hidden, and we're not going to be the ones responsible for showing it to you.[3]

Well-known presenter Martin Fowler has a great suggestion he called *HalfSize Composition*,[4] which suggests that you always keep your slide size at 50 percent when you are designing your slides. Anything that looks too small in the designer at 50 percent will look too small to the audience when projected. This is a nice trick because it forces the designer (you) to see all your slides from a virtual distance.

Don Box of Microsoft, in a candid interview about preparing for technical talks,[5] suggests using 14-point fonts for source code demos—a surprisingly large font to some readers but still small from our perspective. We recommend an 18-point font for most code samples and have been known to go as large as the slide, resolution, and screen real estate permit. Don also uses a specific font face, Lucida Console, which is universally installed on Windows machines. With today's ease of access to thousands of fonts, many of which are free, we recommend Inconsolata,[6] a TrueType font that is compatible with both Windows and the Mac.

Known Uses

Corporate C-level updates, earnings reports, and quarterly team briefings seem to be the primary implementers of this pattern. This reflects a culture of document creation and a misguided sense of how to consolidate information. However, leaders in the data-visualization space such as Edward Tufte have consistently told us for several decades, "The minimum we should hope for with any display technology is that it should do no harm." It's hard to reconcile that advice with monstrosities such as the official slide shown in Figure 3.5.

Related Patterns

Slideuments frequently consist of many pages of information crammed into bullet points.

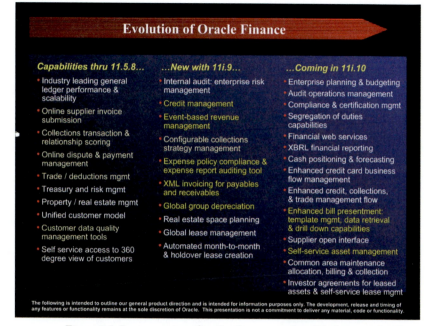

Figure 3.5 Representation of an Oracle status-update slide featuring Ant Fonts

Heavy users of the Bullet-Riddled Corpse antipattern have an apparent affinity for this antipattern as well. As the presentation tool lets them conveniently keep adding to bulleted lists, the fonts become smaller and smaller.

Be careful when creating an Infodeck that you don't allow the fonts to become too small to read when the deck is published as a PDF.

Antipattern: Fontaholic

Also Known As	Ransom Note, Crazed Typographer, Font Hangover
Definition	A Fontaholic is someone who doesn't know when to say "enough" when using fonts. The font-face options all look so awesome when you browse through them.
Motivation	You need to "jazz up" your presentation. What better way to do that than to add some fun fonts and maybe even some clip art? Wow! That looks better. But if one additional font made it look a little better, then nine fonts will make it simply awesome!
Applicability/ Consequences	This antipattern is applicable any time you have a boring presentation that needs that extra "punch."

After you've used four, six, or even nine font faces, both you and your audience get the headache equivalent of a hangover from looking at your slides. Audiences will be talking for days about how many fonts you used in your presentation. Various expletives may be laced into those water-cooler recaps.

Mechanics To implement this antipattern, open up the Fonts control panel on Windows or the Font Book on Mac. Randomly choose five or more fonts from the vast list of faces that have been progressively installed by your operating system and software, in addition to ones you've downloaded from the Internet. If the first five don't seem to produce enough variety when placed in your slides, iterate and add another five until you are satisfied. Also consider mixing three font faces in a single paragraph to score the font equivalent of a hockey hat trick.

An example of a fontaholic slide can be seen in Figure 3.6.

To avoid this antipattern, pay close attention to your fonts. For most of your presentation, select a sans serif font. A common set preinstalled on many systems and available for purchase include the following:

- Helvetica
- Arial
- Verdana

Studies have shown *FHWA Series Fonts*[7] to be one of the most legible from great distances. Our less formal audience surveys have shown a

Figure 3.6 A slide designed by a Fontaholic

Figure 3.7 Slide designed by an adept font user

popular variant of Helvetica called Helvetica Neue to be the most decipherable at a distance.

Figure 3.7 shows an example of proper font selection on a slide.

Known Uses
- Church presermon announcements
- Ransom notes
- Class materials created by new professors at community colleges
- Sales collateral created by salespersons who are struggling to close deals

Related Patterns   A Photomaniac tends to like lots of fonts, trying sometimes to match font styles to random pictures. Unless you're a professional typographer, you probably shouldn't attempt this matching and instead stick with a few clean and simple font faces.

Antipattern: Floodmarks

Also Known As   Death by Advertising, Marketing Mania, Kudzu Logos

Definition   Floodmarks represent extraneous background imagery featured on every slide. If one logo is a watermark, then Floodmarks represent too many watermarks. This includes company logos, conference sponsors, and even recurring graphical elements like background images and swooping lines.

Motivation   For business presentations, many corporations impose a hideous slide template rife with Floodmarks.

Independent presenters at conferences are under relentless pressure to plaster their slides with sponsor floodmarks. Conferences frequently try to impose a common slide template on all presenters, featuring tons of Floodmarks, as in Figure 3.8.

Conference organizers feel that every extra dollar brought in makes the event more viable, offers more decoration and staffing options, and doesn't harm the event (much). We've overheard a conference organizer say, "The more sponsors the better. I just have to keep them from knowing about each other because of dilution concerns until the last possible moment." In short, money drives the desire for sponsorship. Sponsorship drives the pressure for branding. Conferences push the branding from the hallways into the most personal of materials—the presentations themselves.

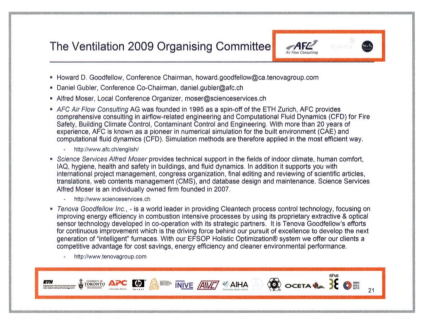

Figure 3.8 Floodmarks eat a lot of space in this representation of a conference template

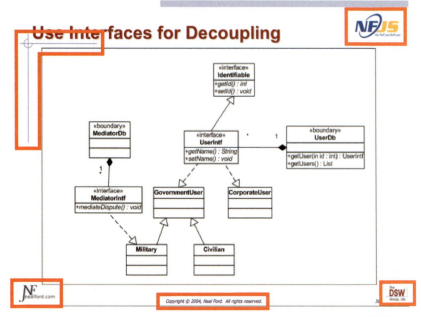

Figure 3.9 Image compromised to fit within Floodmarks

Applicability/
Consequences

Any presentation or event that has a sponsor behind it needs to *get that message out there*. The sponsors paid for the platinum sponsorship package, which means that the hallways will be filled with their banners, booths will be serving demos of their wares, your slides will be branded with their logos, and your firstborn will bear the corporate emblem as a tattoo, inked on even before the little one is released from the hospital.

Overuse of branding has a numbing effect, making Floodmarks nothing but unnecessary background noise. Floodmarks also make it difficult to use the entire canvas of the slide. Do you squeeze your image between the cruft (an onomatopoetic software term describing useless, tacky decoration), or do you take the chance of partially obscuring the floodmark? Figure 3.9 shows a hideous example from Neal's naive past.

In Figure 3.9, Neal had so many Floodmarks on the page that he was forced to size his image to avoid them, compromising the quality of the image and therefore the presentation.

Even the seemingly innocuous graphic elements like swooping lines and swirly boxes represent Floodmarks. In Figure 3.10, the presenter is faced with a no-win situation. To make the image big enough for the text to be legible, the presenter must make it overlap the line that borders the title. Even if the presenter were wise enough to choose (or create) a template without a title, the company logo Floodmarks still haunt the

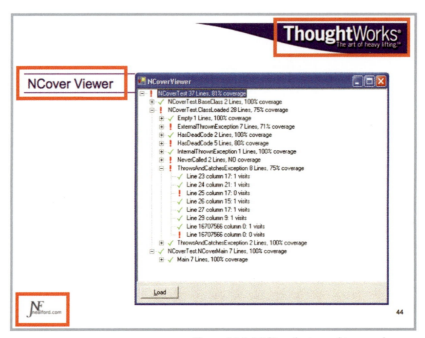

Figure 3.10 Making the image big enough to see overlaps the Floodmarks in an unattractive way

upper-right corner, which would still prevent the image from filling the entire slide without overlap.

Knuckling under to either your company or a conference to use its Floodmarks-ridden templates hurts your chances of creating a compelling presentation; it is difficult to use a Unifying Visual Theme on top of Floodmarks. Using the same visuals as everyone else in the company or conference makes it hard to stand out. We recommend Defying Defaults instead.

We include copyright notices on each slide as Floodmarks. We're not legal experts by any stretch, so if your company forces the issue, we have no legal ground to override them. However, we think the danger of someone stealing your slide and using it for nefarious purposes is less likely than annoying your audience by bombarding them with useless information. Does your audience really need to know that every single slide is under copyright protection?

Any repetitive element is either ignored or irritating, neither of which is good for your presentation.

Mechanics   Our distaste for branding elements isn't universal. We understand the utility of corporate branding. Use link Floodmarks in abundance on the Bookends if your company or conference insists. However, for most slides, we prefer all our templates to be Floodmarks-free. It's much easier to add graphical elements to blank backgrounds than remove pervasive elements later to avoid overlaps and other visual clashes.

For public presentations, the audience will likely know who sponsored the show and your talk because most vertical surfaces within the encompassing square mile include conference posters with sponsor lists. Use the supplied Floodmarks on the first slide, and then revert to your well-considered Unifying Visual Theme.

Related Patterns

Using Floodmarks automatically makes you a Fontaholic if you use different fonts on your slides from the ones that the Floodmarks use. Mixed fonts used for any reason create an unsettling effect.

If you do feel compelled (either by corporate mandate or conference organizer guilt trip) to incorporate some Floodmarks into your presentation, the safest place to do so is on the Bookends, where they interfere the least with detailed content.

Refusing to use Floodmarks is an implementation of the Defy Defaults pattern and one that exemplifies the benefits of that pattern. By refusing to brand your material like everyone else, you automatically stand out.

Antipattern: Photomaniac

Also Known As

Random Clip Art, Random Stock Photos, Death by 1,000 Photos

Contributed By

Martin Fowler, Chief Scientist, ThoughtWorks[8]

Definition

Vainly attempt to use random stock photos to make your boring presentation appear less boring.

Motivation

PowerPoint has provided a horde of free clip art for over a decade. For its day, it served a good purpose, but now clip art is hopelessly outdated, and it has the same effect on your presentation. The new graphics-heavy trend in presentations is to use stock photos such as those offered by microstock agencies like ShutterStock,[9] iStockphoto,[10] Flickr,[11] and Corbis,[12] to name just a few. It's easy to find killer stock photos that are rich and vibrant, regardless of the fact that they don't match the narrative. The temptation is great to stretch the bounds of good taste or sanity to try to use them. No presentation is bad enough that a few poorly chosen stock photos can't make it worse.

Applicability/ Consequences

You've fallen victim to the Photomaniac antipattern in any presentation in which you use attractive but essentially random stock photos in place of a real Unifying Visual Theme.

Using high-quality images on Bookends and Intermezzi that match and amplify your Unifying Visual Theme is a great idea. We aim to establish metaphors that strengthen or amplify our message. Using images with a specious connection to the topic at hand has the opposite effect. For example, in Figure 3.11, the slide refers to *nesting* methods in a programming language (calling one method from inside another). This concept has nothing to do with a bird's nest except the spelling of the word *n-e-s-t*. It should be no surprise that using random photos makes your presentation feel random to the audience.

Mechanics   Implementations of this antipattern begin with a visit to any of the aforementioned stock-photo agencies and a search for keywords tangentially related to the topic of the presentation. For cost-saving reasons, there is a motivation to purchase the images in the lowest resolution possible and just expand them in the presentation software. The insufficient resolution photos will inevitably pixelate. Audience members, even if only subtly, will feel that the quality of the presentation is like that of a low-cost television commercial. Instead, consider a presentation an investment in the education of the audience and be liberal in your spending to acquire a few relevant and sufficient-resolution images that support your Unifying Visual Theme.

If using Creative Commons photos from sources like Flickr and Google Images, a Photomaniac may violate the license by "saving time" and not

Figure 3.11 Conceptual clash between subject and (very pretty) stock photo

crediting the photographer. Some presentation authors justify this by saying, "The photographer already knew it was going to be an uncredited effort and it really isn't that hard to take a good photograph." Presenters who value the creativity that goes into building their Narrative Arc should equally value the creativity of others that produced visual elements upon which they are building.

Avoid this antipattern by choosing images that match your Unifying Visual Theme, using them sparingly, and avoiding use of irrelevant images solely as Brain Breaks.

Known Uses Salespersons are the most common implementers of this pattern. The pure facts about a product can feel boring to someone intimately familiar with them and thus inspire an unsettled feeling of a need for more visual spice. This trap leads to use of random stock photos as a crutch. The better compensating techniques include breaking up the presentation into more lively pieces via Talklet and providing comfortable points of brief reflection with Brain Breaks.

The most prevalent application of the Photomaniac antipattern is at the conclusion of presentations. Audiences and presenters alike have been coached that we should shake hands and agree on something after a talk. That imprinting makes it easy to wrongly believe that a photo of that western cultural habit of a handshake will increase our chance of

Figure 3.12 Slide suffering from Photomaniac stock photos

agreement and sales success. Avoid the trap; removing the handshake photo is always a net improvement.

Related Patterns   When quickly building Bullet-Riddled Corpse presentations, authors frequently also use randomly selected photos. In the process, they become both a virtual murderer *and* thief.

A strong Unifying Visual Theme will help you avoid this antipattern. Even if you create a picture-heavy presentation using a pattern like Vacation Photos, a Unifying Visual Theme precludes randomness, letting the images enhance rather than detract from your message.

Pattern: Composite Animation

Definition   Layer two or more animations on top of one another and run them simultaneously. This creates the appearance of new animations and a unique special effect.

Motivation   A significant portion of your audience has seen the use of every animation and transition in your presentation tool of choice. To make something stand out, you can create an entirely new animation by layering existing effects one on top of another.

Applicability/   A composite animation is applicable in any presentation in which a simple
Consequences   animation will not accomplish the effect that you're seeking. The more simple the presentation tool's animation capabilities, the more likely it is you want to use a composite animation. A composite animation makes possible what others thought the presentation tool was incapable of doing.

Even with this inspiring new set of animated combinations, please govern your use of motion. Every presenter ends up with their favorite set of animations and transitions and overuses them until they realize the distraction they can create and moderate their use. The whole point of building a unique animation is its novelty and scarcity of application.

The "don't overdo it" rule has one exception: when you use the same composite animation repeatedly to make the same point. For example, in his *Functional Thinking* talk, Neal wants to illustrate lessons that nonfunctional programmers can learn from functional languages. He built a composite animation that appears when one of the lessons is driven home but at no other time. The audience quickly learns that when they see the unique animation, the words that follow have special emphasis.

Mechanics   The real trick to implementing this pattern is to identify two or more animations that work together well. For example, you can't really do a left-wipe *appearance* animation, which reveals the element gradually, alongside a typewriter-type animation, which animates the appearance of each letter. They look so similar that the effect will be lost.

In general, this pattern is much better supported in Keynote than PowerPoint. Keynote simply has a richer supply of animations, and they look smoother when running.

Composite
Animation in
Keynote

Presentation tools allow only a single *build in* animation per element, which this pattern "fixes" by tricking the tool into allowing you to add several complementary animations on what looks like a single element. This pattern is both easy and attractive in Keynote because several of its animations work nicely together. For example, Neal used a combination of *shimmer*, *convergence*, and *flame* to create a composite animation that really stood out.

1. Place a slide element (such as a text box) on a slide.
2. Add your *build in* animation of choice for the element.
3. Copy the element and place the copy exactly over the top of the original.
4. Change the animation to a compatible one.
5. Repeat for as many elements as you want to layer.

The interaction among slide, element, and inspector is illustrated in Figure 3.13.

Composite
Animation in
PowerPoint

Presentations tools allow only a single *entrance* animation per element, which this pattern "fixes" by tricking the tool into allowing you to add several complementary animations on what looks like a single element.

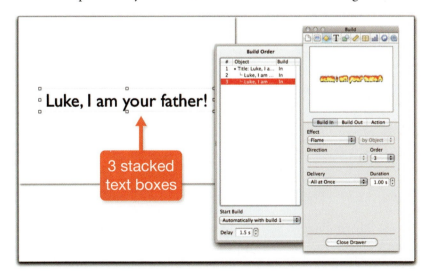

Figure 3.13 Composite Animation in Keynote

Figure 3.14 Composite Animation in PowerPoint

This pattern is a little tougher to implement in PowerPoint. It simply doesn't have as many animations that work well together when layered, so you need to be more judicious in your animation selection.

1. Place a slide element (such as a text box) on a slide.
2. Add your *appearance* animation of choice.
3. Copy the element and place the copy exactly over the top of the original.
4. Change the animation to a compatible one.
5. Repeat for as many elements as you want to layer.

The interaction among slide, element, and inspector is illustrated in Figure 3.14.

Related Patterns   The Emergence pattern discusses building tension by slowly revealing elements via animation. A Composite Animation may well be the climax of your tension-building exercise, adding to the surprise because you're using a visual effect no one has seen before.

Mark's Massive Pattern Pile

Mark Richards, a well-known speaker on the No Fluff, Just Stuff conference circuit, is known for both his enthusiasm and his wealth of material. Because the No Fluff, Just Stuff conference series is regional, the speakers encounter different audience experience and knowledge levels in different locales. Mark struggled to identify the correct mix of material for a talk on software antipatterns. Making matters worse, he had a huge amount of material that he couldn't fit into the allotted time. In several cities, the worst-case scenario happened: He misjudged the audience experience level and prepared his most advanced material for audiences of novices, who were lost.

Mark and Neal were commiserating over drinks about this seemingly intractable problem. Mark had the idea to customize the talk by preparing enough material for all contingencies and letting the audience decide. Together, he and Neal figured out how to make this pattern work in Keynote, and the Á la Carte Content pattern was born.

Pattern: Á la Carte Content

Also Known As Jeopardy, Choose Your Own Adventure

Definition Poll the audience at the beginning of the talk (and possibly along the way) to construct an impromptu agenda. In contrast to a typical linear presentation, this pattern gives the audience multiple opportunities to choose what comes next in the talk, helping you tailor the content more exactly to the audience.

Motivation Presentations are typically prepared and delivered with a rigid structure, which can lead to audience boredom, especially with technical content. And if most of the audience is already familiar with much of your content, your presentation will not only bore them but also waste their time. One way to engage audience members more meaningfully is to have the audience choose the next piece of the talk. The attendees vote for their most desired topic. This raises their interest, the talk's applicability, and likely, the attendees' assessments and ratings of your presentation.

If you can't cover all your material in the allocated time, the talk organically distills to its most desired form. Even if you'd intended to cover all the content, you can smoothly remove content if necessary. You don't even need to address the missing content (see the Going Meta antipattern); the audience will think that you aimed to cover only a subset of the offered segments.

Applicability/ Consequences This pattern works particularly well when you are required to deliver the same content to different groups with different knowledge levels. It's particularly useful for business presentations. Time is critical in companies, and nothing is more annoying than a presentation that drones on forever about known facts. Building your presentation with the Á la Carte Content pattern enables the meeting attendees to narrow their interest quickly, wasting the least amount of time.

This pattern also works well if you are doing a Live Demonstration, particularly for product demos and other showcases. Be careful, though, not to let it slip into being a Dead Demo.

The downside is you must prepare a significant amount of additional material. On the other hand, this pattern works well when you already have an excess of material and would rather let the audience decide. Use the excess material to create a Coda for your presentation.

Tell the attendees up front how much time you anticipate each section will consume, helping them to manage their time most effectively. Armed with that knowledge, they may well opt for, say, two topics that will fit into the allotted time rather than an initially more interesting longer one.

Mechanics | The strictness of the structure depends on you and the audience. One way to implement this pattern is via the Talklet pattern, wherein you have coarse-grained chunks of mostly unrelated content. Another variant is the "Build Your Own Adventure" style, in which you give your audience a listing of possible topics and let them choose the order. Each of these chunks tends to be smaller—generally from 5 to 15 minutes in length—than one designed as a Talklet. Finally, following a suggestion by Erik Doernenburg, you can present a tag cloud of possible topics, giving the audience complete control over the content.

Both Keynote and PowerPoint allow you to add hyperlinks to elements, and those hyperlinks can point to other files. For this pattern, create a "home" page of icons or text boxes with hyperlinks to the beginning of the pertinent content. At the end of each section, place a hyperlink back to the "home" page.

Á la Carte Content in Keynote | Create a slide that will serve as your "home" slide, including images and/or text indicating categories. For each of the categories, add a hyperlink to the element, as shown in Figure 3.15.

Select each category element in turn and use the hyperlink tab on the inspector, as shown in Figure 3.16.

Á la Carte Content in PowerPoint | Create a slide that will serve as your "home" slide, including images and/or text indicating categories. For each of the categories, add a hyperlink to the element.

In PowerPoint, hyperlinking an element works identically to all the other Microsoft Office products. Select your image or text box. PowerPoint won't allow you to hyperlink some grouped elements, so if you have grouped an image and text box for convenience, you may have to ungroup them to apply the hyperlink. Right-click on the element and choose to edit the hyperlink, as shown in Figure 3.17.

Known Uses | Venkat Subramaniam[13] uses this pattern for a *Programming Language Puzzlers* presentation at No Fluff, Just Stuff. He offers increasing point values for the increasingly complex choices the audience can make. Audience members "prove" themselves to others in the audience by shouting out a selection. Subramaniam then clicks on the cell and a correspondingly

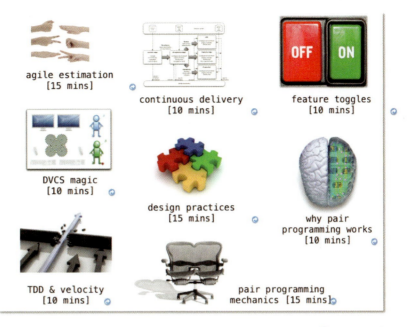

Figure 3.15 The "home" slide from Neal's Á la Carte Content *Agile Engineering Practices* presentation

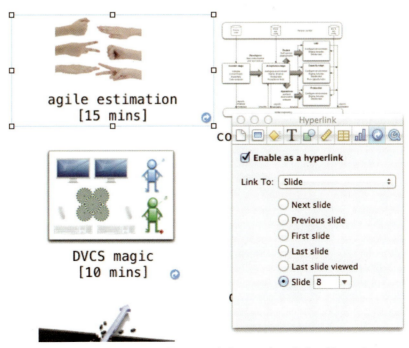

Figure 3.16 Setting a hyperlink in Keynote's inspector

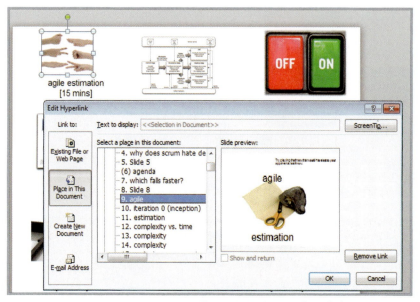

Figure 3.17 Setting a hyperlink in PowerPoint

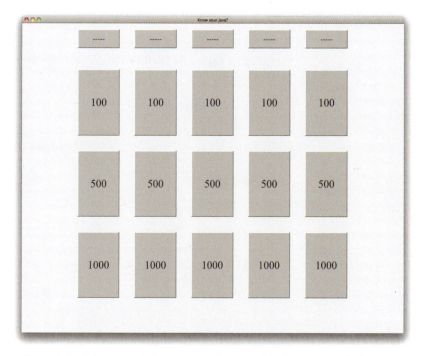

Figure 3.18 Subramaniam's Programming Language Puzzlers game on the home screen

Figure 3.19 Subramaniam's Programming Language
Puzzlers game with a question opened

detailed question comes up on the selected topic. The opening screen of his puzzlers application appears in Figure 3.18.

Once an audience member has chosen their topic, Venkat's application highlights the question, as shown in Figure 3.19.

Related Patterns   A Talklet makes a great individual piece that you can offer as Á la Carte Content.

Pattern: Analog Noise

Also Known As   Handmade (via Nancy Duarte), Vintage, Classic

Definition   Place visual elements in your presentation that *don't* look polished and perfect.

Motivation   Standards of beauty change over time. In the eighteenth century, being fit and tan was considered unattractive because it implied that you spent your time toiling in the sun. Now it means that you get away from indoor lighting occasionally. Aesthetic standards for presentations change too. When computerized presentation tools came out, it was a marvel that you could produce clean, pretty fonts and straight lines without a ruler. But over time, the polish has become tiresome. Adding some Analog Noise to your presentation creates visual interest and makes things stand out.

In a widely published study, scientists Daniel Oppenheimer and two colleagues, Connor Diemand-Yauman and Erikka Vaughan,[14] study demonstrated that readers retain *more* information when it is shown to them in a font that is hard to read. This suggests that the most important items in your talk should include some noise.

Applicability/
Consequences

Use Analog Noise any time you have a message or element that you want to stand out in a definitive way.

If used correctly, Analog Noise adds visual punch to your presentation, giving you another tool to drive your points home. If overused (which is easy to do), it becomes a visual irritant. Use it either sparingly or consistently. If you want to decorate an otherwise polished presentation, use it only to emphasize your most important points. If it's part of your visual theme, make sure you use it consistently. (For example, in Figure 3.25, we show an example of using an analog-noisy font throughout a presentation.) Because analog noise is so visually distinctive, inconsistent use becomes painfully obvious.

Mechanics

Using analog-noisy fonts is easy in both Keynote and PowerPoint: Both supply a ready number of good fonts for this purpose. Figure 3.20 shows an

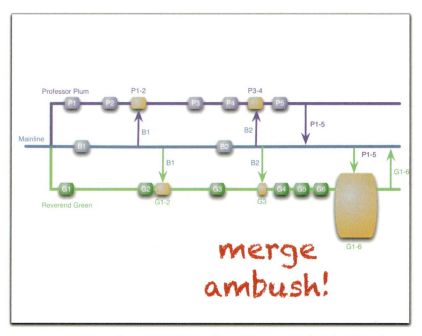

Figure 3.20 A noisy font nicely contrasts the refined line drawing

example that creates a nice contrast between an information-dense line drawing and a noisy font to drive the point home.

The level of noise needn't be so high as to be noticeable. Rather, it can act as a highlight for existing content. For example, consider the slide in Figure 3.21.

Drawing lines with analog noise is a built-in modifier in Keynote: When you choose any shape from the palette of built-in shapes, you can change the *stroke* property in the Graphic Inspector portion of the inspector, as shown in Figure 3.22.

Noisy graphics offer a nice contrast if you have lots of clean graphics. You can also use noisy lines to indicate that something is less sure. For example, Figure 3.23, from Neal's *Emergent Design* talk, implies that time moves forward and that the learning that takes place isn't nice and orderly but valuable nevertheless.

Another way to use analog noise is to feature it as part of your visual theme. For Neal's *Functional Thinking* presentation, he wanted to leverage everyone's experience with math class and chalkboards, so he chose a dark background and used the font named *ChalkDuster* as the main title font and another noisy font as the standard text font. One of the slides appears in Figure 3.24.

A visual element can take on semantic meaning. Neal's *Functional Thinking* talk is about the ways in which constructs in a programming paradigm unfamiliar to the attendees manifest in one that is familiar to

Figure 3.21 The added fringe focuses the picture around the important part, fuzzing out the rest

Figure 3.22 The stroke property for lines in Keynote

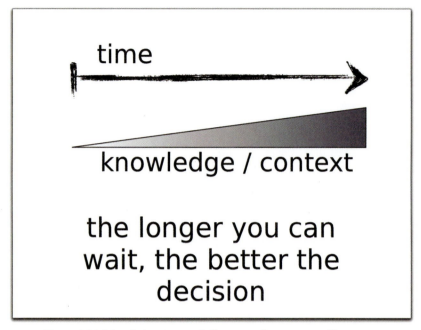

Figure 3.23 Noise helping nonverbally convey the messiness of learning over time

Figure 3.24 Purposeful use of noisy fonts and lines

Figure 3.25 Allowing the user to "pick up" the chalk

them. One of presentation's main goals is to encourage attendees to explore the new conceptual territory. The chalk-and-blackboard theme blends effectively into the content when Neal exhorts the audience that they too can do this, with the slide in Figure 3.25 as the visual backdrop.

PowerPoint doesn't include a way to create noisy lines and shapes, but a burgeoning third-party market exists for hand-drawn lines and other artifacts we would classify as analog noise.

Known Uses Neal loves this pattern and uses it to the brink of overuse. The pattern shows up embedded in the standard templates of presentation tools more frequently with each release.

Related Patterns Using Analog Noise is an excellent way to Defy Defaults, especially if you are trying to lower the stuffiness level of the typical presentation within a particular environment.

Pattern: Vacation Photos

Also Known As   Backdrop, Last-Minute Preso, A Thousand Words

Definition   On your presentation slides, use full-screen, high-quality images and very few (or no) words.

Motivation   Images are powerful, and the right one conveys a tremendous amount of information in a small space. It seems you can't swing a power cable these days without hitting a slide deck with images in it; some presentations are nothing *but* pictures. Pictures convey emotions more readily than words, and a well-crafted graph communicates data more quickly than a table of statistics. The audience can't *read* pictures, so the verbal focus stays on you and your message.

Applicability/
Consequences   This style works best for presentations that are primarily storytelling, such as keynotes, where the pictures add nuance without distraction. This pattern also works well for high-profile speakers who aren't entirely comfortable with speaking and worry about using the presentation tool. A backdrop of thematic pictures enables them to talk without distractions.

Images carry emotion and, when chosen with care, grab people's attention. But they have to fit your talk. If attendees can't see how a picture relates, they'll spend their precious attention trying to figure out the puzzle you unintentionally placed before them. Lingering on an image can also backfire. Just because a picture is worth a thousand words doesn't mean you should spend half your talk sitting on one picture. People will naturally look back at the image and think, "There must be a reason this image is still here . . . did I miss something?"

Mechanics   Thanks to sites like iStockphoto, which offer a nearly infinite variety of reasonably priced stock photography, adding images to a slide deck is easy. Good keyword search and regular content updates mean you'll probably find something that will fit your needs. However, beware of a bit of a backlash against what some people call the "smiling lady" pictures. Nearly every corporate website is guilty of using photos of people who are clearly not employees (and yes, they're always smiling). Instead of humanizing the company, these images project a notion of the company as unauthentic and plastic.

Although it may seem like the Internet really does have everything, in some instances it's worth the time and money to get the exact shots *you* want. These images will be fresh, and they'll be exactly what you're looking for. However you acquire your images, make sure you have the proper copyright to use them as you wish.

Using images from the same set or that have the same feel serves as a powerful theme in a talk or across a series of talks. In fact, some collections are so iconic, people link them to a particular brand. A popular image has a tendency to show up in multiple places, which diminishes its power in your talk.

First, identify images that fit your talk. You can do this any way you wish: brainstorming, mind mapping, polling your peers, sketching, whatever helps you capture a slew of ideas. Ask people what they think of when they hear X from your talk. Go for quantity, not quality. Think about any infographics that would help you tell your story. Would a graph help illuminate a point better than a table?

Once you have a decent set of ideas, start plotting where they might fit within your slide deck to have the most impact. Mind maps or outlines are very helpful, but if you're injecting images later in the process, use big-picture views of your slides like Light Table in Keynote. Experiment with different placements until you get the feel you're looking for. Start winnowing your set of images to the ones with the most impact.

At this stage, it's time to procure images. Stock photography sites are a great place to start, but also look around the Creative Commons licensed images on Flickr. There are literally millions of images that you can use with limited restrictions. (Make sure the license works in your situation; some cannot be used commercially.) Odds are, you'll have more than a few pictures to choose from; pick the ones that fit the best. Ask your friends and family if you're not sure.

Related Patterns   You still need a strong Unifying Visual Theme (or your presentation will lean toward the Photomanic antipattern). Using only photos doesn't relieve you of the responsibility of telling a good story.

The opposite of this pattern in many ways is the Photomaniac antipattern, implementations of which often use inappropriate stock photos.

Architect Abe's Arbitrary Astronomy

A well-known software architect, Abe, was asked to give a keynote at a major developer conference. One of Abe's well-known presentation quirks was to impart random astronomy trivia, such as the age of the universe. Considering that he was speaking to software geeks, it resonated with the crowd, and he became well known for it. Abe was also known for his evangelical style, which involved strutting around the stage throwing papers and generally causing a ruckus, to the great enjoyment of the audience. People asked him so often why he didn't use the perfectly good projection system on the stage that one year he came up with a "solution" that combined both tendencies.

Rather than add presentation-appropriate slides, Abe used his computer to display random, cycling astronomy pictures while he was talking. The goal was to provide a generic backdrop, but because the images had nothing to do with his subject, they were a constant distraction. It was hard to pay attention to Abe for long periods because of the beautiful space pictures spinning and whirling on either side.

If you're going to use photos, make sure they amplify your story rather than distract and detract from it. More generally, make sure that the visual channel doesn't detract from the auditory one.

 # Pattern: Defy Defaults

Definition   Don't choose the default settings for any part of your presentation, whether they're supplied by tools or by event organizers.

Motivation   One of your goals should be to differentiate yourself, and using default colors and fonts doesn't help that cause. Try to avoid anything that homogenizes your presentation.

Applicability/ Consequences   Over time, you develop an identifiable style, using a combination of fonts, colors, backgrounds, and so on.

Mechanics   The themes and templates provided by modern presentation software are impressive, and they help with a very hard job: coming up with complementary visuals, fonts, animations, transitions, and so on. You should start with a truly blank slate only if you have a good visual sense and know what you are doing. But you also shouldn't choose the first theme that comes up when you launch the tool. If you use the same old template as everyone else, it becomes hard to differentiate your presentations from others.

Many corporations have a "standard template" that includes a catalog of antipatterns. Even if you can't avoid it entirely, perhaps you can move some of the Floodmarks around or make a small change to one of the fonts, keeping it in the same font family but with small differences.

Most conferences try to force presenters to use a standard conference template, rife with marketing and other conference information, frequently manifested as huge Floodmarks on each slide. The big technical conferences enforce draconian penalties if you don't use their template. This policy makes sense for presenters who don't have any distinctive style; an imposed style is better than none. However, we always push back on this requirement. Part of the reason the conference invited you was your unique take on a subject, and that should include presentation elements. Most conferences will relent if you insist.

If you are forced to knuckle under to default slides, see if you can use them only on your Bookends or Intermezzi, at least keeping ugly defaults away from real content.

Remember, sometimes it's better to beg forgiveness than ask permission. The visual distinctiveness of your work is important, so carefully weigh how much deviation you can afford.

Related Patterns   Default slide templates from corporations and conferences alike always include Floodmarks.

Defying JavaOne

For years, the most popular programming language for many big companies was Java, and the biggest Java conference on earth was JavaOne, held in San Francisco every summer. Everyone in the Java universe came to this event, both for the conference and for the hallway meetings.

JavaOne was notorious for trying to force homogenization on every talk. The organizers issued a hideous template every year and had a staffer check your work to make sure you complied with it. After you submitted your talk, you could make changes to it only onsite at the conference, in the presence of a JavaOne staffer and a lawyer, to make sure you didn't add anything libelous.

One side effect of this policy was uniformly awful presentations. Everyone had the same color scheme, the same bullets, and the same palette of five possible slide types. It seemed as if the organizers were trying to make the visual part of each talk as lame as possible.

One year Neal noticed a loophole. Because JavaOne is a technical conference, many of the talks consist primarily of demonstrations, most of which are so complex that it's virtually impossible to run them all from a standard computer setup. For that reason, the organizers allow you to drive the presentation and demonstrations directly from your own laptop.

For the next JavaOne, Neal submitted a very minimal slide deck with about five slides, each using the standard conference "Demo" slide. Onsite at presentation time, he told the room attendant that he would mostly demonstrate techniques and drive the few slides from his own computer. Neal proceeded to give his normal hour-long presentation for that topic, which consists of slightly more than 100 slides. After that point, he never used the JavaOne template again.

Not only did Neal go unpunished for this rebellion, but he was also rewarded. JavaOne each year releases a list of "JavaOne Rock Stars," the top 20 speakers as scored by attendees' evaluation forms. After Neal started defying the defaults, he won six JavaOne Rock Stars awards. But in a way, he was cheating: Everyone else at JavaOne used the hideous template; Neal's couldn't help but look better by contrast.

Antipattern: Borrowed Shoes

Also Known As   Other Person's Presentation, Bowling Shoes

Definition   You're presenting someone else's work.

Applicability/Consequences   Whether you chose this antipattern or it was forced upon you, presenting someone else's material is surprisingly difficult. Although you might not realize it, your individual presentation style becomes imprinted onto your materials. Even with adequate preparation, presenting someone else's slides feels wrong—as if you can't find the right rhythm, or the words and slides are not in quite the right order. It's about as comfortable as wearing someone else's shoes.

The main consequence of this antipattern is a terrible presentation. Watching someone struggle through a slide deck is one of those rites of passage in the business world that most of us would just as soon skip.

Mechanics   The best thing to do is to bite the bullet and rework the presentation into your style. Yes, this is going to take a long time that you don't have. The next best strategy is to reserve some extra practice time so that you gain a better feel for the material you'll be presenting, as discussed in both the Carnegie Hall and Crucible patterns.

The mechanics of the presentation are the easy part. What if you've inherited a slide deck that has serious deficiencies? For example, you are expected to fill in for the ill comptroller and give a compelling talk to the board of directors, but the slides dropped in your lap are just a dry recitation of facts. You're sure the comptroller had planned to tell some wonderful stories, but they're nowhere to be found in the slides or the speaker notes. In this case, you're going to have to take the time to retrofit the presentation into some sort of reasonable shape. At the very least, add a Narrative Arc so that you're telling a story rather than listing facts.

If you're a subject matter expert who finds the slides you've inherited to differ too jarringly from your normal presentation style, consider doing the talk with very minimal slides or perhaps a lowly whiteboard. If you let everyone know that you're a last-minute stand-in, they'll forgive an analog presentation with rough edges. Slides that make no sense to you won't make sense to your audience either; if you try to struggle through them, you won't come close to fulfilling the presentation's original purpose.

If you have been given a crappy slide deck and no time to do anything about it, then don't do the presentation. Doing a terrible presentation is worse than doing none at all. In the best-case scenario, delay the presentation long enough that its original owner can deliver it after all.

Related Patterns

Borrowing a slide deck typically doesn't afford the presentation undergoing the refining fire of the Crucible.

Borrowed presentations also commonly lack the critical Narrative Arc that makes the presenter and the presentation have maximum impact.

CHAPTER 4

TEMPORAL PATTERNS

LEVERAGING TIME TO ADD A FOURTH DIMENSION TO presentations is a recurring theme throughout the book. This chapter shows patterns that take advantage of time to add life to presentations. As a side effect, we also uncover a way to create attractive presentations as both slide shows and handouts.

We discuss one of the unfortunate realities of corporate life in this chapter, the Slideuments antipattern, a presentation that also attempts to be a document. Because many of the patterns in this chapter manipulate time during the presentation, they help solve the common problems presented by Slideuments, with solutions such as Gradual Consistency and Charred Trail.

Mary's Dilemma

With great opportunities come great problems. Mary the Marketer has both. She's in charge of putting together and delivering the presentation for the rollout of the new product that everyone is sure will revolutionize the industry. Mary's debut happens at the big trade show, where everyone concerned will be present . . . almost. For those not present, Mary's presentation must act as a stand-alone document that's just as compelling as her live presentation. How can one thing (her presentation) serve two such radically different purposes (live on-stage presentation and brochure)? It turns out she's being asked to create Slideuments.

Antipattern: Slideuments

Also Known As	A Deck for the Boss to Flip Thru
Definition	Garr Reynolds defines this antipattern in *Presentation Zen* (see Resources) as a presentation also used as a readable document. We adamantly agree with him that either you can create a presentation to deliver live, or you can use a presentation tool to create a document. *You can't create one artifact that works well in both cases!*
Motivation	Slideuments are an attempt to combine two incompatible vehicles for delivering information—a *presentation* and an Infodeck—under the misapprehension that they are compatible.
Applicability/ Consequences	It's possible to create Slideuments, but the outcome is rarely good. The tool diminishes or corrupts the message you are trying to convey. Slideuments are worse than either of the alternatives (only a presentation or only a document).
Mechanics	You can create a marginally better form of Slideuments by building a presentable presentation and adding comprehensive speaker notes for the prose portion of the document. When you print the slides, print the speaker notes too. Distribute the document as a PDF rather than in its native slide format. That way the recipient doesn't need to have the presentation tool that you used. (Everyone has a PDF reader.) And you force people to look at more than the slides because each page exists in only one format. Distributing a slide deck in native format with important information in the notes is risky because many viewers won't even think to look at the notes.

The approach we've just described has two major drawbacks. First, it's mechanically difficult to write prose in the speaker's notes sections of presentation tools. These tools weren't designed as word processors, so their |

support for creating attractive content is poor. Second, people have a strong tendency to use the slides as the outline for the items they talk about in the notes, forcing the outcome toward the Bullet-Riddled Corpse antipattern.

Ideally, either create a presentation without worrying about how it will look when printed, or use another tool to create a real document. To repeat, presentation tools make crummy word processors.

Known Uses Slideuments are a pervasive antipattern in most large corporations: All deliverables that don't have an inherent format become slide decks. When Neal was part of a group doing an architectural assessment at a large company, the group was told that the deliverable must be a PowerPoint slide deck because "the CEO is really good at flipping through slide decks really fast!" That wasn't a big selling point for Neal and his coworkers, and they refused. Instead, they delivered a written document because the nuanced messages they needed to include were impossible to force into slides (see the Cookie Cutter antipattern).

Related Patterns Slideuments are the evil twin of the Infodeck pattern. Frequently, people think they want Slideuments when what they really want is an Infodeck. Infodeck captures the best part of the Slideuments antipattern's intent (portable information that isn't prose) without all the negatives of trying to make it a presentation too.

The Bullet-Riddled Corpse antipattern shows up in conjunction with Slideuments; they are both common antipatterns encouraged by presentation tools.

Now that we've ranted against this antipattern, the remainder of this chapter shows several patterns that make it more palatable, including Charred Trail, Gradual Consistency, and Soft Transitions. We live in the real world too, and we realize that sometimes this isn't a battle that's worth fighting (especially if you are concurrently fighting other battles).

Merlin Mann's Token Transactions

Merlin Mann is a frequent speaker on productivity and Getting Things Done (GTD) techniques. An interesting presentation that he gave a few years ago, *Time and Attention*,[1] noted that one company handed out wooden tokens for employees to use to purchase meeting attendance. Yes, *purchase*. Employees had to use these scarce tokens in increasing quantities to get other employees to attend their meetings. This created a tangible measurement of the otherwise hidden cost of widely attended meetings, and it raised awareness of alternative, asynchronous forms of sharing and reviewing information. More knowledge workers should consider and take advantage of asynchronous forms of communication to maximize the amount of work they and their collaborating colleagues can accomplish in a workday—for example, an Infodeck!

Figure 4.1 Merlin Mann giving his *Time and Attention* talk at Google

 Pattern: Infodeck

Contributed By	Martin Fowler, Chief Scientist, ThoughtWorks[2]
Also Known As	Death by PowerPoint, "A Deck"
Definition	An Infodeck is a document created with presentation tools that is intended to be distributed—and never presented before an audience—to convey information.

There is an important, subtle distinction in this definition. We're not talking about a slide show running in kiosk mode, in a continuous loop, although there are similarities. An Infodeck isn't meant to be displayed as a slide show; rather, it is meant to be consumed by a single person—either at a computer, on a printout, or on an alternate display like a tablet computer—as a series of discrete narrative elements.

An Infodeck delivers information without the aid of a presenter delivering it. Thus an Infodeck is a standalone document, much like a spreadsheet.

Motivation   There are certainly legitimate reasons for creating an Infodeck. Just make sure you are doing it on purpose—not accidentally by creating an anemic presentation.

Martin Fowler, who found this pattern in the wild rather than creating it, lists three advantages to creating Infodecks:

- You can use spatial layout to help with explanation. Frequently, presentation tools have better drawing support than word processors, and slides evoke "canvas" more readily than a blank word-processor screen.
- They discourage long prose that people don't read. If the bullet points convey all you want, leave it at that rather than write a lot of purple prose around your bullet points.
- It's easy to include diagrams as primary elements in the communication or let the diagrams, rather than prose, lead the narrative.

Applicability/   As long as you can avoid allowing an Infodeck to become Slideuments, pre-
Consequences   sentation tools are effective ways to craft succinct communication. However, the desktop-publishing features of most word processors do this job better without some of the limitations of a tool used counter to its original purpose.

In many ways, this pattern itself is a litmus test. If you set out to create a presentation and end up with an Infodeck, something went wrong. The subtle advantage that presentations have over other communication media is the control that you as the presenter have over the rate of knowledge exposition. Don't surrender that control lightly.

Don't try to present an Infodeck: Because you have put no effort into transitions or animations, you'll present a series of textually dense slides, utilizing none of the features that make presentation tools effective.

Mechanics   None of the rules we've laid out in the book change when you create an Infodeck. Those in the Creativity Patterns chapter are especially apt.

Don't use transitions and animations for these types of slide decks. Rather, spend your time on concise and informative layout of information.

You can create compelling presentations using the Infodeck style. In particular, if you have compelling visuals that accompany your topic, showing them during your presentation aids it without the use of transitions or animations. However, if you've used no transitions or animation on any of the slides, you've purposefully ignored the time element of the presentation. If you have a word-heavy slide deck with no time manipulation, you risk allowing your Infodeck to tend toward becoming an antipattern.

Known Uses   Every corporation that hasn't explicitly banned the Infodeck uses it.

Related Patterns   Slideuments are usually a failed attempt to create an Infodeck. Decide early if you need a presentation or an Infodeck; don't try to create both.

The Cookie Cutter antipattern applies acutely to the Infodeck: Don't allow the *slide* to become the unit of thought.

- Just because you are creating an Infodeck, you shouldn't ignore Creativity Patterns like Narrative Arc. Being allowed to avoid transitions is one benefit of this pattern, but don't throw everything out the window.

Developer Dan's Density Dilemma

Developer Dan wanted to become a better presenter, so he attended seminars that focus on speaking style, poise, diction, and the myriad other qualities that make a compelling speaker. But he received some contradictory advice. One seminar told him never to use slides or other presentation tools because slides draw audience attention away from the speaker. Another told him to use slides but never to convey more than one thought per slide. So he tried using the Takahashi pattern, but the boss, who printed the presentation to read on the flight, yelled about the high number of pages.

How can Dan reconcile this conflicting advice? He needs slides so that he can show technical artifacts such as code, but he doesn't want to kill a forest. He needs a way to add information *density* without adding *size*. It turns out that he needs two patterns, Exuberant Title Top and Gradual Consistency, that add emphasis to elements via time rather than space.

☁ Pattern: Gradual Consistency

Definition

When presenting information, you have an extra dimension that's unavailable in a written document: *time*. Use time wisely in your presentation, building intelligently toward the final form—which could be Slideuments.

Motivation

When you produce Slideuments, don't feel compelled to show the "finished" version of the slides right away. With Gradual Consistency, the slides will eventually look like the printed version, but it takes some time (and intermediate versions of the slides) to arrive at the final version.

Applicability/ Consequences

Gradual consistency should be used in most Slideuments presentations. Because you are forced to print out your presentation, your slides hold little surprise when you present them. Gradual consistency helps emphasize the fact that time is sometimes very important in interpreting information, and it adds motion back into your presentation.

Gradual Consistency enables you to turn the disadvantage of Slideuments into an advantage. If forced to print out a copy beforehand, you can now leverage each audience member's sense of narrative on each slide, illustrating via time how you reached the conclusion they now see cast in stone before them.

Mechanics The mechanics for this pattern have more to do with *how* you construct each slide's narrative than with a particular set of tool techniques. Instead of showing tools, Neal will deconstruct a complex slide from one of his technical presentations.

In Neal's *Emergent Design* presentation, he defines a concept called *idiomatic patterns*, which is an alternate way of looking at a well-known concept in the software-development community—*design patterns*. He starts by talking about patterns but as a grand concept: Patterns with a capital P, as shown in Figure 4.2.

For the first animation, he wanted to deflate the concept of design patterns a bit, so the first animation changes the uppercase P to a lowercase one, as shown in Figure 4.3.

In this case, Neal replaced the entire uppercase "Patterns" with another text box with the lowercase "patterns"—partially because the "patterns" text box has a complex further life on this slide. An interesting alternative would be to replace only the first letter, implemented by creating two text boxes: one for the first letter and another for the remainder of the word ("atterns"). That would allow a different animation for just the first letter, which would support the presentation's goal of making a subtle distinction between the two different types of patterns.

The next animation builds in the word "idiomatic," further separating Neal's conception of patterns from the traditional one, as shown in Figure 4.4.

Neal then converted these two words into the slide's title, thereby implementing the Exuberant Title Top pattern: Make a major point, then use the body of the slide to provide extra examples or nuance. This effect is shown in the next intermediate version of the slide, which appears in Figure 4.5.

The next animation shows the two categories of idiomatic patterns—"technical" and "domain"—as shown in Figure 4.6.

Figure 4.2 Gradual Consistency:
Introducing the "Pattern" concept

Figure 4.3 Gradual Consistency:
Changing only the first letter

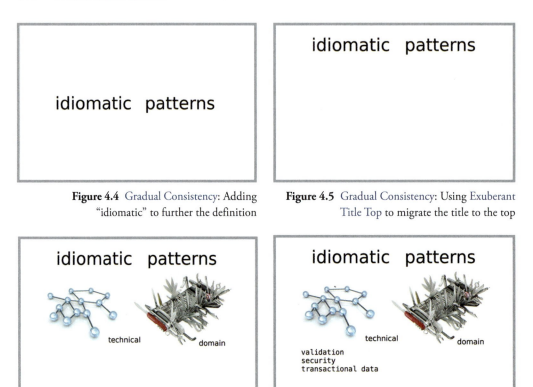

Figure 4.4 Gradual Consistency: Adding "idiomatic" to further the definition

Figure 4.5 Gradual Consistency: Using Exuberant Title Top to migrate the title to the top

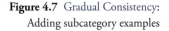

Figure 4.6 Gradual Consistency: Adding two subcategories

Figure 4.7 Gradual Consistency: Adding subcategory examples

These categories are important, so Neal added some abstract but representative images to highlight the fact that there are two and that they are of roughly equal importance. The next animation starts adding examples under each of the idiomatic-pattern subcategories, as shown in Figure 4.7.

Each of the three examples resides in a separate text box. He used a *click* animation trigger for the first example and then built the others automatically using the *build after previous* option. By making the examples appear gradually, he emphasizes the fact that multiple examples exist. But because he had only a couple of sentences' worth of material for each example, he didn't want to make the second and third examples' appearance as formal as it would seem via a *click* action. The order and manner you use to animate elements either highlights or hides something about that element, which is very effective when used well.

The next animation shows the examples for the other subcategory, as shown in Figure 4.8.

The last animation provides the final definition nuance for this concept, which appears at the bottom of the slide, as shown in Figure 4.9.

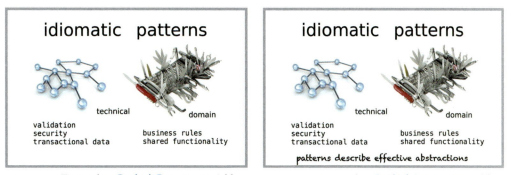

Figure 4.8 Gradual Consistency: Adding examples for the other subcategory

Figure 4.9 Gradual Consistency: Adding the last definition nuance

This last bit of text appears on an already crowded slide, but Neal wanted to make sure he added that last supporting statement. To make it stand out a bit, he used a bold font (later changed to an Analog Noise font for even more emphasis) and used a Composite Animation rather than his usual *dissolve* animation.

All the animations on this single slide illustrate patterns and techniques that appear throughout this book (and more than typically come into play at one time). Getting the elements in the right place for Slideuments purposes required a bit of invisible, pre*appearance* moves. For example, Figure 4.10 shows the build inspector in Keynote, with the "pattern" text box highlighted. It does a pre*appearance* move underneath the other "Patterns" text box (the one with the capital P) so that it can replace it when Neal emphasizes their difference. It then moves back up to the top of the slide as an Exuberant Title Top.

Figure 4.10 Gradual Consistency: The slide inspector in Keynote highlighting the complex life of the "pattern" text box

This final built version of the slide corresponds to the print version in the Slideuments. If your audience members are following along as you do the presentation, this is what you're building toward. Gradual Consistency provides a way to add some dynamic interest to your talk. When you start with this slide, your audience can see the common elements, which creates a bit of tension: What's missing, and what's going to be added? That tension translates into interest, especially if you also remove some things along the way as Neal did in this example (changing "Patterns" to "patterns").

Related Patterns   This pattern works particularly well with the Slideuments pattern, as you frequently want to slowly build toward the printed version.

Exuberant Title Top is a specific implementation of this pattern.

Mary's Handouts

Mary understands the perils of the Cookie Cutter antipattern, so she wants to make sure each slide in her presentation conveys a single thought. However, she also has to consider what the size of the handout will be. Although it looks fine to flip quickly through 200 slides during a presentation, no one wants to do that with paper.

How can she meet the simultaneous goals of a quality presentation and a concise printed equivalent? Bulleted lists meet the goal of conciseness, but they lead directly to the Bullet-Riddled Corpse antipattern. Single slides with just a few words make presentations more engaging but hinder conveying significant amounts of information in a compact printed space. Mary needs the next few patterns, which allow the presenter to control the exposition rate precisely.

Pattern: Charred Trail

Also Known As   Highlighted Bullet, Single Line of Focus

Definition   When printed, a Charred Trail slide is a complete slide. In presentation mode, items on the projected slide appear one at a time; as each one appears, the previous one grays out.

Figure 4.11 shows a slide in the designer (which is how it will print), and Figure 4.12 shows the same slide during the presentation.

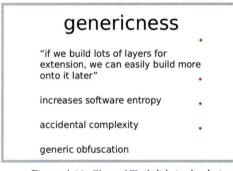

Figure 4.11 Charred Trail slide in the designer

Figure 4.12 The same slide during presentation

Motivation

This pattern works nicely for audiences accustomed to presentations featuring many Bullet-Riddled Corpse slides because when printed it appears to be in the same format. However, it also provides the highly desirable presentation quality of highlighting each point as you discuss it.

If you must create Slideuments, this pattern enables you to create a printed page that contains high-level talking points. As you present, only the item you're focusing on shows on the screen with full contrast.

A charred trail provides a good sense of where you are within the slide, making it a version of a Context Keeper, but with the scope of a single slide instead of the entire deck.

Applicability/ Consequences

This pattern enables you to produce a concise printout that still provides a reasonable presentation format at the expense of a nontrivial amount of additional effort.

This pattern is applicable any time you are forced to create a Slideument and need to control the exposition pace. It is also a useful organizational principle that enhances readability yet presents well.

This pattern works nicely with Exuberant Title Top.

Mechanics

PowerPoint includes this pattern as one of its features, although it has one annoyingly hidden property required to make it work properly. Keynote implements this feature directly, making it easy in both tools to create a template slide featuring this technique.

PowerPoint

PowerPoint allows you to implement this pattern by setting animation options for *entrance* animations such as *fade*. Once you've placed your elements in a text box in the *animation* pane, select the topmost element, click in the *animation* pane, and select *effect options . . .* , as shown in Figure 4.13.

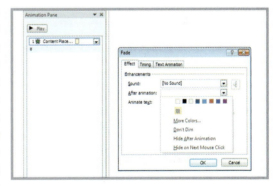

Figure 4.13 *Effect options* dialog in PowerPoint

One of the options is what color you would like to set the element after animation; to create the Charred Trail effect, set it to a transparent version of the original color.

You must take one more step to make this implementation palatable when you present the slides. By default, each of the elements in the text box will dim their color after the subsequence animation, which is the behavior you want . . . except for the last element. For our implementation of Charred

Trail, the last element isn't "charred"—in other words, the next thing that should happen after the last element on the slide isn't to make the last element transparent but to transition to the next slide. By default, PowerPoint will dim the last element, requiring you to click an extra time to get to the next slide.

To eliminate this annoyance, expand the *animation* pane to show each individual element, and select the last element you'll show. For that element, set the *effect options . . .* to *don't dim*, which will make the last element behave correctly.

Keynote   Keynote implements this pattern directly, as shown in Figure 4.14. Choose any *build in* animation you like, and then choose the *delivery* option of *by highlighted bullet*. Unlike the PowerPoint version, you don't have to do anything special to avoid "charring" the last element; Keynote acts correctly, allowing the last animation ("charring" the last element, which you don't need) to perform the slide transition instead.

Related Patterns   This pattern is a form of Context Keeper for an individual slide: It helps the audience focus exactly where you want it to, keeping the current context within each slide.

This pattern works nicely with Exuberant Title Top.

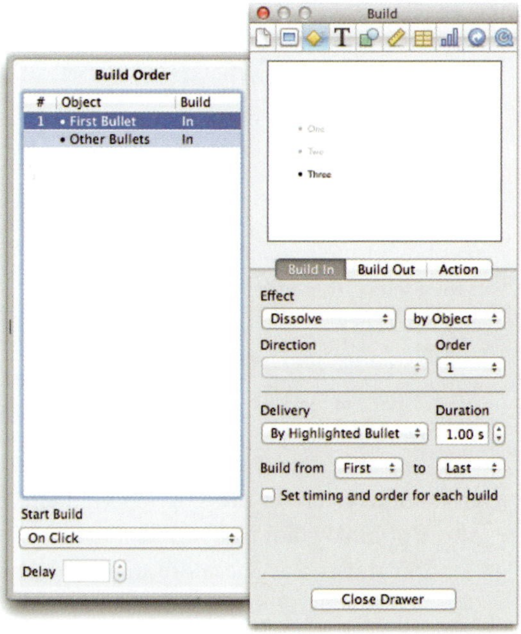

Figure 4.14 Slide inspector showing *by highlighted bullet* approach for Charred Trail

Pattern: Exuberant Title Top

Definition   An Exuberant Title Top is a slide title that starts in the middle of the screen and then migrates to the normal top position before exposing the remainder of the slide elements. An example of the beginning state of the slide during the presentation is shown in Figure 4.15.

The first animation moves the title to the top of the slide, as shown in Figure 4.16.

During the presentation, the title appears first, driving it home as the most important point. Then, upon the first animation, it migrates to the top, making room for all your supporting evidence.

This pattern works especially well when combined with other slow-exposition patterns such as Charred Trail, as shown in Figure 4.17.

Motivation   On a presentation slide, you can emphasize something in two ways: the size of the information and how long it lingers on the screen. Exuberant Title Top enables you to have an element with "normal" information density in printed form but emphasize it during the presentation. By adding time as a dimension, you can emphasize the important points during the presentation yet still generate a familiar slide layout.

Startling Title!	**Startling Title!** First bit of supporting evidence Second bit of supporting evidence Even more supporting evidence What?!? Even more supporting evidence Sure hope you're convinced by now

Figure 4.15 Exuberant Title Top (beginning position)   **Figure 4.16** Exuberant Title Top with body

Figure 4.17 Exuberant Title Top + Charred Trail

This pattern applies strongly to Slideuments because it bridges the gap between attractive printouts and effective presentations but can be a useful technique in any presentation.

A slight negative reaction to this pattern can arise when people in the audience are following along (an antipattern that goes hand-in-hand with Slideuments). Because Exuberant Title Top exposes your full slide content slowly (especially when used in conjunction with patterns like Charred Trail), it sometimes takes a long time for the presented slides to match the printouts. This can create a bit of tension (especially for audience members accustomed to following along) that you might want to mitigate early on with an explanation.

The basic mechanics of this pattern have you play with time in the designer as much as during the presentation. Slideuments should be readable when printed, meaning that the printed version should mirror the slide in the designer. You want the title in its "normal" place at design time, but you want it to start life in the middle of the slide when presented. The key realization is that *build in* doesn't need to be the first animation activity by an element on a slide. Exuberant Title Top works by moving the title element to the center of the slide as its first animation. Only then does the *build in* animation fire, followed by another move of the title back to its home at the top of the slide.

General Recipe

1. Place the title on the slide where you want it to appear in the printed version of the Slideuments.
2. Create a *build in* animation for the title.
3. Create the first of two *move* animations. The first moves the title from its finishing spot to the location where you want it to appear initially. In the animation inspector, change this animation so that it occurs before the *build in* animation.
4. Create the second *move* animation, symmetrical to the first, moving the title from the initial location to the final location.

1. The slide shown in Figure 4.17 appears both in the designer and when printed out as Figure 4.18.

   But when you click on the title itself in the designer, you see the real trickery at work here, which is shown in Figure 4.19.

   Most people think of *build in* as the first possible animation for an item on a slide, but that's not the case. For the design-time view (and consequently the document you're going to print) to remain pretty, the title box must be in its final position, at the top. However, for the effect

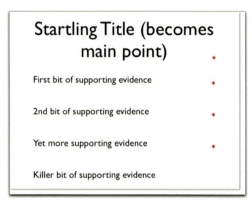

Figure 4.18 Exuberant Title Top slide in designer

Figure 4.19 Exuberant Title Top slide in designer

to work, the title must appear in the middle of the slide and migrate to the top. The complete slide in the Keynote designer along with the inspector appears in Figure 4.20.

2. When the slide transitions in, the title's first animation moves it to the middle of the screen. Then the title's *build in* animation fires. The first move to the middle is set to happen as the slide transition occurs, and the duration is set to the minimum time (0.01 seconds).

3. The *build in* build makes it appear. The next click performs a second *move* build to get it back to its original location while the rest of the slide content starts to appear. Generally, the first supporting-evidence item should be set to build *after* the second move, which gives the appearance that the title is being pushed upward by the supporting facts. If you use the *with* build, you'll see some overlap between the migrating title and the first element.

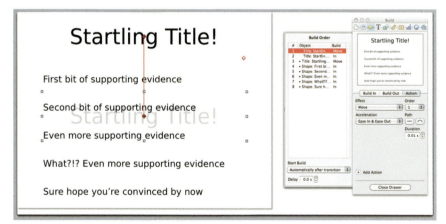

Figure 4.20 Exuberant Title Top slide in designer

Keynote will fight you a little on setting up this pattern because it assumes that the first thing you'll want to do to a slide element is make it appear. Consequently, if you add a *move* build and then add an *build in* animation, Keynote reorders the builds to make the *build in* occur first. It's a simple matter to repair the misguided help by manually moving the *move* build above the *build in* build; Keynote won't bother it again.

Exuberant Title Top
in PowerPoint

1. The slide in Figure 4.21 shows an Exuberant Title Top slide in the designer, along with the *animation* pane.

   Most people think of *entrance* as the first possible animation for an item on a slide, but that's not the case. Because the goal of Slideuments is to create a presentation that looks nice when printed, you must keep the design-time view clean. That means that the title box must be in its final position at the top. However, to get the effect to work, the title must appear in the middle of the slide and migrate to the top.

   When the slide transitions in, the title's first animation moves it to the middle of the screen. Then the title's *entrance* build kicks in. The first move to the middle is set to happen as the slide transition occurs, and the duration is set to the minimum time (0 seconds). Once that happens, you can now allow the title to appear as it normally would.

2. The *entrance* animation makes the title appear. The next click performs a second *move* animation to reset the title back to the top of the slide. Generally, the first supporting evidence item's animation should be set to *start after previous*, which gives the appearance that the title is being pushed upward by the supporting facts. (If you use the *start with previous*, you'll see some overlap between the migrating title and the first element.)

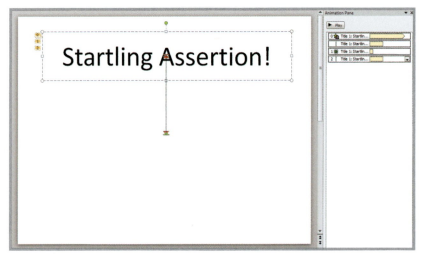

Figure 4.21 Exuberant Title Top in the PowerPoint designer

PowerPoint will fight you a little on setting up this pattern because it assumes that the first thing you'll want to do to a slide element is make it appear. Consequently, if you add a *motion path* animation and then add an *entrance* build, PowerPoint will reorder the builds to make the *entrance* first. It's a simple matter to repair the misguided help by manually moving the *motion path* animation above the *entrance* build; PowerPoint won't bother it again.

Related Patterns   This pattern is frequently used with the Slideuments pattern as you build slowly toward the printed version of the slide.

Charred Trail and Exuberant Title Top make an attractive combination because they work well together to provide good information density and controlled exposition.

This pattern is a specialization of the Gradual Consistency pattern; the title eventually goes to the top to match the final version of the slide.

 Pattern: Invisibility

Also Known As   Hidden Treasure

Definition   Use invisible elements and surprise animations to restore some mystery and surprise to your presentation. Those invisible elements may be blank slides that you place at strategic points in the presentation to force the audience's focus back to you, the presenter.

Motivation   Surprise is an excellent technique for creating and maintaining interest. Yet when you are presenting from Slideuments, the audience usually has a copy of your presentation. They know all your surprises, which ruins them. This pattern suggests that you use hidden images, phrases, or other invisible (to the handouts) elements to restore intrigue.

By the same token, you sometimes want some preparatory time to set up the subject of the next slide. Allowing the old slide to remain shows stale content. You can create a slide that uses animations yet starts in a completely blank state. You effectively keep elements invisible until you want to show them.

Applicability/
Consequences   This pattern works in any Slideuments setting. Some may think this is too showy for office presentations, but we disagree. Those presentations tend to be among the dullest, and anything that adds interest is welcomed by everyone in the room (presenter and audience alike). Business presentations must frequently implement the Slideuments antipattern; this pattern is a good complement.

One negative consequence of this pattern is less consistency with the printed version of the Slideuments. You must weigh the benefit of using a few surprise elements to spice up the presentation against the erosion of consistency.

Another consequence of this pattern appears at design time for your slides. To make Slideuments attractive, you must pay attention to your slides' appearance in the designer because that is the view that prints. If you have invisible elements on the slide, it's easy to forget they are there and accidentally work on the slide. Keynote adds little diamonds to indicate hidden elements with builds, as shown in Figure 4.23. PowerPoint shows the animation order number on top of each element. Neither mechanism is great; it's easy to not see the invisible element when you have lots of other elements on the slide. Neal uses a little indicator on the speaker's notes for the slide: If the characters "(-)" appear at the first of the notes (it's supposed to look like an eye), he knows that there's something invisible on the slide and to tread carefully when making changes.

A little of this pattern goes a long way. After you've sprung a surprise on your audience once, they'll automatically pay more attention in case you do it again. As long as you plant one early, you can use very few yet benefit from this effect. Conversely, if you use it too much, it loses its surprise factor and becomes annoying.

Mechanics   The Invisibility pattern is simple to implement in both Keynote and PowerPoint, but each utilizes a different tool feature. The short version: In Keynote, you make the image invisible by setting its opacity to zero and then use an action to set the opacity to 100 percent. In PowerPoint, it's more difficult to set the opacity initially, so you can use a slide-sized white image with no border as a curtain. To make the image appear, you "drop" the curtain. The curtain effect will work in Keynote as well, but our current implementation is easier.

Here is an example of this pattern from one of Neal's presentations. He's trying to show some options for a technical solution to a problem, and the first suggestion works but is considered suspect by other developers (for good reason). For completeness, Neal wanted to show the option but also convey that perhaps it isn't the optimal solution. The slide sequence appears in Figure 4.22.

The designer view is the view you get when you print your Slideuments. When you look at this slide in the designer, the background image doesn't seem to appear. Figure 4.23 shows the designer view for this slide.

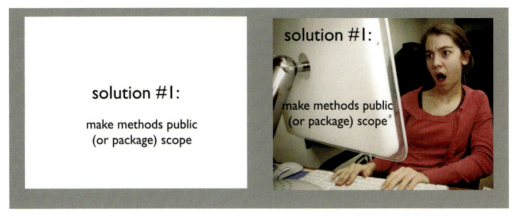

Figure 4.22 Invisibility slide as presented

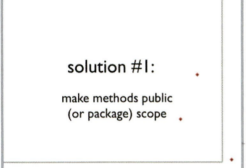

Figure 4.23 Invisibility slide in the Keynote designer

Figure 4.24 Ghost image of the invisible element

Notice the red diamonds in the designer view, which is Keynote's indicator for hidden animations. Clicking on the bottom-right diamond shows a ghost view of the image whose opacity you have set to zero, as shown in Figure 4.24.

As you can see in Figure 4.24, the image exists but won't appear until its appearance animation happens. In this particular example, Neal also moved the text to fit into convenient spots on the resulting slide. He wanted the main point to show up centered on the slide and only make way for the surprise element. You may also notice that part of the image "hangs off" the slide in the designer, which is perfectly OK. Neal needed to get the image aligned with the text and ended up using just the part of the picture that fit nicely with the text.

Alignment with the surrounding text can be tricky. You want the text to look unassuming, which adds more impact to the surprise element. When you place the invisible image on the slide, set its opacity to 10 percent until you get everything the way you want it. Then set it to zero for the final effect (and find a way to remind yourself that invisible things now lurk on your slide the next time you make changes).

Invisibility in Keynote

1. Choose a suitable image or phrase that you want as your surprise and add it to the slide.
2. Set the image's *opacity* to 0 using the inspector, as shown in Figure 4.25.
3. After you have all the other elements in place on the slide, add an *opacity* action that restores the image to 100 percent.
4. You can use the reappearance of the image as the *build in* animation if you like. However, if you're really going for surprise, set the *duration* of the *opacity* action to 0.10 seconds, and add a *build in* animation for the image. When you add the *build in* animation, Keynote will always place the *build in* animation above any existing *actions* you might have in the slide's build order. You have to change the order manually only once; Keynote will stop fighting you on this subject.

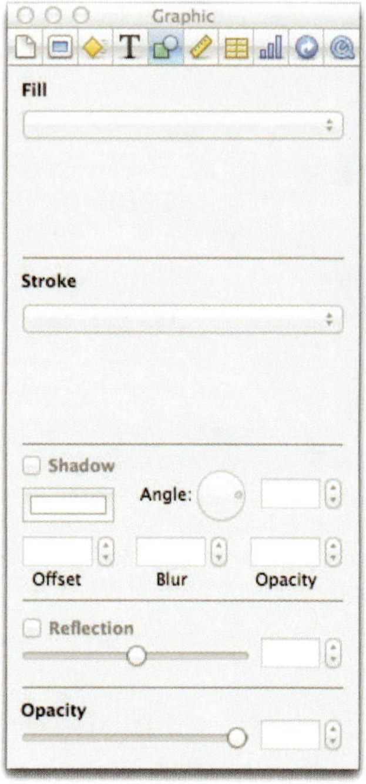

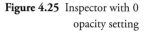

Figure 4.25 Inspector with 0 opacity setting

Invisibility in PowerPoint (Also Known as the "Curtain Trick")

1. Choose a suitable image or phrase that you want as your surprise and add it to the slide.
2. Insert a borderless shape that covers your surprise element. It can be as small as a box that covers a phrase or big enough to cover the entire background of the slide. (See Figure 4.22 for an example.) You'll have to play around with the layering order to get it so that it covers your surprise element but doesn't cover other text that you want to see on your Slideuments.
3. At the point on the slide's timeline when you're ready for the surprise, create an *exit* animation for your shape with zero duration. Removing the curtain will make your image appear. If you want more bang for your surprise, add an *entrance* animation immediately after you *exit* the curtain; the *zoom* entrance works nicely.

Related Patterns

This pattern works well in Slideuments to add a bit of presentation time pizzazz.

Pattern: Context Keeper

Definition   A Context Keeper reveals a presentation's structure. An organizational technique, it uses a presentation device (such as an animation or transition) to reveal the talk's structure temporally, by subject matter, or via some other context meaningful to the audience.

Motivation   Context Keeper imposes a visible structure on a presentation that might not be obvious enough from the content.

Applicability/ Consequences   This pattern applies when the following occur:

- The presentation subject matter naturally consists of discrete chunks
- You have a complex subject and need to identify potentially confusing parts explicitly
- You want to help the audience understand the Narrative Arc of your presentation with some visual guidance

Mechanics   You can implement this pattern in many ways, including Breadcrumbs, but the pattern goes beyond a simple concrete technique. A Context Keeper ties a series of slides together within a larger subject area. Erik Doernenburg, a well-known technical presenter, suggests using a different slide color background for each section—a nice, simple way to implement this pattern.

An excellent mechanism for Context Keeper is the *magic move* animation/ transition in Keynote. With *magic move* as the slide transition, the elements that appear on both slides smoothly animate from their location on the first slide to their location on the subsequent slide. The elements never leave the screen; they just magically migrate from one position to the other.

Context Keeper in Keynote via Magic Move   An example will illustrate how this Keynote feature can implement Context Keeper. Neal did a talk for the Clojure developer community called *Neal's Master Plan for Clojure Enterprise Mindshare Domination*. Neal knew that he couldn't come up with better ideas than the community itself could; the real purpose of the presentation was to provide scaffolding for the community to categorize its already good ideas. Thus the Narrative Arc of the talk provides categories of approaches, with exposition and examples of each.

To introduce each category, Neal used the *anvil build in* animation; it falls from the top of the slide and lands by stirring up "dust." After he introduced the category (using Twitter-style hashtags), he used *magic move* to keep the hashtag on the screen for the entire duration of that topic. Consider the slides in Figure 4.26.

The *#packheat* hashtag anvils in from above, and *magic move* keeps it on the screen while that category is current. When the category is complete, Neal uses the *anvil* entrance animation for the next hashtag, *#befriend*.

Figure 4.26 Using a hashtag + *magic move* as a Context Keeper

Figure 4.27 Fading recurring element to keep it from becoming a distraction

Although using a recurring element like the hashtag in this example ties your context together nicely, it can be a distraction if it becomes a Floodmark. A technique Neal uses allows the *magic move* to be the context keeper and then gradually fades the recurring element away on subsequent slides. When the context shift is new, he enhances the noticeability of the Context Keeper by leaving it at full color and then gradually reducing its opacity on subsequent slides, as shown in Figure 4.27.

Context Keeper in PowerPoint

As of this writing, PowerPoint doesn't include this powerful feature. You can mimic the effect with some effort, but the end result isn't as nice.

To partially emulate *magic move* as a Context Keeper in PowerPoint, do the following:

1. *Entrance* animate the first element in whatever way you like.
2. For the *exit* animation, choose one like *fly out* or *wipe*.
3. For the next slide, the first animation after the transition should be the symmetrical *entrance* animation. For example, if you chose *wipe* as the *exit* on the previous slide, choose the *effect options* to wipe left to right.
4. On the *entrance* animation on the subsequent slide, choose *wipe* with the option for right to left.

Using transitions and animations as a Context Keeper creates a visual bridge to the previous slide by using symmetrical animations. This doesn't look as nice as Keynote's *magic move* because you still "lose" the element as the slide transitions. The magic of *magic move* is that it can display things at times not allowed using standard transitions, such as *between* slides.

Related Patterns

The Breadcrumbs pattern is a specific implementation of this pattern.

You need an identifiable Narrative Arc to provide the context this pattern preserves.

Pattern: Breadcrumbs

Also Known As   Agenda, Roadmap

Definition   Place slides at critical junctures within your presentation to give the audience checkpoints that indicate where you are in the overall presentation.

Motivation   When you give a long talk, it's easy for attendees to lose track of the narrative flow, especially if the topic is highly technical or the material is new for the audience. Showing checkpoint slides along the way makes it easier for the attendees to see the overall structure of your material.

Applicability/ Consequences   This pattern works best in situations in which you are

- giving a lengthy presentation;
- covering complex technical subjects; and
- presenting a very abstract, "hand-waving" kind of talk.

On the downside, you must sacrifice some of your presentation time to a metapresentation concern—namely, elucidating the talk's structure. If you find yourself always using this pattern and your subject area isn't overly technical, perhaps you should rethink your presentation's organization. If the attendees can't figure out the organization, perhaps you should revise the organization to make it clearer. You don't want the audience to miss your important points because they can't readily figure out what context a point belongs in. Getting the organization right is sometimes tricky but always improves the clarity of your presentation.

We've seen some evil VBA (scripting code for Windows-based applications) code on the Internet that enables you to embed a "live" progress bar in your presentation, showing precisely what percentage you've completed. We dislike real-time progress indicators because they distract from your message by introducing too much metapresentation information (see the Going Meta antipattern). You want the audience to proceed within a context of *ideas*, not just elapsed time. Your audience will start noticing the progress and, just like a user waiting for a document to save, start hoping for a merciful end.

Mechanics   This pattern has many different implementations; a common one is to replicate the agenda slide throughout the presentation. You can use presentation-tool tricks like highlighting the upcoming section or dimming the completed ones à la the Charred Trail pattern.

You don't have to use bulleted agendas to implement this pattern; it's difficult to get many levels of indentation unless you resort to Ant Fonts.

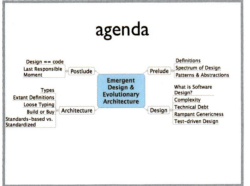

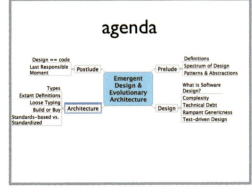

Figure 4.28 Representation of a mind map providing a good breadcrumb overview

Figure 4.29 Highlighting the breadcrumb to make your location unambiguous

Neal sometimes uses a mind map to show the overall structure in a single image, as shown in Figure 4.28.

Showing an entire mind map might not be the best way of automatically notifying your attendees where you are within the presentation. You can always improve the static view of the mind map with a little bit of highlighting, as shown in Figure 4.29.

During the presentation, Neal has a *dissolve* entrance animation on the highlight box so that the audience sees the overall agenda for a moment; the next topic of conversation then slowly highlights. An alternative approach he has also used is to reduce the opacity on the elements that aren't the current topic.

Related Patterns   This pattern is a specific implementation of the Context Keeper pattern.

You can combine Breadcrumbs with Bookends, placing your agenda elements within the other content.

Breadcrumbs serve to illuminate the structure of your talk, but be careful to avoid Going Meta by telling your audience too much about the structure and other things you find fascinating but are decidedly peripheral to the subject of the presentation.

Pattern: Bookends

Also Known As	Opening and Closing Curtain, Previews and Trailers
Definition	Place similar or identical slides at the start and end of your presentation deck, often for the purpose of advertising yourself or your presentation.
Motivation	The following are various motives for using Bookends:

At the Beginning

The front bookend slide reassures audience members that they are in the correct room with the correct presenter. It is also a form of guilt-free advertising for the presenter that entertains the waiting audience and consumes none of the allocated presentation time.

Additional attendees, including some who may be highly interested in your topic but unaware of your talk, might be enticed into the room by the first advertising slide. Persons wandering by the open door of the room who see the slide might think, "That's catchy. I think I'll sit in on this." Just as usefully, the front bookend slide might turn away attendees who are already in their chairs. Perhaps they now realize they're in the wrong talk or that they'd misunderstood the single-sentence abstract that had led them to attend. The net result is that your audience is now a set of more interested attendees. The energy of the room, the volume of questions, the intensity of interaction, and the feedback scores will all be heightened by this process of natural but aided audience selection.

At the End

The concluding bookend slide is often identical to the opening one. It offers one more opportunity for audience members to jot down your phone number, website, e-mail address, or other contact information. It can also serve as a reminder to the audience to tweet a positive (or occasionally critical) comment about your talk while mentioning your Twitter handle.

A final bookend slide serves one more important purpose: It lets the audience know that your presentation has concluded. This may seem like a trivial benefit, but think back to presentations you've attended in which you were uncomfortably unsure if it was polite to leave. Is she done? Is there more? This should be crisply clear—not be a matter for conjecture. A bookend slide politely says, "We're done, and you are free to leave or ask questions."

Applicability/ Consequences	Every presentation that allots time for the audience to get settled and doesn't immediately transition to another presenter at its end should apply this pattern. This includes corporate, boardroom, internal, informal, and special interest group presentations. No matter how

familiar the group, almost certainly someone in the audience will know how to reach you only from the contact information on your talk's bookend slides.

If stylistically permissible, this pattern should be applied even to unique formats such as Ignite and Pecha Kucha, which are popular styles that implement the Lightning Talk pattern.

Making your contact information clear increases the chance of contact for future interest, which might be good for business if you're a professional speaker (but a curse if you get too much useless contact).

Feedback will be more transparent about your performance. If your social media links, such as a Twitter handle, are posted as part of the bookend slides, you can expect more candid feedback—some complimentary, some constructive, some passive, and some downright mean-spirited. Social media books such as *The Backchannel*[3] offer insights into how to harness and shape this new avenue of instant commentary.

If you're speaking with an opportunity for feedback via evaluation forms, be sure to remind your audience on your final bookend slide to fill them out. Receiving useful, actionable comments on your presentation is both rare and valuable, and it's essential to applying the Crucible pattern correctly.

Mechanics   *At the Beginning*
The bookend slide can contain as much or as little information about the presenter as desired. The following are frequently used items:

1. Speaker's full name
2. Speaker's business title or position
3. E-mail address
4. Twitter handle
5. Blog URL
6. Company name
7. Company website URL
8. Copyright information (or perhaps Creative Commons License)

At the End
The concluding bookend slide might differ from the opening one by including "Questions?" in a large font. This signals not only that the presentation has ended but also that questions are now welcome.

The final slide might also differ by including a link to where your slides can be downloaded. In the age of digital distribution, it is increasingly common to deliver a supplement or the slides themselves digitally, eschewing the printed handouts model of yore.

The concluding bookend slide often contains the following:

Figure 4.30 An opening Bookend slide

Figure 4.31 A closing Bookend slide

1. Slides download URL
2. Talk and presenter feedback URL, such as a link to SpeakerRate.[4]
3. A repeat of many or all the items on the opening bookend slide

Related Patterns   An advanced implementation of this pattern is embodied in Preroll—an animated, embedded movie that loops through several slides.

A similar mechanism to Bookends is the Intermezzi slides, which serve as transitional buffers between subject matter shifts. Generally, we are more likely to allow Floodmarks and other distractions on Bookends than Intermezzi.

Pattern: Soft Transitions

Also Known As   Slow Fade, Fade to Black, Crossfade

Definition   Use subtle slide transitions (such as *dissolve*) to avoid always being forced to show exactly one slide's material at a time.

Motivation   As we discuss in the Cookie Cutter antipattern, using the *slide* to define the unit of size for your thoughts is a bad idea. Some thoughts require more than one slide to explore them fully. Don't fall into the trap of allowing the presentation tool to define the scope of information flow. Instead, use the tool to its advantage, controlling the information flow via slide transitions and animations.

Transitions, defined as moving from one slide to the next, implement your narrative flow. If you use no transitions (in other words, are presenting an Infodeck), all information arrives in slide-sized chunks. Using consistent, subtle transitions is one way to unify your topic visually across multiple slides.

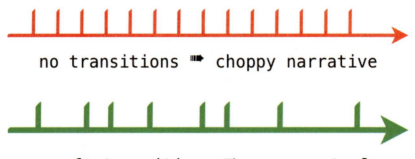

Figure 4.32 Transition styles help define narrative flow

Applicability/
Consequences Liberating yourself from the choppy nature of the Bullet-Riddled Corpse antipattern helps you to relax and focus on telling a compelling story alongside the information you must convey. This is illustrated in Figure 4.32.

When you use transitions effectively, they enable you to control the information flow rather than rely on the arbitrary amount of information you can cram onto a single slide.

Mechanics The key to effective transition use is consistency and subtlety. Use a consistent transition while you are exploring a particular topic and then use a strikingly different one to signal movement to a new topic or digression. For example, Neal is a big fan of using the *dissolve* transition in Keynote (*fade* in PowerPoint) as a subtle way to move between topical slides and then using *cube* (perhaps *push* in PowerPoint) to signal movement in the agenda.

As a general rule of thumb, you should choose complementary transitions and animations. For example, Neal uses both the *dissolve* transition and animation in many of his talks. Because he builds up content slowly using the *dissolve* animation and he transitions slides using the same effect, the presentation has an overall consistency. In another of his presentations, he uses Keynote's *move in* transition, with the *left to right* option, which makes elements appear moving from right to left. He then used the same animation with the same option for each slide element. The overall effect was that everything (both slides and individual parts of slides) rushed in from the right, creating a forward motion effect throughout the presentation. Using similar transitions and animations allows you to hide the difference between them, further blurring the line between slides.

When you use this technique in conjunction with Intermezzi slides, no one will doubt that the subject has changed.

Related Patterns This pattern ties in well with the Emergence pattern when you are building a multislide narrative.

This pattern also facilitates multislide implementations of the Gradual Consistency pattern.

Use the Soft Transitions pattern to help avoid the Cookie Cutter antipattern.

Pattern: Intermezzi

<table>
<tr><td>Also Known As</td><td>Digital Entr'acte</td></tr>
<tr><td>Definition</td><td>Use a color change, thematic shift, or outline introduction to clearly signal the beginning or end of each logical part of your presentation's narrative structure.</td></tr>
<tr><td>Motivation</td><td>Presentations should be composed of logical parts in the form of a Triad or Narrative Arc. Intermezzi, like Breadcrumbs, are a form of Context Keeper that helps you to set your presentation's organizational context.</td></tr>
</table>

When audience members are sitting through a lengthy presentation, they need *hooks* to reset their understanding of where you are taking them in the overall story. Small, graphically creative cues—sometimes supplemented by a list of points or words describing the *next big idea*—can help align audience minds with your presentation direction.

Applicability/ Consequences

This pattern is useful for long expositions, deep topics with many tentacles, and tutorial-style talks. Any presentation over 15 minutes in length can benefit from it. It is especially recommended for talks in the 50- to 90-minute range because they can cover so much ground that the audience needs to be gently kept in mental lockstep with the presenter.

If done poorly, these demarcation slides can cause a slight visual interruption of the narrative. But if you are careful to keep them within the Unifying Visual Theme, they can reinforce your overall message rather than detract from it.

Mechanics

You can use many techniques to implement this pattern, such as the following:

- Color change from main presentation
- List of items to be covered (opening)
- List of items just covered, inviting questions (closing)
- A visual element or picture that represents the next group of ideas
- A loaded question that raises or renews interest in the next section

Another common way to delineate section changes is to use obvious graphical slides, generally tied to the Unifying Visual Theme. Neal uses this technique often, as illustrated by the red boxes in his *Emergent Design* presentation in Figure 4.33.

In Figure 4.33, the subject of the presentation is the agile software development engineering practice of *emergent design*, and the Unifying Visual Theme is a series of struggling sprout pictures Neal found on a stock-photo site. The talk naturally segregates into sections, and the obvious sprout slides make it clear to the audience that Neal is changing topics.

Known Uses

Matthew applies this pattern to his GitHub Git Workshop,[5] which consists of seven hours of daily classroom time. Intermezzi provide context to the delivery of a segment of the materials—in essence, a preview of the grouping of subtopics. It silently cues students as to the most appropriate times to ask questions. This smoothes Matthew's delivery and better interleaves the questions and resulting discussion with their associated materials.

Related Patterns

Bookends is a specialized version of Intermezzi, generally with more Floodmarks-like content.

Intermezzi are a specific implementation of the Context Keeper pattern.

Figure 4.33 Using sprout pictures to separate major sections and create a Unifying Visual Theme

Pattern: Backtracking

Contributed By   Martin Fowler, Chief Scientist, ThoughtWorks[6]

Definition   Backtracking is a Context Keeper technique that enables you to reestablish a narrative context by purposefully repeating slides.

Motivation   Many talks naturally feature a primary narrative stream with necessary digressions along the way. Backtracking helps you safely venture off on a tangent and then immediately reestablish the previous context. The duplicated slides remind the audience where you left off and also establish a new context for the next few slides.

This pattern provides benefits beyond structural convenience. Returning to a familiar spot is a familiar narrative pattern. Comedians call this a *callback*: returning to a punch line delivered earlier in the show to elicit a new (sometimes even bigger) laugh. People are accustomed to navigation clues in stories and movies; you can leverage that innate knowledge for your presentation.

Applicability/ Consequences   This pattern applies to presentations that feature digressions.

Be careful when implementing this pattern because it forces you to violate the *DRY* (Don't Repeat Yourself) principle: If you change any of the slides you're using as backtrackers, you must remember to change all copies of them.

Mechanics   No special tool support is required to implement this pattern. When you identify a trail off your main narrative, copy the slide that you show just before you start your digression and paste it at the end of the digression.

Use a distinctive slide transition to indicate you are venturing into a digression. Neal loves the *cube* transition in Keynote, flipping to the *right* to start the digression and *left* to return.

This pattern is different from using the slide tool to revisit an earlier slide as a reminder. The Backtracking pattern purposefully duplicates slides to act as visual placeholders. As in the Invisibility pattern, Neal always places a special character in the speaker's notes (in this case, it's "#_#") to remind him that this is a duplicated Backtracking slide and to be careful to only change the original.

Related Patterns   This pattern is a specific implementation of the Context Keeper pattern.

Intermezzi make a great backtracking destination; they exist in the presentation to provide an anchoring point, which is generally where you want to return after digressions.

Pattern: Preroll

Definition Preroll is an advanced animated implementation of Bookends that automatically loops through two or three slides while the audience is still filtering into the room and getting situated.

Motivation If your opening bookend slide is crowded with too much information—an antipattern of the highest order—you can gain more canvas and decrease information density by splitting it into two or three slides and implementing Preroll.

When other presenters in your circle have adopted the static Bookends technique and you want to raise the bar again, this animated variation gains attention and comments.

Applicability/ Consequences This technique applies to any presentation that needs more advertising space for the presenter's contact information or a list of points describing *who will enjoy this talk.* . . .

Preroll requires you to maintain additional files and use additional tools. Implementing it is much more time-intensive than traditional static Bookends.

Mechanics You typically apply this pattern only to the opening bookend slide. Animation at closing is less effective than a static slide in communicating that your presentation is finished.

Preroll is not built into the Keynote or PowerPoint applications. You can implement it in one of two ways. One is more flexible but creates a second file. The other is embedded in the master presentation but requires a second tool.

The two-file approach: Simply create a second Keynote or PowerPoint file, store it in the same directory as your core presentation, and set several settings uniquely on this preroll file:

1. Include an interesting, attention-grabbing transition such as *cube* or *fall*.
2. Automatically advance the slides on a timed basis.
3. Loop the slides continuously when the last slide is reached.

The embedded-movie approach: This implementation requires both a slide-presentation tool and video-recording software. It requires all the preparatory work of the two-file approach but embeds the result into your core presentation. After creating the second Keynote or PowerPoint file using the two-file approach, you must do the following:

1. Play the preroll presentation you just created.
2. Record a screen-capture video of the full sequence of preroll slides.
3. Trim the recorded video to start with the first slide and end with the last (because you might have captured a bit too much with the screen-recording tool).

4. Set your movie export preferences to your presentation-delivery resolution.[7]
5. Export to a native format that your presentation application can embed natively. Keynote understands MOV and M4V. PowerPoint understands AVI and WMV.
6. Embed the finished (exported) movie file in the first slide of your presentation.
7. Set the properties of the embedded movie to loop until the slide is advanced.

Related Patterns   Preroll is a specific implementation of the Bookends pattern.

Pattern: Crawling Credits

Also Known As   *Star Wars* Credits Crawl, Closing Credits

Contributed By   Nancy Duarte, CEO, Duarte Design Inc.[8]

Definition   As in Crawling Code, text continuously and slowly scrolls upward, fading the oldest text into the distance. But this nuanced variation applies solely to the closing credits of a presentation.

Motivation   As presentations become more elaborate, more contributors—be it to the stock photos, prose, research, quotes, illustrations, or sample code—tend to be involved. You can list contributors (and, optionally, your contact information) in a fun and animated style through a slow automatic crawl of text on the presentation's closing slide.

Credits should be large enough for all to see and visible for long enough so that audience members can record any of interest. Crawling Credits enables you to meet both criteria when your credits won't fit on a single slide. It's often easier to have a single, static bookend slide to signal the end of your presentation, but if you must expand to more than one, mimicking the visual style of movie credits lets you pack in more information while still conveying a clear sense of ending.

Applicability/ Consequences   An animated closing can be a strong visual differentiator from less polished presentations. If construed as unnecessary eye candy, it can be a negative differentiator. The stodgiest of audience members might think an animated closing is pretentious. Perhaps it is. But if they remember it, and it's done tastefully, it is yet one more way to make your presentation memorable.

If you use an embedded-movie approach to craft the Crawling Credits, editing the text is complicated for even the smallest of updates. Plain text in a slide takes just a click and edit to revise.

Audience members who write or type slowly or are not focused on the screen when the credits begin scrolling can miss all or part of an item of importance to them. You can mitigate this potential problem by creating a static bookend slide that includes the most-critical URLs and displaying it after the scrolling credits have concluded.

Mechanics   The easiest way to implement this pattern uses a single static image that is much too *tall* for the slide. In other words, the content hangs significantly off the top if you place the bottom of the image aligned with the bottom of the slide. Then use an animation such as *move in* and set the direction option to *bottom to top* and the duration to a long interval. As the image animates on the slide, it will slowly move "up" the slide, like movie credits. Crawling Credits can also be implemented as a mashup with the techniques described in the Preroll pattern.

Related Patterns   This pattern has similar implementation to but different uses from the Crawling Code pattern.

Crawling Credits generally appear on or just before a final bookend slide.

In many ways, Crawling Credits is the symmetrically opposite effect of the Preroll pattern.

Mary's Presentation

In Mary the Marketer's case, the primary deliverable is the big product launch at the trade show. She double-checked with the organizers, and it turns out that only 60 percent of the target audience will be there, the rest receiving the news via a PDF of the Slideuments.

Having a "printed" version suggests a higher information density so that you don't waste paper for someone who might print it out. Mary decided to start the presentation using the Cave Painting pattern to illustrate the trials and tribulations of getting the product to market. She then created a tight series of Slideuments, using Exuberant Title Top and Charred Trail to maintain audience interest in the live presentation but keep information density high.

Because of the large number of people who will consume her deliverable in nonpresented form, Mary considered creating an Infodeck, but they work poorly for live presentations, and she wanted to make sure that both experiences worked as well as possible.

This is a good example of using our patterns as *nomenclature* about presentations. Notice how much knowledge about Mary's presentation we managed to cram into the preceding paragraphs because we can now communicate via a pattern shorthand.

CHAPTER 5

DEMONSTRATIONS VERSUS PRESENTATIONS

ALTHOUGH PRESENTATIONS FREQUENTLY INCLUDE demonstrations, presentations and demonstrations are not the same thing. A *demonstration* is designed to show directly how something—generally either a tool or a technique—works. A *presentation* presents information *about* something; the something could be a tool or technique that you discuss with or without demonstrating it. The patterns and anti-patterns in this chapter clarify this subtle but important (and often missed) distinction.

It is common to build a presentation around the output of a tool such as spreadsheet software or a programmer's integrated development environment. Although you can embed the output directly into the presentation, we show several better patterns (Traveling Highlights, Crawling Code, and Emergence) that add veracity and remove risk.

Project Manager Pam's Perfectly Putrid Performance

Pam's team has been working like mad for the last three weeks, realizing the new client vision for one of its software products with blood, sweat, tears, pizza, and overtime. The team has performed beyond its potential and hit the deadline. All that's left is the showcase, where Pam will demonstrate all the new killer features. The client knows this is a brand-new code and might have a few bugs, but the new functionality is vital to the vision for the product. Unfortunately, along with Pam's team, Murphy (and his law) showed up for the showcase. Even though the new features worked brilliantly over and over when Pam practiced them, the showcase was a disaster. Pam didn't get a chance to show the new business vision because the bugs (which would have been gone by the following week) sabotaged her.

Pam didn't yet understand the distinction between a *presentation* and a *demonstration* and inadvertently ended up implementing the Dead Demo antipattern. She wanted to *present* the new features to get approval, but she ended up *demonstrating* bugs and imperfections. She thought she wanted to demo the new product, but it was not ready yet: She would have been better off building a presentation and using a pattern like Lipsync, which would meet her goals exactly.

Shoeless Subramaniam's Spectacular Show

Venkat Subramaniam, a well-known speaker on the software-developer conference circuit, is famous for his talks' style as much as their content. He talks about highly complex subjects, yet the closest thing to presentation software he uses is a text editor, which holds his agenda. He dazzles the audience by typing code and explaining as he goes, incrementally building software and running it periodically. To the outside observer, this is the most obscure entertainment imaginable: 100 people with their eyes glued on a screen with scrolling text, having the time of their lives, entranced.

Subramaniam has been doing this for years because he has mastered the skill of talking and typing at the same time, and he has the concentration ability to hold that complex context for hours at a time. In a talk Neal attended that involved an incredibly complex tool and many multilevel steps, Subramaniam built an impressive artifact in about 45 minutes, explaining what he was doing and why. A few unexpected things happened along the way, but he handled them adroitly, explaining what had happened and how to solve that type of problem. When he was done and showed the finished artifact, the audience gave him a standing ovation. His performance was a tour de force of concentration and skill. Like a professional athlete, he makes the difficult appear easy.

Oh, and he always takes his shoes off before his talks. That helps him to relax—and is the inspiration for the Shoeless pattern.

Tester Tom's Tragic Hotel Wi-Fi Trust

Tom is an adrenaline junkie. He doesn't jump off skyscrapers or hurtle down a frozen luge track on ice skates. No, Tom likes to give presentations that require an Internet connection. In fact, he's infamous for copying a URL from his slide deck, pasting it into a browser, and then waiting for the page to load. This task is usually accompanied by a series of apologies and curses. Nothing drives an audience to their smartphones faster than watching a web page fail to load. Tom is convinced the attendees won't believe something is real unless he actually demos it live. That might be the case in certain circumstances, but a shred of doubt is better than the annoyance of watching a status bar.

Despite what you may think, some hotels (and conference centers) actually *don't* have Internet connections at all! Tom learned this the hard way after flying halfway around the world. As you can guess, his talks required an Internet connection. He'd given the talks successfully many times in a variety of venues, and he'd grown complacent. The night before his presentation, he was told that the conference center did not have an Internet connection. Tom worked through the night implementing an emergency Lipsync pattern, recording his demos via hotel Wi-Fi. Needless to say, he hit the espresso hard the next day.

Hotel (and conference center) Wi-Fi is completely untrustworthy. Someday we'll live in a world with ubiquitous high-speed Internet connectivity, but until then, just assume you won't have a Wi-Fi connection. Even if you do, the odds that it'll function at a level necessary for your talk are not good.

Pattern: Live Demo

Also Known As   Live Tool Use, Live Coding

Definition   You demonstrate in real time how something works or how to do something as part of your presentation. Successful implementation of this pattern can turn a demonstration into performance art.

Motivation   The motivation for demonstrating something within a presentation varies widely. At its most noble, it shows the audience members something they want to know in an interesting, entertaining context. Perhaps it seems like less work to throw together a few Bullet-Riddled Corpse introduction slides and then demonstrate the tool or technique in an ad hoc way. At its worst, it boosts the presenter's ego while lacking information quality and density. We identify this as a dangerous pattern to be used by advanced presenters only. We've seen many presenters who *think* they are delivering a great demonstration but are actually just annoyingly stroking their own egos.

Live Demo can be a life saver if you don't have enough material to make a compelling presentation in the time you have. Interacting with a tool is a great time sink and—if done to encourage audience interactivity—a benefit to the audience as well. (But see the Dead Demo antipattern for the dark side of this motivation.)

Applicability/ Consequences

Live Demo works particularly well when the following occurs:

- The presentation consists of instructional material *about* a tool or technique.
- The topic is completely new to the audience, and you want to start from a known context to lead them toward new ideas.
- The focus of the talk is the interaction with the tool or application of the technique.
- The technique is something the attendee is expected to mimic, in whole or in part, either in real time or later.

This is an effective pattern when the focus of the demonstration is a tool or technique. It becomes the Dead Demo antipattern when that's not the case. It's extremely difficult to perform well—and trivially easy to do so poorly that the audience checks out completely. Performing a Live Demo well takes an enormous amount of practice (see Carnegie Hall pattern), deep knowledge of the subject, bravery, and calm in the face of the unexpected—along with the ability to speak in well-considered, articulate sentences while performing a complex and error-prone task in front of a large group of people. You might want to consider the Lipsync pattern instead.

When performing some intricate technical feat such as writing source code, you'll make mistakes, no matter how well you've practiced. One of the benefits of live demonstrations is the contextualization for the audience members: They empathize when something goes wrong. It makes the presenter more human and provides the opportunity to discuss important tangents. However, the worst part of this pattern also manifests in this situation: It can destroy or at least seriously harm the presenter's reputation if an unrecoverable error or mistake occurs.

Mechanics

You must be effective in ad-libbing with the tool you are demonstrating (with). The most difficult aspect of this pattern is the immense level of audience concentration the presenter must maintain. It's boring to watch someone use a tool and excruciating to watch someone backspace over mistakes repeatedly, so most presenters keep lively banter going at the same time. That's hard enough to do when things go well and extremely difficult when unexpected variations arise.

Make sure you have a firm agenda. It's OK to stray from it at the audience's request, which is one of the benefits of this approach, but you don't want to be seen as fumbling around. Make sure you have goals in mind and keep on track. Be willing to say no to audience requests if you think they'll provide a poor Live Demo experience.

Practice is essential. By demonstrating something in front of a group, you are an expert on it, no matter how much you might disclaim otherwise (which never helps—see the Going Meta antipattern). You must look polished in your demonstration and should be able to answer questions as you go. Your knowledge must significantly exceed that of others in the room so that you can answer questions gracefully.

One way to reduce risk if you do undertake a Live Demo is to create intermediate versions or snapshots beforehand of what you'll be demonstrating live. If something goes terribly wrong, you have a known good place to restart and hopefully regain your composure.

If you do want to show the audience the mechanics of something via a Live Demo yet don't want to incur the ongoing risks, you can start the presentation with a few Live Demo examples then switch to a safer pattern like Lipsync.

Known Uses   Nikon, on the release of its D4 DSLR camera, had a situation in which it was imperative to give a live demo.[1] To prove that an innovative remote-control

Figure 5.1 The Nikon D4 live demonstration

feature was already in the camera hardware (not an implementation of the Lipsync pattern), the presenter turned the camera on the audience members and displayed live pictures of them. The presentation gave credibility to the feature and assuaged any of the audience's concerns that it was technological vaporware.

In 1994, Bill Gates decided to do a live demo of Windows 95 and its Plug and Play capabilities. He performed a move that had likely been practiced dozens of times—connecting a scanner—and snap, the dreaded "blue screen of death" appeared.[2] Gates tried to deal with the situation as well as possible, but the audience lost its focus on the talk's real goals and laughed hysterically. The snafu made the news on many local TV stations around the world—not exactly what Gates was hoping for.

Related Patterns   The Dead Demo antipattern is the evil twin of Live Demo.

The Lipsync pattern is a common way to replace a Dead Demo with a presentation.

Developer Dave's Dazzling Code Show

Developer Dave worked on his killer demonstration for the Lunch-and-Learn all month. He found some awesome examples of the new web framework and built a significant piece of the current system in very short order using this new technology. As the meeting approached, he honed his examples to a fine edge.

But Dave didn't count on the meeting taking place in the black hole meeting room, where you can never get a good Internet connection via the wireless network. During the demo, Dave realized with growing distress that none of his examples work without Internet access. What should have been a fantastic victory—convincing everyone that he has found the correct tool to solve all their problems—instead left everyone with a sour impression, both of Dave (for wasting their lunch break) and of the demonstrated technology, which doesn't seem to do much.

Murphy (of the eponymous law) always shows up at important meetings, even though he's never on the invitation list.

☠ Antipattern: Dead Demo

Also Known As	Live Tool Use, Live Coding, Live Demo
Definition	Use a lengthy demonstration of a tool or technique as a time sink to counterbalance a lack of compelling presentation material.
Motivation	Motivations for this antipattern (which is all too common in the software world, where all the authors reside) include the following:

- The presenter has only enough prepared material for a portion of the allotted time, so he or she uses the remainder to "riff" with the tool.
- The presenter wants to show off his or her skills with a tool or technique—not the tool itself.
- The presenter knows the rest of the presentation is a dull recitation of bullet points and that watching paint dry is more interesting.

Some presenters believe that, by the strength of their demonstration of a tool or technique, they can create something entertaining, informative, and meaningful beyond what's possible in a normal presentation. They are almost always incorrect. Not to mention that Murphy always attends your most important presentations and sits in the front row.

Applicability/ Consequences	This antipattern manifests whenever you threaten to distract from the content of your presentation via flashy showmanship or cover up the fact that you aren't saying anything new.

A Dead Demo often aspires to be a proper Live Demo but falls short because of the daunting difficulties inherent in implementing the Live Demo pattern well.

Many conference attendees like—or even prefer—the Live Demo style and will frequently tolerate a Dead Demo, mistaking one for the other. But any such preference is based on an invalid comparison. When comparing someone using a tool poorly to reading a Bullet-Riddled Corpse presentation, people will prefer any sign of life to abject boredom.

Another consequence of this antipattern is a compression of the amount of material you can cover. Inevitably, demonstrating the tool consumes some of the presentation time—time that could be packed with more information. We estimate that even outstanding technical demonstrators who employ this technique cover at most only 60 percent of the volume of material that could be done as a presentation. A well-done presentation that uses some of the patterns appearing later in this chapter (e.g., Lipsync or Traveling Highlights) can cover more material in more detail with significantly less stress on the presenter. Information density is the primary trade-off when you use this antipattern.

Watching someone backspace over mistakes is grueling. Most people don't type in front of an audience, and they don't realize it'll be harder than doing it at their desks. When typing as performance, typists tend to speed up because they have a palpable sense that people are waiting, which causes more mistakes, which causes even more speedup to compensate for increasingly lost time. Neal tells nascent presenters that he'll gladly watch them live-code computer software if they are proficient enough to allow him to remove their backspace key.

Known Uses   Virtually every conference that has even the slightest technical content includes some presentations that succumb to this antipattern.

Related Patterns   The Live Demo pattern is the symmetrical good pattern to this antipattern.

Lipsync, Traveling Highlights, and Emergence all illustrate techniques for avoiding this antipattern.

Experienced Expert's On-Stage Meltdown

This interlude is based on a true story. A well-known conference speaker with years of experience on the tech circuit was notorious for his off-the-cuff, coded-on-the-fly programming demos. He accepted an invitation to keynote a major industry conference.

During his talk, nothing went right. He had connectivity issues, firewall configuration problems, you name it, and nothing worked. He tried taking another path only to be stymied there as well. About 25 minutes into his 45-minute keynote, he stopped in midsentence during his latest crashing demo, paused for an increasingly awkward 15 seconds and then mumbled, "I'm sorry, but I'm done." Then—to the shock and chagrin of the conference organizers—he walked off the stage.

The next day, in a smaller setting, he successfully performed the demo that had crashed and burned so spectacularly the day before.

Doing live demonstrations in unknown environments is risky, and the importance of the talk amplifies the risk.

Designer Davis Delayed in a Ditch

Web designer Davis was thinking, "I've done a bunch of live demos and I've got the skills to pull it off," but he discovered (the hard way) that past performance is no guarantee of future success. His talk was riddled with live-coding examples that work by accessing an external website. Live coding is hard enough, but relying on things outside your control is begging for trouble. He'd given the talk successfully *many* times before but didn't realize that the service he relied on had changed since the last time he'd delivered the presentation.

Needless to say, his talk didn't go as he'd expected. Though familiar with the typical mistakes and typos of live coding, he was unable to adjust to the service's changes on the fly. Sure, it would have helped if he'd reviewed his talk the night before. But had he instead relied on the Lipsync pattern, the changes to the external service would have been irrelevant. His decision to live code marred his presentation's message and left him stuck, trying to illustrate concepts that really had nothing to do with his broken demonstration yet relied on it working.

Developer Dave's Dragging Demo

Developer Dave has figured out a unique combination of two tools to assist in software debugging in a way that will blow developers' minds. He puts together a presentation for his local special interest group, aiming to present it at a conference eventually. The combination of tools is tricky to set up, requiring lots of ancillary tools to run.

At the special interest group, one of the required support tools was reluctant to start correctly, causing Dave to fiddle with it during the presentation. He explained what was happening along the way in broken sentences, in between trying to fix the problem. He eventually repaired it, but more than two-thirds of the audience had slipped out and gone home. The punch line was great, but it took so long to get to it that the audience was bored (and left) before Dave could deliver it.

Programmer Pam's Impossible Dream

Note: Most of our interludes are made up; this one is based on a true story that led to the identification of the antipattern and the solution, the Lipsync pattern. We've changed the names to protect the guilty (and still on the lam) party, Programmer Pam.

Penultimate Software worked hard on the next-generation connectivity suite to enable all applications of all types to talk with one another seamlessly and magically. Unfortunately, the big sales conference happened before the technology was finished cooking. Programmer Pam was tasked with demonstrating the new functionality during the opening keynote. It failed.

The next available time to demonstrate the killer product was the noon keynote the next day. It failed again. The president of Penultimate Software was irate: You can't sell people software that clearly doesn't work! The mandate comes from on high, directed at Pam: It *must work* for the final keynote on Thursday.

Pam has a serious problem. Because the software is still immature, it is also very unpredictable. How can she show the vision for the software that will eventually work flawlessly but isn't quite there yet?

Back in her hotel late into Wednesday night, she worked on the demo. She would run it successfully a half dozen times, and then it would randomly fail. In desperation, she came up with a risky but brilliant plan. Using screen-capture software, she recorded her full-screen interaction with the tool, capturing one of the good runs.

On stage on Thursday, Pam acted as if she were using the tool, but she had really launched her recorded performance. At one point, the other Penultimate employee on the stage asked Pam something about what she was doing, hoping to get some exposition about the tool. He didn't realize that Pam, once he started the recording, couldn't stop for ad-libs! Pam brushed him off and, despite a slight video hiccup at the very end, she pulled off the demo, to great applause. The technology works!

At the speaker's dinner that night, Pam confessed to the other speakers what she had done, to much laughter and joking. She was henceforth known as Milli Vanilli[3] on the conference circuit. However, it was an effective trick, lowered her stress in an impossible situation, and served the purpose: showing the *vision* for the software despite the current bugs. We've captured Pam's trick as the Lipsync pattern.

 ## Pattern: Lipsync

Also Known As   Milli Vanilli

Definition   Live examples may sound like a great idea, but they too often lead to the Dead Demo antipattern. Instead of demonstrating a tool or technique live, record your interaction with the tool beforehand as video and play it back during your presentation.

Motivation   Recording a demo has a raft of benefits over doing it live:

- You can edit for time, speeding up necessary but boring sections or compressing the length of long-running processes.
- Instead of concentrating on getting a persnickety example to work, you can talk over the top of the running demonstration with full concentration.
- You can pause or replay confusing parts or purposefully come back to a branching point. Frequently when showing tools, presenters need to show variations in workflow based on contingencies such as errors. Lipsync demos give you full control over the tool in the preparation stage and enable short snippets of video to explain small nuances. Using the demonstration itself as a Context Keeper works well because it automatically contextualizes the point you've returned to.

- Because the recorded demonstration is running inside a presentation tool, you can overlay all the animations, transitions, and decorations you could ever want atop the video, adding even more context.
- In your lab, you can construct and capture complex scenarios that you can't predictably produce live (such as specific but rare error conditions) and then dissect them for your audience.
- Live Demo is one of the most difficult presentation patterns to implement well.
- Recording the demo reduces stress dramatically; if you make a mistake, start over or edit the recording. Although some attendees genuinely appreciate watching a presenter "get out of the ditch," that adds pressure to an already stressful situation, especially if you never intended demonstrating ditch-escaping tricks in your presentation.
- Lipsync reduces any dependencies your talk has on technology such as Wi-Fi, a troublesome piece of software, or complex multiapplication or machine requirements. The more moving parts a demonstration needs, the more parts that will break in front of a crowd.
- Lipsync works especially well when you want to want to show technology that frequently changes. You can expose features without worrying about the technology's stability.

Applicability/ Consequences

It's a mistake to use Lipsync to fake a live demonstration because doing so will destroy your credibility if the audience catches on. Instead, use it as an advantage. The audience can see that communication channels are available when the presenter doesn't have to concentrate on talking and coping with a live demo simultaneously.

One possible negative consequence of Lipsync versus the Live Demo pattern is the inability to improvise your demonstration based on audience requests. If this is an important requirement, it might lead you toward Live Demo. However, we suggest an alternative that requires a bit more setup work but gives you the stability and stress reduction of Lipsync with the improvisation of Live Demo, especially for easily versionable things like source code.

The goal is to save the state of the tool being demonstrated at various checkpoints along the way. The tool and what it's used for will determine how these snapshots manifest. For example, for a written document, you can create numbered folders with saved versions. If you are writing source code, use the same version-control tools you use for projects to save tagged versions of your demonstration. If the audience asks for some variations in the recorded demonstration, check out tagged version of the code that corresponds to that demo and turn the presentation into a demonstration. This technique gives you the best of both worlds because you're free to wander as far as you would like to satisfy the audience yet can resume the presentation at the point where the digression started.

Mechanics   If the tool or technique you're showing is computer-based, screen-capture software might be built into it. Otherwise, it's available for all platforms either for free or at a low cost. The only requirement is that it be able to record some or all of the screen as video; the fancier screen-capture applications allow you to choose whether to include audio, the cursor, highlighting, and so on.

Once you've recorded your demonstration, it's trivial to add it to a slide in your presentation tool; all modern tools support embedded videos, along with a variety of animations for appearance, disappearance, and effects. For showing a software tool, we prefer a full-screen capture that completely fills the slide. While the demonstration is running, it would appear to a casual observer that the application itself—not a recording of the application—is running full-screen.

Make sure you know the capabilities of the presentation computer or tablet and the projector(s). Running video can tax hardware heavily and sometimes reduce a beautiful demo into a flickering mess.

When you "shoot" the screen capture, turn off all notifications and close distracting applications. Irrelevant pop-up notifications and the like make a video look slipshod. You should also hide the "lint" from your desktop, such as the task tray on Windows or menu-bar services in OS X. If you don't, audience members will start wondering which applications you have that they don't. It's a needless distraction.

If something distracting does occur and you can't get rid of it, use the duct tape of presentation tools: the borderless white box. A carefully placed box can hide all sorts of things, either temporarily or permanently.

Related Patterns   The Dead Demo antipattern is the motivation for this pattern.

Neal's Furious Downpouring Arguments for Lipsync

Neal, Matthew, and Nathaniel live in a world in which Dead Demo talks are quite common. Some speakers at software events even seem to feel that it's a sign of weakness not to slog through all the accidental complexity of writing code live. It's so pervasive that Neal had to convince Matthew that Lipsync isn't a crazy idea.

On a drive to the airport in a memorable spring downpour after a conference in Des Moines, Neal and Matthew started talking about the benefits and hazards of writing code live in front of a group. Matthew was dumbfounded that he would make such an argument;

live coding is a staple of talks at technical conferences. But Neal kept countering Matthews point against Matthew's increasingly fraying objections. By the end of the trip, Matthew agreed to try it and has since become a huge advocate.

Business Analyst Barb's Bouncing Balances

The meetings have met, the accountants have counted, and the analysts have analyzed. Months of effort culminate in the big evaluation: which parts of the company stay and which go. Barb's team was the lucky winner chosen to put together the analysis. The slide template and most of the other content was dictated by the consultants; Barb was just building a few individual slides.

The problem came down to the big summary slide, which shows the sums and summaries from all the raw data, which is maintained in a spreadsheet. As is always the case, the numbers in the spreadsheet fluctuated up until the day of the meeting. The presentation went well, but Barb got a cold feeling down her spine about an hour into the presentation. She'd spent the last hour of slide-preparation time translating numbers from the spreadsheets into the tables on the slides. What if she'd missed some? Do the numbers all add up?

✈ Pattern: Traveling Highlights

Definition   Use graphics, opacity, and other emphasis tools to decorate something you are discussing or demonstrating.

Motivation   This pattern is a Slide Construction pattern, but it and the following two patterns appear frequently in presentations that illustrate features and details about a tool, procedure, process, or other concrete artifact.

Displaying numerical data or source code while you talk about it is visually dull. Traveling Highlights helps you to focus audience attention on specific parts of the screen while leaving the rest obscured but visible to provide consistent context. And it encourages creative use of animations and transitions to add visual effects to otherwise static screen shots. Like bullet points, it also serves as a reminder to the presenter that something in particular needs attention.

This pattern increases the information density of your slides. You can cover more information in one slide by using Traveling Highlights than by

Figure 5.2 Traveling Highlights in source code

showing single-screen shots on multiple slides. This is an advantage for presentations forced to implement the Slideuments antipattern because it keeps the slide count (and therefore page count) down.

Applicability/
Consequences This pattern is useful if a presentation uses many detailed artifacts—source code charts, spreadsheets, tool output, and so on—that you want to show in varying degrees of detail while keeping a larger context available.

Mechanics This pattern is easy to implement in a variety of ways in all modern presentation tools. Figure 5.2 shows how a tutorial presentation illustrates computer source code using this pattern.

In Figure 5.2, a single slide (shown here as six animated steps) builds source code as the presenter talks about it and then highlights a particular part on subsequent animations.

To create this effect, don't start by displaying source code in a text box or numeric data in a table. Instead, use screen shots of the software tool that the code or numeric data comes from, and show them full-screen. For computer source code, take a screen shot from a development environment. Software developers are accustomed to seeing computer source code colored in specific ways by their tools, so representing code as plain text would look odd to them. Similarly, if you're showing data that comes from a spreadsheet, use a screen shot of the spreadsheet. Your audience is accustomed to seeing the data in a spreadsheet anyway, and now you've got one less transcription to perform.

For the effect shown in Figure 5.2, follow these steps:

1. Capture just the region of the development environment's screen that encompasses the source code you want to show, not the rest of the tool. A developer audience will recognize the context from the tool's built-in syntax highlighting alone. (For screen captures from a tool like a spreadsheet, you might want to include more of the tool's user interface to provide context.) Many of the screen-capture tools enable you to capture a fixed region and will preserve that region between subsequent screen shots.
2. For the first portion of highlighted code you want to show, highlight those lines and recapture the screen shot, using the exact same region.
3. Place the new image directly over the old one, using the presentation tool's rulers and guides to help you line it up.

4. For the presentation, use a *dissolve* entrance animation: Because you've captured the exact region both times, only the highlighted portion changes, and the highlight seems to "grow" around the part you're trying to emphasize.

The highlights don't have to be in color. Consider the slide shown in Figure 5.3.

Generally, we would shun a slide with as much information as Figure 5.3, preferring to deliver it in more meaningfully sized chunks (see the Cookie Cutter antipattern). However, perhaps the audience is accustomed to this status-report format, and it really represents the agenda of the meeting. By using Traveling Highlights, you can keep this whole thing on the screen and highlight interesting parts, as shown in the four serial slides in Figure 5.4.

Notice the use of the Analog Noise pattern for both the lines and text to distinguish presentation-added text from the original source. When used

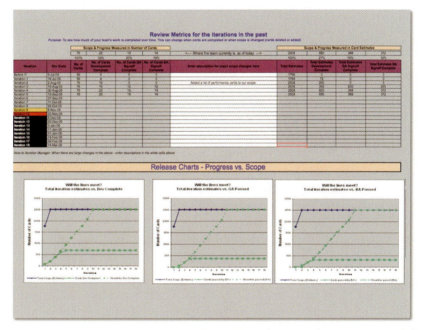

Figure 5.3 Information-dense status-report slide

Figure 5.4 Using boxes and lines as Traveling Highlights

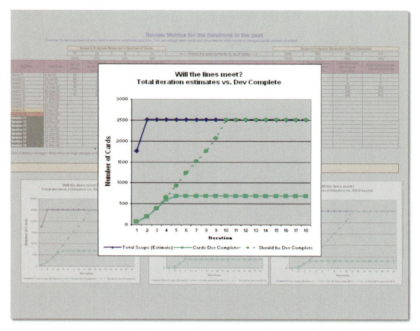

Figure 5.5 Using zoom and opacity for Traveling Highlights

in this way, Traveling Highlights serves as a Context Keeper, enabling you to return to a familiar context between each drill-down into detail.

You don't even have to use graphic elements to implement this pattern. Consider the version shown in Figure 5.5.

In this version, the original image stays in the background while the presentation uses a combination of opacity, movement, and scale to emphasize each part in turn. This version looks nice because each chart "grows" out of its original position, centering itself while the rest of the spreadsheet dims.

To implement this pattern, you must carefully layer animation effects. Consider the Keynote Inspector shown in Figure 5.6.

In Figure 5.6, the overall image (named Status_spreadsheet) has its opacity set to 30 percent. At the same time (using an *automatically with transition* to start the build), the overlaid graph is transitioned in at its size and position on the original. Then, using an *after* transition, it moves to the center of the screen and grows to 200 percent at the same time. The visual effect makes it appear to "grow" out of its position on the spreadsheet. To move to the next element, *dissolve*-transition the current focused element and "grow" the next one. You don't need to "put it back" afterward: Making it appear in its original location and move to the center has a much greater visual benefit than doing the reverse. Instead, spend your visual budget on the item you'll talk about next.

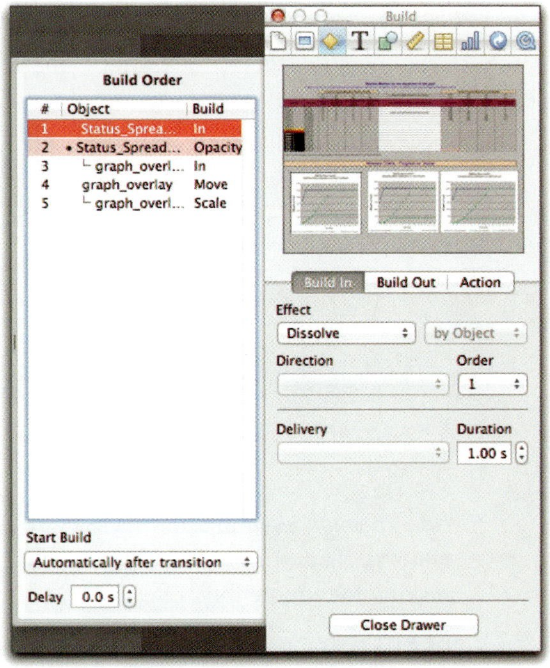

Figure 5.6 Keynote Inspector for size, motion, and opacity settings

Be careful to test the presence and performance of any advanced animations and transitions if you plan to deliver your presentation on a tablet such as an iPad. The version of Keynote for the iPad is severely limited compared to the desktop version, so plan accordingly.

The same series of animations appear in the PowerPoint version of the same pattern, as shown in Figure 5.7.

The implementation details of Traveling Highlights differ in detail but not concept in PowerPoint:

1. Start with the summary slide. This will be the slide you return to after each emphasized item. It serves as your Context Keeper.
2. Paste the full-size embedded image (in this example, the chart) onto the slide and then make its size and position the same as the summary image's. Pasting the full-size image and then resizing it generally results in a higher-quality image. The alternative—pasting a small image and telling PowerPoint to scale it upward—generates image noise.
3. Set an *entrance* animation to make the embedded image fade in.
4. Add a *motion path* animation. PowerPoint has a huge number of these, tracing all sorts of patterns, most of which we think look pretty bad. For animations like this, simpler is often better. In this case, we chose a straight line.

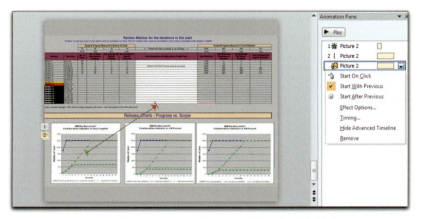

Figure 5.7 Traveling Highlights in PowerPoint

5. Add an *emphasis* animation such as *grow/shrink* and set it to *start with previous*. This lets the movement and growth occur simultaneously, making for a more fluid effect.

Be sure to test this sequence under real-world conditions. PowerPoint isn't forgiving of inadequate hardware, which manifests as ugly, jerky animations. If that's the result you get, you'll create a better audience experience by eschewing fancy effects in favor of a simpler approach, such as simple appearance animations rather than ones that rely heavily on motion.

Related Patterns   This pattern works well for text (and images) that fit in a single slide. If a chunk of text that works as a unit is too large for one slide, Crawling Code might be a better choice.

Pattern: Crawling Code

Also Known As   Sliding Code, Viewport

Contributed By   Nancy Duarte, CEO, Duarte Design Inc.[4]

Definition   A block of text slowly reveals itself from the bottom of the screen and scrolls off the top—on cue, not continuously. Only the portion of the block under discussion is visible on the screen. The audience member's mind keeps the context of the adjacent but invisible portion in its periphery, thus creating a mental illusion of a larger canvas displaying the complete block of text.

Motivation

Slide text should always be in a large enough font that even people in the back of the room can read it. But when you have a multiline chunk of text that works as a unit, you can't always fit all the lines on one slide at a readable size. However, you'd prefer not to split it across multiple slides.

Applicability/
Consequences

Any presentation that shows programming code, lengthy formulas, a long step-wise process, or a significant quotation can use this pattern to give the audience a fluid and comfortable reading experience with mental context.

Implementing this pattern requires a significant time investment. You need to craft the right transitions precisely so that each block shows up in the right order, has all appropriate lines on screen, and grows and shrinks the blocks in perfect harmony with the text movement.

Because you expose the text in a predetermined order, you have less room for spelunking through the material during the question-and-answer session. You can handle questions in a free-form manner by also having the text in question ready to display via a text-editing or word-processing program.

Mechanics

If you have a long string of text to display that needs to stay with the other lines for context, keep it together in one long text field. Pump the font size up to 22 and let the lines of text exceed the bottom of the slide. Lots of lines can fall off the slides. Then highlight the parts of text that you plan to talk about—either by colorizing the text or drawing boxes around it. If you draw boxes around the text, be sure to group the boxes with the text block. After you have your massive text field, use path-based animation to move the text block slowly up the slide. You can move it up as many times as necessary to scroll through as you share your insights.

Known Uses

Matthew uses this technique for every presentation that shows long blocks of programming code. The most dramatic application is in the *Encryption Boot Camp on the JVM* presentation. Rather than show a chunk of the program and flick rudely to the next chunk on the following slide, he makes the code smoothly scroll up the screen. This presentation includes sample programs that are up to 100 lines long, each with blocks of three to eight lines that need to be studied at a time. The small blocks relate to the overall structure of the program, so seeing them smoothly scroll, occasionally in a nonlinear order, helps the audience understand the program. If an audience member asks Matthew to reiterate any given segment, he can easily reverse to it via his presentation software's back-navigation feature because the segments' order is wired into the presentation.

Related Patterns

This pattern is similar to the Crawling Credits pattern but used within the body of the presentation.

Pattern: Emergence

Also Known As Animation for Learning

Definition

Use motion, transitions, highlights, and other presentation effects to gradually reveal pieces or details of the big thing you're ultimately going to show.

Motivation

Seeing all of a large, complex entity at once is overwhelming. By revealing it a small part at a time, you can discuss each piece in turn, building up to the whole to clarify the grand objective.

Applicability/
Consequences

If you have the feeling that "this is a big thing to talk about"—and the big thing is portrayed in diagrammatic, photographic, formulaic, or programming-code form—your presentation deserves application of this pattern. Using Emergence, a presentation can take small, digestible steps toward revelation of the whole.

Audience members will stay attentive during the piecewise revelations because you'll provide an interesting piece of exposition for each detail. At the end, they'll have a good grasp of the big picture.

Mechanics

The implementation for this pattern is the same for both Keynote and PowerPoint: Use animations and transitions to obscure part of the entire context, gradually revealing it by removing the obscuring elements. The most popular device for this purpose is the "duct tape" for presentations: the borderless white box.

If you are required to create Slideuments, be forewarned that this pattern will require extra work. A goal of Slideuments is to be able to print the final state of your slides. When you use Emergence, most of the elements are obscured in the beginning state. To be able to print the final version of the slide yet still use Emergence, you set up the slide in the way you normally would and then add some additional animations to control what the elements look like when printed:

1. Place the boxes or other obscuring elements in place as you normally would.
2. Set the opacity of the obscuring elements to 0 percent, rendering them invisible. You now have the printable state of the slide.
3. Add an animation for each box, setting its opacity to 100 percent. Move these animations *above* the *entrance* animation for the main subject of the slide and set their duration to be as short as possible. Basically, you're sneaking an animation in before the main subject shows up, making the obscuring elements opaque again. When your main subject appears, it will be behind the now visible obscuring elements, which you can animate away when appropriate.

You can implement Emergence in Keynote by using *magic move* to move a large box as the slide or interslide transition. It will glide gracefully from the piece you're showing to the one you reveal next. You can also implement it with a white or partially opaque block that hinders, blurs, or otherwise obscures the portions of the full entity that are yet to be revealed or are not currently under discussion.

Related Patterns   Traveling Highlights has a similar objective: highlighting parts of a bigger picture one piece at a time.

David Geary's Undo-Driven Demonstration

A well-known technical speaker, David Geary, confided to the authors one of his tricks for doing flawless live demonstrations of sometimes tricky source-code writing. Shortly before the talk, he builds his demonstration and then uses the *undo* feature of his code-editing tool to "back out" his changes, back to the starting point.

During the presentation, he hits the *redo* key to gradually "retype" the code he wrote a little while earlier. This is a form of the Lipsync pattern but more interactive and much harder (and more labor-intensive) to set up.

Pattern: Live on Tape

Also Known As   Videogram, Recorded Presentation, E-Mailing It In, Screencast

Definition   When travel issues, time conflicts, or budget constraints prevent you from delivering a presentation onsite, video-record your talk as if you were giving it to a live audience.

Motivation   Sometimes your (or your company's) schedule or budget won't permit you to deliver a presentation in person. Recording the presentation and delivering it in an asynchronous manner to others is a sign of respect for their schedules above yours. And your recorded materials can reach a much wider audience than a live talk. It's difficult to get additional people to attend a live presentation at a given time in a given location. It's trivially easy to forward a link to useful recorded material.

Applicability/ Consequences   It's easy to think of Live on Tape as a mere replacement for an in-person presentation. But this pattern can also fit the bill for a wide variety of smaller-scale and less-considered presentation forms. These include demonstrations of products to managers, of ailments to physician coworkers, of testimony to attorneys, or of defects to technicians and programmers. Rather than expensively colocating critical individuals in a conference room at a specific time, you can send the video file for consumption at any free moment each recipient might have. It's much easier for them to make maximum use of their small available moments with a portable video file than it is to gather at a predetermined time to watch a live demonstration.

Live on Tape is easiest to implement for presentations in which most of the action takes place on the slides and in the audio channel. The pattern becomes increasingly challenging to leverage the more physical objects the presentation uses—for example, evidence that audience members are expected to examine manually. It would also be difficult to implement for presentations that use interactive imaging-display technology (to rotate and fully observe an MRI or CAT scan image in its three-dimensional richness, for example), although you could approximate such a sequence through embedded use of the Lipsync pattern.

Live on Tape enables you to deliver a higher-fidelity experience than a mere flat file would impart to your audience. You can communicate more nuanced information in an impressive, multisensory (auditory plus visual) way. Any audience expecting a lifeless, static PDF of your presentation will be delighted by the better experience they derive from your recorded live performance.

A Live on Tape version of your talk can be slightly disappointing if the audience expected to see you in person. But if you're careful to manage such expectations—especially advisable if your schedule is complex and volatile—you can mitigate the risk of audience disappointment.

Mechanics   You can implement Live on Tape in a several ways. We describe them here in order of least time-consuming to most time-consuming.

A portable solution—available for use in just about any location and situation—requires only a phone stand and a modern smart phone that offers high-definition resolution video recording.

For a more crisp form of application demo or presentation recording, use the camera built into desktop monitors or the lids of notebook computers simultaneously to capture user actions on the desktop. Render your final presentation as a picture-in-picture of the presenter in the corner of the larger desktop capture. Operating systems generally include native applications to capture video from these prevalent built-in cameras as well as video of a user's desktop interaction. Third-party screencasting applications are generally required to composite the two video streams.

As in the Lipsync pattern, make sure you cover, remove, and hide any distracting elements on your desktop that don't relate to the presentation.

A solid color desktop wallpaper works best and actually aids the compression (size reduction) and download speed of the final video.

Known Uses

Apple often has a very limited number of seats at its announcement events, especially those held on the Cupertino campus. In a twist of Live on Tape, the presentations are crafted to suit two audiences simultaneously—the one in the seats at the venue and the Internet audience that consumes these informational sessions as soon as they hit the web. Numerous events of this style are hosted on the Apple Events site,[5] as shown in Figure 5.8.

Related Patterns

This pattern is an application of the Lipsync pattern to an entire presentation rather than just a portion of it.

Live on Tape is often a compromise alternative to a proper Live Demo.

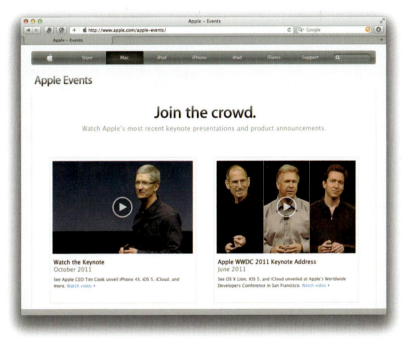

Figure 5.8 Apple's page for Live on Tape videos

PART III
DELIVER

AFTER YOU'VE BUILT THE KILLER PRESENTATION, NEARLY all that remains is to *deliver it*. This section highlights techniques to make your actual "standing in front of the room" presentation better, along with common pitfalls to avoid.

Stage Prep covers important details you must cover shortly before you present, including some techniques to help sway the crowd.

In this book's first two parts, we intermixed patterns and antipatterns to suit each chapter's context. However, performance antipatterns are a special case; they can undermine even your best preparatory efforts and frequently manifest as bad habits. Thus we devote a full chapter to Performance Antipatterns—things you should avoid during the performance part of your presentation.

After we cover all the things you shouldn't do, we finish with Performance Patterns—techniques for dealing with questions, ways to pace yourself, innovative tricks for difficult audiences, and lots more.

CHAPTER 6

STAGE PREP

ELIMINATING SURPRISES IS ONE OF THE SECRETS TO effective presentations, and the most plentiful sources of surprise are the time when and space where you'll give your presentation. This chapter covers the mental, physical, and environmental preparation you need to do for an upcoming presentation. It also includes some strategies for helping tip the audience's opinions in your favor.

Pattern: Preparation

Also Known As	The Time Is Right, Dress for Success

Definition   You've prepared and practiced your material, and you Know Your Audience. But there's yet more essential preparation to be done.

Motivation   Giving a talk without proper preparation is, at best, risky. At worst, it's a complete nightmare for you and your audience. Hard drives fail, cell reception is spotty, and any number of other glitches can derail your presentation if you're not ready for them. Unless you are asked to fill in at the last minute, there's no excuse for being ill-prepared.

Applicability/ Consequences   A prepared speaker is a relaxed speaker. One of the keys to giving a great talk is eliminating variables, and there's no substitute for strong preparation. You will still feel the butterflies, but at least you'll know you've done everything you can to deliver a great talk. Show respect for your audience and they'll return the favor.

Being prepared can turn a potential disaster into a minor nuisance. Hard drives fail and batteries die; it *will* happen to you. Five minutes of planning can prevent calamity.

Mechanics   When speaking at a conference, be aware of the schedule; some conferences allow 30 minutes between talks, but the changeover time can be as short as five minutes. The next speaker deserves time to set up, and the audience needs time to change rooms.

In many ways, a presentation is a form of theater. Talks often have a Narrative Arc, and many speakers utilize theater training as a way of preparing for a talk. Improvisational training is a lifesaver in moments when things don't go according to plan.

Dress comfortably. Presentations are stressful enough, so don't compound the discomfort with shoes that hurt your feet. What you wear is a reflection of who you are, so don't be afraid to show your personality. Some speakers wouldn't dream of giving a talk in anything short of dress pants and a button-up shirt, others love ironic T-shirts, and some render themselves Shoeless as soon as they get on stage.

That said, dress appropriately for your audience. Just as costumes can make a huge difference in a play or a movie, what you wear when you present is almost as important as what you say. We're not saying you need haute couture to be a good presenter, but you do need to be aware of your audience and its expectations. If you're presenting to a group of doctors, lawyers, or senior executives, your trusty Phish T-shirt, cargo shorts, and

Birkenstocks might not be the best choice. By the same token, showing up at the average technical conference in a three-piece suit sends the wrong message too.

If you're not sure what's appropriate, talk to the organizer or other speakers. Check the show's website for pictures from last year's event. The venue can also provide useful hints. A conference hosted by a law office will have a different feel from one at the local community college. If you're still not sure, you're better off being slightly overdressed.

Pack your laptop bag the night before and double-check that you have everything you need. Better, spend a few dollars on duplicate power bricks, USB cables, and whatever else you can't live without, and *leave them in your laptop bag*. A hundred dollars' worth of electronics buys an awful lot of peace of mind. Print out any important information and put a copy where you won't forget it (in your laptop bag, for example).

Make sure your presentation material is backed up to at least one other location (on the Internet, a USB flash drive, a portable hard drive, or all three). If you have to get up early, be sure your alarm is set (and if you're using your cell phone as an alarm, plug it in), and allow plenty of time to get your rest. If you can't live without your morning coffee, leave time to get your fix. The moral of the story? Give yourself *plenty* of time.

Hydration is critical. You'll be surprised how much fluid you use while speaking. Verify you have liquids that will be available during the talk. One well-known technical presenter would never begin before he had two full glasses of water; the belt and suspenders version of ensuring hydration.

If you're going to speak all day, whether teaching, presenting at a conference, or driving a long meeting, consider including electrolytes when you hydrate, either via drinking a sports beverage or eating a banana. Drinking only water all day will keep you hydrated but can imbalance your minerals; adding electrolytes helps. This is a hard-won lesson from years of speaking all day at tech conferences!

Related Patterns   The Know Your Audience pattern is the obvious precursor to this one; you must understand the audience you present to before you can prepare properly.

The Carnegie Hall pattern is our Creativity pattern that suggests preparatory exercises.

Pattern: Posse

Also Known As	Friends, Support Network, Shills
Definition	Arrange for some friends to attend your presentation. They'll support you and give you applause.
Motivation	You're not gaming the system if you have friends cheer you on during a presentation. Well, maybe you are—but in a legitimate way. Having a front row of supporters means having people you can make positive eye contact with. Supporters making assuring noises and nods of the head spread their aura, causing a harmonized effect in the strangers in the room. The strangers will have a better experience, be more inclined to rate the presentation positively, and engage more frequently with you.
Applicability/ Consequences	All talks benefit from this pattern, with the following three types gaining the most:

- A talk you have never delivered before.
- A talk you give in a semihostile environment to an audience that is notably skeptical of your topic beforehand. This is particularly true in office settings, where audience numbers sometimes translate into political gain.
- A talk you give in an environment that's foreign, either literally or figuratively: locale, audience, subject area, or format.

Note that we are *not* suggesting some sort of stunt, like a comedian or magician: Don't hide someone in the audience to ask a question at a particular time or laugh at your jokes. If the audience or meeting attendees sense that you've done this, it will likely cause a backlash. We're just trying to even the playing field.

A traveling buddy? "What a waste of money!" you might exclaim. But a Posse isn't just a fix to insecurity. It gives you the knowledge that someone can help you if equipment malfunctions and that someone in the audience will clap for you. That changes your entire mindset as a speaker, even before you utter the first word.

If you're considering a travel-required event and are proposing to bring a few colleagues along, it might be hard to get that approved at first. To justify the added cost in a corporate environment, correctly frame this as a marketing opportunity. Your company should want the room to be packed, the response to be positive, the feedback to be stellar, the attendees' memories to be of a high energy experience, and the interaction to be frequent and sincere. Having a Posse measurably enhances all those facets.

Mechanics   Plan your speaking events, especially your early ones, with prejudice toward those that let you bring along a friendly colleague.

Known Uses   GitHub has a corporate policy of sponsoring an employee to be a conference speaker . . . and sponsoring a colleague to attend the conference with the speaker.

Related Patterns   The Greek Chorus pattern suggests adding friendly advocates, but it suggests doing it within the presentation itself rather than inviting a real Posse along.

Developer Dave Stacks the Deck

Developer Dave was ready to pitch his ideas for the next generation of the product to the management group. He'd done his homework and crafted his slides with the care of an artisan. He knew that the bosses would base their decision, in part, on the opinions of their key staff. In addition to practicing his talk, Dave discussed his ideas with the influencers, incorporating their feedback into his remarks.

Dave knew he'd be nervous; it's not every day that he pitches the VP. To ease his nerves, he included a few friendly faces among the invitees. He also made sure that those who supported his ideas were seated front and center. Arriving with plenty of time to set up, Dave spent a few minutes glad-handing the crowd. Sure, it was just idle chit-chat about last night's game, but a few smiles and a laugh calmed his nerves.

Dave's talk was a hit, and the company adopted his new ideas. He's now seen as an up-and-comer in the technical ranks, and many of the VPs seek out his opinions on new technology.

 # Pattern: Seeding Satisfaction

Also Known As   Meet and Greet, Handshakes, Smiles, Preheating, Backstage Pass, Small Talk, Opening Band, Warm-Up Act

Definition   Rock concerts and comedy shows usually start with an opening act that warms up the crowd before the headliner performs. You need to be your own warm-up act and engage the audience before your talk. No matter how compelling a speaker you are and how incredible your story, it helps to preheat the audience. Boost the enthusiasm by getting out there and shaking some hands.

Motivation   A few minutes chatting with audience members before a talk has numerous benefits. It humanizes you to the attendees and them to you. You're no longer a stranger; even if you just chat about the weather, you're making a connection with someone in the crowd—and even one friendly face in a crowd can make all the difference during a talk. It also gives you a chance to gather a bit of knowledge about your audience. Why did they choose this talk? Are they enjoying the conference? What is their skill level? With this knowledge, you can subtly shift the material if needed or even direct people to a more appropriate talk.

A little small talk can do wonders to settle your nerves. Instead of stewing about your slides or how you'll hit the right tone, you can crack a joke or just discuss the news of the day. A pleasant minor distraction can help the butterflies fly in formation.

Applicability/Consequences

Every talk benefits from a little preheating.

When you spend a few minutes talking with people, they get to know you, even if just a little bit. No longer are you just a biography; you're a mom, a runner, a lover of fine espresso. You're a person. It's a lot harder to write a snarky comment about someone you have a connection with.

Small talk is appropriate in most cases, but be aware of the culture. If you're in Boston, expect to run into Red Sox fans!

Mechanics

It's important to Know Your Audience, and nothing beats talking with individual attendees. Instead of generalities, you'll have real data that will help you tailor your talk to the room. If your audience is more advanced, you can go deeper; if they're new to the cause, you know to gloss over the complexities. It also gives you a chance to see which areas are of particular interest to your crowd. You won't be able to change your talk completely, but you can apply the right emphasis.

Seeding Satisfaction helps you to build rapport. You can even do a bit of promotion, perhaps mentioning another talk that people might like. This is also a great chance to distribute handouts, make sure everyone has what they need for the presentation, answer questions about your abstract, or clarify what the talk covers. While chatting with an attendee, you can point out aspects of your talk that are pertinent to that individual or give someone a pointer that might not come up during the normal course of your talk.

Arrive at your venue early and get everything set up. Some speakers wait near the door and greet attendees as they enter. Be respectful and read their body language; don't push if some are busy checking e-mail or don't seem inclined to be sociable.

This time also gives you a chance to warn off people who might be in the wrong talk for their interests or abilities. Be alert to skills mismatches when you chat with your audience. Bad reviews are often linked to unmet expectations. If your talk isn't right for someone, *tell them*. You'd rather have people walk out of your talk and attend something they'll enjoy than sit through your spiel, suffer, and give you a poor rating. Many people are grateful when you tell them the talk isn't a good fit, especially when they can do something about it.

Related Patterns   When you apply the Know Your Audience pattern, you make certain assumptions so that you can guide your material. Seeding Satisfaction before the talk helps you verify your assumptions and tailor the presentation's pacing and exposition level.

Pattern: Display of High Value

Also Known As   Alpha Dog

Contributed By   Tim Berglund, August Technology Group[1]

Definition   Audiences automatically confer high status on presenters and expect them to live up to it. Whether audience members are attending your talk voluntarily or as a requirement of employment, they believe that they stand to benefit if you have valuable things to say and take your role seriously. Willingly adopt the mantle of status and use it to serve your audience.

Motivation   Many new presenters struggle with self-confidence, and even seasoned professionals can get the jitters when presenting new material that they haven't practiced sufficiently. Only relentless practice can solve this perennial problem (see the Carnegie Hall pattern), but you can blunt its force in the short term by remembering the status differential between yourself and your audience. A typical audience assumes that presenters have valuable things to say and are high-status members of their profession or community. The relationship between you and your audience becomes more comfortable if you're willing to occupy a high-status role for the duration of the presentation. This is appropriate even if the audience is composed entirely of your peers or superiors; you are presenting to them because you have something of high value to offer them.

**Applicability/
Consequences**   This pattern describes a mental frame and a set of techniques applicable to all presentations, regardless of the status differential between presenter and audience in effect before or after the presentation. It is especially useful when you need to respond to problems beyond your control, such as troublesome audience members or equipment failures.

The implicit symmetrical antipattern is *Display of Low Value*, which finds expression in apologies for lack of preparation or technical difficulties, and excessive deference to the expertise of the audience. Through uncomfortable humor and contrived humility, you frame yourself as unimportant and only marginally worthy of standing in front of the audience. Although this may seem virtuous on its face, it actually insults the audience members by implying that they would waste their time listening to someone with nothing to offer.

In some unfortunate cases, presenters adopt Display of High Value to inflate their status at the expense of the audience rather than for its benefit. Weak presenters who become comfortable displaying high value may begin to use audience members as props, abusing them with insulting comments in order to appear strong in front of the group. This tragic misuse of the pattern will only lead an audience to conclude the opposite of what the pattern intends to reinforce. Remember that your goal in all cases is to serve your audience. You can do this more effectively by being willing to display high value but not by affecting abusive pretensions to high value.

Appropriate use of Display of High Value sets an audience at ease and makes it more receptive to your message. You'll also be more likely to take appropriate command of the room during interactive presentation formats, accepting helpful levels of audience input while remaining in control of the presentation timing and narrative—a practice for which audiences are always thankful.

Mechanics The primary way to execute this pattern is to adopt a mental frame of being comfortable with your position of high status relative to the audience. This is not an external technique but an internal decision to believe certain things about yourself and your work as a communicator. Especially if you're a new presenter and doubt your speaking ability or your acceptability to your audience, remind yourself that displaying low value is actually insulting to the audience you want to serve.

A few concrete techniques—many of them variations on admonitions in the Going Meta and Hecklers antipatterns—can help you display high value:

- Don't apologize for lack of preparation or problems with audiovisual equipment; do move on as if you are offering value to your audience that they are willing to receive in whatever way they can.
- Don't let audience members hijack your presentation with overlong questions or debate; do answer questions concisely, and tersely end debate before it starts. If possible, make yourself available one-on-one after the presentation for personal follow-up with the debater.

- Don't be concerned if an audience member asks a question you can't answer; do acknowledge the value of the question and quickly suggest ways to follow up later.

The pattern is especially useful when a heckler is trying to control the room or derail your presentation—a rare case in most professional and higher-academic settings and one we cover in the Hecklers antipattern.

Known Uses   The very mention of certain presenters in the technology space evokes thoughts of their intelligence, their insight, and the benefits of hearing what they have to say. A select few include Rich Hickey,[2] Martin Fowler,[3] and Kent Beck.[4] In the legal space, that same position is held by Lawrence Lessig.[5] In the arts, Ralph Fiennes. In science, Hans Rosling.[6] In mathematics, Stephen Wolfram,[7] In education, Sir Ken Robinson.[8]

Related Patterns   A sure way to derail this pattern is to implement the Alienating Artifact antipattern.

This pattern and the Know Your Audience pattern are closely related because you must discern what your audience's perception of high value is.

Be careful to avoid Going Meta during your pretalk credentialization; it's tempting, but it never helps.

Be a Boy Scout

Be Prepared is more than just a Boy Scout motto; it's incredibly useful advice. The unexpected will happen during your talks, and it's your responsibility to be ready for it. Your laptop bag should contain spare batteries, your laptop power brick, a presentation remote (or two), USB cables, pens, paper, and anything else that helps you be at your best. A recent backup of your hard drive can be an absolute lifesaver.

During a long stretch on the road, Neal discovered that his laptop hard drive was failing. For many people, this situation would have been met with white-knuckle panic, but Neal was a Boy Scout: He had a full backup on an external hard drive. Though the external drive made his laptop a bit sluggish, his presentations weren't affected; in fact, the audience was none the wiser because he never mentioned it (see the Going Meta). During one conference, Matthew's laptop died, but a backup to a portable drive enabled him to deliver all his talks using borrowed laptops.

We *strongly* advise that you have a (recent) backup of your laptop on an external drive. At a minimum, you should have all your presentation material on one other storage medium, such as a USB thumb drive. Store your slide deck in "the cloud" via services like Dropbox for another layer of redundancy. We hope you never need to rely on it, but having a backup is cheap insurance and can easily prevent disaster.

Being prepared isn't limited to hardware failures. Know the schedule, the venue's location, and where your room is. Give yourself ample time to arrive, even if you've been there before; Matthew and Nathaniel once rode a metro bus to the end of the route because they missed their stop in heavy fog. In addition to an electronic version, have a physical copy of any important data: schedule, location, organizer contact information, and so on.

Taking a few extra minutes to prepare can make all the difference between a bump in the road and a complete disaster.

Squatter Steve, Going Long

Nathaniel attended a conference presentation at which, to put it politely, the speaker was oblivious to both his time slot and his surroundings. At about the two-thirds point of the talk, the speaker realized he was behind schedule. In such circumstances, most presenters quicken their pace and potentially skip sections, but not this guy; he was going for broke. If anything, he slowed down. In rare cases, speaking outside your slot is at best a minor inconvenience. At worst, it can impact the entire conference.

This case was an instance of the latter, in spades. Some conference centers have a ballroom where meals and panels happen, with most of the talks occurring in breakout rooms. Alas, in this case, the ballroom was broken into thirds for regular sessions and then converted back to a ballroom for meals. This particular orator had the coveted slot before lunch, and he was squatting in the middle room. *No one* could eat lunch until he wrapped up. Nathaniel recalls how painful it was to watch this speaker continue to drone on while hotel staff did everything but throw a chair at him to get his attention. The conference organizer almost had to drag him off the stage. Needless to say, it was a memorable talk . . . but not for the right reasons.

Some speakers seem oblivious to their surroundings. At a major international show a few years back, Matthew had to nearly drag the speaker immediately preceding him off the stage. The talk was one Lightning Talk in a series with very little time between speakers, which exacerbated the impact of running over. The speaker overstayed his welcome and proceeded to answer audience questions from the stage. Matthew started to set up, yet the interloper showed no signs of moving it along. Eventually Matthew grabbed the lingerer's laptop and moved it to the side table. That got his attention.

Antipattern: Shortchanged

Also Known As	Overtime, Squeezed, Pressed for Time
Definition	You have a scheduled time slot at a conference or you've reserved a meeting room for the big presentation, yet when you show up someone else is still there, speaking over their allotted time.
Motivation	It happens to all of us. You've prepared, you've arrived early, and you're ready to set up. Unfortunately, the previous speaker is still going. How you react to this situation can mean the difference between a minor hiccup and a disaster.
Applicability/Consequences	Any time there is a schedule, someone will break it. Typically, this antipattern happens with inexperienced speakers or those who aren't familiar with the schedule. Some speakers revel in going over their allotted time, though. It happens constantly within companies, where meeting rooms are often the rarest commodity.

In the most extreme cases, you'll be left with less time than expected. You'll feel rushed, maybe even a little panicked. Instead of the five or ten minutes you planned for setup, you have a minute or two. You'll have to forego Seeding Satisfaction, and you might need to use some Expansion Joints; it's even possible you'll have to skip an entire section. Resist the urge to Go Meta and call attention to it.

In more typical situations, you might have to venture outside your comfort zone and politely (but firmly) assert yourself, which is a variation of our Display of High Value pattern. You and your audience have every right to the amount of time the organizer intended for your talk; don't be afraid to take it.

Mechanics	First, don't panic; it won't help matters. Second, don't be afraid to push the previous speaker out of the room, metaphorically. Most speakers will start to get the hint, especially if you invade the presentation space. If they are still lecturing, hover conspicuously by the exit. If the speaker doesn't miss a beat, approach the front of the room (preferably via a side route). Be polite but firm; you have a job to do. If someone is squatting in a meeting room, the gathering crowd at the door will exert increasing schedule pressure.

If the speaker is answering questions, start setting up. Most people will understand their obligation to a fellow speaker and move things along. Unfortunately, some speakers are oblivious; help them pack up. It may seem overly aggressive, but moving someone's laptop can get his or her attention.

Be prepared to interrupt a conversation. If the preceding presenter is answering questions at the podium, be bold and speak up. In the *rare* cases when these steps don't work, contact the organizer or a surrogate and have them play the heavy. They have a vested interest in keeping the trains running on time.

Keep a close eye on your gear. Speakers have been known to grab a similar-looking remote or a power brick accidentally. Some even assume that everything on the table is theirs.

It goes without saying: Don't be the speaker someone has to kick out of a room. It is your responsibility to know how much time you have and fit your talk to that constraint. Do not assume the talk slots are the same as yesterday's or that every slot is the same length; they can and do vary. If you see someone hovering by the door, double-check that you're not running long. When you've completed your talk, start breaking down and get out of the way of the next presenter. If people have additional questions or want to continue the conversation, politely ask them to take it outside to give the next presenter a chance to set up.

We know you think that every slide, anecdote, and joke is crucial to your presentation. However, when you're crafting a talk, think through which material is really crucial and which is merely nice to have. You hope you never need to cut a thing, but you should always have at least a notion of where you can make up some time should the need arise. In extreme cases, this will mean hiding or deleting some slides. Become proficient at skipping over slides during a presentation using your preferred tool, which all have keyboard shortcuts that allow you to gracefully edit on the fly. Another advantage of the heads-up display mode (discussed in the Weatherman pattern) is the ability to resequence your slides on the fly. Don't leave the slides in place and zoom past them during the presentation. People always notice a slide you skip over, and some will spend precious attention trying to decipher what you omitted.

Related Patterns   The Preparation pattern helps calm you when your nervousness escalates as you watch the clock. If you know that you are well-prepared, you stress less about unexpected environmental factors.

Make sure that you avoid Going Meta by explaining why you're starting a bit late. The audience can see what is happening. Throwing the last speaker under the bus because he or she had an enthusiastic crowd and couldn't handle questions well seems rude.

The Expansion Joints pattern helps if you suspect you'll end up in this situation, enabling you to compress your talk to accommodate preternaturally shortened time slots.

CHAPTER 7

PERFORMANCE ANTIPATTERNS

WE'VE ARRIVED AT THE MOMENT OF TRUTH: THE PERFORMANCE.

Before you can apply patterns, you must make sure you haven't developed bad habits, or antipatterns.

Frank's Frankly Fatuous Fumbling

One of Neal's colleagues, Frank, was a terrific speaker. He could hold a business meeting in the palm of his hand because he was articulate, charming, and knowledgeable. But when he got nervous, he began starting sentences with "Frankly." The more nervous he became, the more "franklys" came out.

The consulting engagement that Neal and Frank were working on culminated in a big meeting. Frank was going to be the master of ceremonies, doing most of the talking and handing off specific sections to specialists like Neal. The specialists were just sitting at the table up front, awaiting their turns. Neal had been teasing Frank about his favorite word before the meeting, so to pass time, Neal started ticking off the number of occurrences on a notepad. Another of the specialists sitting next to Neal took notice and starting nudging Neal any time he missed one.

After the meeting, everyone gathered for a retrospective. Neal asked Frank how he thought he had done with his "franklys" during his 90 minutes of talking. "I don't know—I was pretty nervous," Frank said, "I probably said it a lot, like 10 or 15 times."

The final tally was 53. Frank was suffering from a Hiccup Word.

Antipattern: Hiccup Words

Also Known As	Stuttering, Gap Fillers
Definition	Involuntarily pepper your talk with airtime-filling nonwords used as placeholders for thought (such as *um*, *ah*, and *oh*), or real words overused to the point of ridiculousness (such as *actually* or *frankly*).
Motivation	No speaker means to stammer, stutter, and overuse words, but it's a natural reaction to stress and thought. When speaking to a group, you have a strong sense of the silence you own, compelling you to fill it completely. However, your brain can't supply the correct words to your mouth at exactly the correct pace, so you defensively make bridging sounds toward the next word. A reasonable pause is better, as described in the Breathing Room pattern, but relaxing enough to allow pauses takes practice.
Applicability/ Consequences	All presenters go through phases when they have their favorite Hiccup Words or sounds; Neal's is the overuse of the word *actually*, against which he must keep constant vigilance. Even the most prepared presenters will eventually forget something, and Hiccup Words amplify any perceived lack of knowledge. This antipattern

is insidious because it is noticeably distracting for the audience yet hard for the presenter to identify.

Mechanics Hiccup Words, like real hiccups, seem involuntary to the presenter but can be eliminated with careful effort. You must practice removing them from your speech.

The hardest part of fixing this antipattern is discovering that you suffer from it. You can either get a friend to count your Hiccup Words or record yourself. Hearing how inarticulate you sound is initially shocking, but part of becoming a polished speaker is gritting your teeth and becoming accustomed to hearing yourself speak. You can only fix problems that you can find.

When you're on the spot, a brusque "I don't know" or a strategic "I'll get to that detail later" will buy you time to collect your thoughts. Though abrupt, they are far better than *uh*, *let's see*, and *oops*. Another strategy is to step up to the next higher level of abstraction (although that can still be perceived as a dodge).

Known Uses Rick Perry, a candidate for the US presidency in 2012, gave a pyrotechnic display of Hiccup Words in a debate. When asked the names of the three federal departments he would shut down if elected, he named the first two and then said, "The third agency of government I would . . . I would do away with, the education, uh the . . . uh commerce . . . and, let's see. I can't. The third one, I can't. Sorry. Oops."[1]

If Perry had said, "But the reason I want to shut down several agencies is really the systemic issue of waste and inefficiency," that boring, almost unnewsworthy recasting of the gaffe to a higher abstraction level might have spared him substantial humiliation.

Related Patterns One reason for Hiccup Words is stress about silence being perceived poorly. The Breathing Room pattern is an antidote to that feeling.

The Carnegie Hall pattern, which provides practice strategies, will help you overcome this antipattern.

Antipattern: Disowning Your Topic

Definition   In the course of your talk, decide that you're not meeting audience expectations and make damaging adjustments on the fly.

Motivation   Dozens of things can compete for your attention when you're presenting, and it's easy to misjudge audience reactions in the heat of the moment. For example, you launch into your presentation to a Midwestern audience on the new manufacturing process for widgets. It's the first talk of the day, and the stage lighting prevents you from seeing the audience well. You construe the attendees' silence to mean, "We already know what you're saying." You speed up because you don't want to bore them. In reality, your original pace was fine, but the audience members aren't comfortable in this environment yet, and many of them are unsure of the social conventions for feedback, so they opt for the safety of quiet contemplation.

Applicability/ Consequences   Speeding up your delivery when you present an already complex subject leads to poor understanding, which makes the audience even quieter.

Mechanics   To avoid this antipattern, don't mistake quiet for mastery. Don't generalize the reactions of one animated individual in the front row and end up ruining the presentation for everyone else. Own your topic. Take the time to gauge your audience based on your best information, and build a killer presentation. At presentation time, deliver your material with clarity and confidence, and don't significantly alter your practiced pace.

Related Patterns   If you have a complex subject area and are concerned about missing the audience level, the Crucible pattern is invaluable; apply several rounds of practice and refinement to hone the audience level.

You're less likely to suffer from this antipattern if you've carefully applied the Know Your Audience pattern.

Martin Fowler's Audience Ownership

At the first-ever Ruby on Rails developers conference (RailsConf [2]), Martin Fowler, a well-known figure in the software-development world, presented one of the keynotes. Fowler is known for his ability to catalog software patterns in the most complex domains, and his keynote provided foundational material on how patterns' underlying abstractions work.

Neal was sitting next to a colleague who complained to him throughout that the talk was too remedial and that he wanted Fowler to talk about the advanced topic *he* was interested in.

Yet when the keynote was over, the audience overwhelmingly loved it. It was at exactly the right level for most of the crowd. Fowler had done his homework and knew the experience and knowledge level of most of the audience, and he pitched his talk at that level.

You'll never satisfy everyone in a large audience, so make sure that you understand the audience level, and *own* your topic when it comes time to talk.

Antipattern: Lipstick on a Pig

Also Known As   Wooden Nickel, Perfumed Garbage, Eye Candy

Definition   Disguise lack of preparation and inferior insights by merely making your slides look visually attractive.

Motivation   Presenters want a talk to look great and to hear positive comments echoing in the hallway afterward. The danger is that time constraints prevent you from really working all the way down to the skeleton of the talk. In the final rush to get a presentation ready for tomorrow's symposium and using the few minutes available, you whip out a tube of visual lipstick or eye candy and liberally apply it to the pig.

Applicability/ Consequences   Lipstick on a Pig is frequently employed when time is running short to build or rework the talk but the presenter still has a vested interest in *looking good*.

A talk with attractive slides but otherwise poor content will typically garner a positive initial reception but have almost no long-term impact.

Mechanics   Presentations should have clear structure, logical flow, and fresh insights for the audience—every time. The structure of a presentation serves as a skeleton that determines the quality of animal you've produced. You should expend energy making sure the structure is right before you put the flesh on the bones—not on trying to conceal the fact that all you have is a pig.

As frequent presenters, we typically find it takes 90 or more hours to build a high-quality and well-structured 90-minute talk, leading to an easy-to-remember formula, *plan an hour of preparation time for every minute of presentation time*. We've seen excellent presenters claim to take less than this, but we've discovered they are merely being untruthful to themselves about the total investment. Our 90-hour number includes research, book reading, web searching, thinking, designing, prototyping, implementing, demonstrating, practice, and rework.

Known Uses   Many presenters, seeking to hone their talks with the smallest possible time investment, pick up *Presentation Zen*,[3] or *Slide:ology*,[4] and absorb only the visual examples—even though those books implore you to go further and build great content with great bones and a story arc.

Related Patterns   Closely related is the Photomaniac antipattern; one of the ways to add Lipstick on a Pig is to quickly steal some pictures from the web.

Salesman Spence's Sorry Sales Session

Salesman Spence is a pharmaceutical sales representative who travels and pitches his company's products to physicians. He has honed his pitch to a scalpel's edge . . . for doctors.

As usual, Spence had scheduled a lunchtime sales presentation to a group medical practice, bartering lunch for attention. But the physicians were called away to an emergency, so the receptionist, office manager, and billing specialist sat quietly through the presentation in an attempt to be polite to Spence.

Spence was well aware of the audience change but boldly delivered his original pitch, stating how the chemical bound to certain receptors was such-and-such percentage effective in cases in which the condition had matured for more than 5.5 weeks and risked some unpronounceable side effect only in males of a certain age or blood type. The technospeak-filled talk fell on deaf ears (but at least the office staff had a good free lunch).

Spence would have better served his listeners—and his own cause—by saying that the drug was comparable to, but more effective than and half as costly as, one that this particular medical practice prescribes almost 20 times a week. He would have secured the attention and respect of his audience and quite possibly their purchasing recommendation to the physicians. He needed to speak the revised audience's more pedestrian language, but instead he confused them by deploying the Tower of Babble antipattern.

Ａ Antipattern: Tower of Babble

Also Known As   Technospeak, Technobabble, Acronym Goulash

Contributed By   Nancy Duarte, CEO, Duarte Design Inc.[5]

Definition   Use a highly specialized vocabulary that's familiar to you but foreign and probably incomprehensible to anyone not in your field.

Motivation   Three competing motivations exist for this antipattern in increasing order of sinfulness:

- You simply forget not to use it. It comes naturally because you live and breathe it in your daily work, and all your coworkers talk the same way.
- You intentionally want to use the most articulate language available to your talk's industry domain to communicate your material as precisely as possible.
- You want to flaunt your intellect to the audience. You may think, "This is my big chance to wow everyone with words they'll struggle to understand."

Applicability/ Consequences

Presentations in any semitechnical or technical line of research or practice are susceptible to this antipattern. This can span from computer science to chemistry and from publishing to video production.

Acronyms and other technical terms are a powerful and useful tool for an audience that knows them. They increase information density and help you establish a rapport with attendees of like background. However, you can't always count on everyone in your audience knowing the language that's comfortable and familiar to you. For the layperson or a specialist in an orthogonal field, it's nonsense.

When you use technical terms to exert intellectual superiority, it backfires. Your audience will blame your failure to build and deliver a clear presentation for their inability to understand it.

Mechanics

To be an effective communicator in your field, it's important to moderate your use of specialized language at the right times. Perform the due diligence to learn the composition and background of your audience (see Know Your Audience). Establish an informed level of technical speech that's appropriate for this talk and this audience. Speak the narrow language of your field to your colleagues, but use more accessible terms for more generalized audiences.

Be careful if you are at an event that uses translators. Usually, translators specialize in translating standard language, not the argot of your arcane technical field. When being translated, speak acronyms clearly, slow down around complex technical terms, and maintain awareness that someone else needs to make sense of your words in a different language.

Known Uses

Investor pitches to financiers, software-development briefings to managerial staff, and medical-research presentations to administrative supply-purchasing staff all have been known to implement this antipattern.

Related Patterns

A related antipattern is Disowning Your Topic, which describes the inadvertent tendency to speed up when you fear that the audience already knows your topic.

A sure remedy for this antipattern is the Know Your Audience pattern.

☢ Antipattern: Bunker

Also Known As	Moat, Podium, Mother's Skirts
Definition	Hide from the audience behind a podium, lectern, or desk, or distance yourself by speaking from up on a stage.
Motivation	Some surveys and research results indicate that most people fear *death* less than public speaking—so it's not surprising that nervous speakers find all sorts of ways to hide from the large, scary group in front of them.
Applicability/ Consequences	Hiding behind something doesn't engender your audience's trust. When you speak to a group of people, making a more personal connection with them adds nuance and extra meaning to your presentation.
	The traditional view of this antipattern calls out things that people literally hide behind, but we include stages and other "moats" as well. Speaking from a stage, even if it is raised only a few inches off the ground, has a devastating effect on your ability to connect with the audience. This divide is desirable sometimes, especially in formal settings like keynotes. But a stage encourages a passive viewing mode. If you strive for interactivity, speaking from a stage is tough. Add in the forced separation caused by stage lighting and you've created a perfect storm of bad experience for yourself.
Mechanics	Avoid standing behind a podium or desk. We know it feels awkward and you're not sure where your hands are supposed to go, but that sensation will pass. We think that gentle wandering is preferable, although it can quickly become distracting if overdone.
Related Patterns	This antipattern underlines the importance of the Carnegie Hall pattern: If you've practiced your presentation well, environmental distractions have far less impact.
	If you Know Your Audience, you'll find it easier to gauge your comfort level when presenting.

Tom's Tussle with the Technical Terror

Tom's talk was going great. He was doing a good job Seeding Satisfaction, his message was crisp, and he incorporated the Entertainment pattern and had the crowd rolling. But then Tom ran headlong into a technical bully—someone who believes they know more than the presenter and intends to convert everyone else to the same opinion. It started innocently enough, with the technical bully asking a reasonable question. But Tom's answer didn't satisfy the bully, who then decided to show off his intelligence. Tom had to defuse the situation quickly and decisively or risk losing the audience.

Technical bullies consider themselves extremely bright, and they probably are. Chances are they aren't used to being challenged because they're often in a position of technical authority. When they sense they are "losing" a technical discussion, they'll often fall back on challenging you with some arcane bit of technical trivia, perhaps interjecting some ad hominem attack for good measure. Unless you can trump the technical bully's face card, acknowledge defeat and move on for the good of the audience.

That's exactly what Tom did. He understood he wasn't going to "win" the argument and that there was no point in trying. He thanked the bully for pointing out a new bit of information and dove right back into his talk.

Antipattern: Hecklers

Also Known As
Time Sink, Just One More Question, Technical Bully

Definition
Outright hecklers, attendees who monopolize your time and attention, and technical showoffs can wreak havoc on a presentation.

Motivation
Most attendees genuinely want you to succeed, but every so often you'll run into a heckler. Some are trying to embarrass you; maybe they felt passed over by the conference organizers, the dog bit them that morning, or they're reacting to some perceived personal slight. Whatever their rationale, you must deal with hecklers before they derail your talk.

In addition to outright hecklers, some audiences include a *time sink* or two. In search of free consulting, they try to monopolize your time by asking more than their fair share of questions or they cross the line from pursuing a good follow-up question to dominating the conversation.

In the technical space, beware the showoff (also known as the *technical bully*). There's usually someone in the crowd who loves to ask arcane questions about one-off situations or rare edge cases in an effort to demonstrate a high IQ or the one bit of technical trivia they've absorbed. A technical bully might present you with various "puzzler" scenarios, hoping you'll slip up. Another might regale you with story after story from his or her own experience.

Applicability/
Consequences
Hecklers are most common at public events; the likelihood of their presence increases as the event price decreases and the audience size increases. This antipattern is much less likely but not unheard of in professional settings, where heckling behavior is typically a proxy for other corporate dysfunction.

Much as you may want to, you can't ignore hecklers. At best, they distract you; at worst, they ruin the talk for the rest of audience. Despite their more benign appearance, time sinks are just as deadly. Most of us want to be helpful, but you have an obligation to protect the audience from one of its own. In addition to creating a better atmosphere for your audience, silencing one heckler will often keep others in check.

Dealing with distractions leads to a better talk. You'll be more relaxed, and your audience will be free to focus on you and your message.

Mechanics   Time and attention are limited resources. It's your job to deliver a message to your attendees, which sometimes means you must play the bad guy. We've all been in a meeting dominated by someone who waltzed all over the agenda; don't let someone do that to your talk.

Shutting down a heckler doesn't come naturally to many of us, but confronting them decisively is an important skill for the frequent speaker. Tone will contain some hecklers. Speak confidently; answer the question or suggest that you take it offline. Do not allow the conversation to spiral out of control. If the heckler insists on continuing, don't give in; simply ask that they continue the conversation during the next break. Politely remind the heckler that you have a lot of material to cover and ask them to respect the rest of the audience.

Some hecklers won't be dissuaded by a polite request, and you may need to escalate your approach. You can often silence a heckler by invading their personal space. If the room allows it, walk over to the heckler and get close. Very close. Engage them directly. Most will back down.

Recognize when someone is asking more than their fair share of questions; focus on the message, and don't lose sight of the needs of the rest of your audience. Never be afraid to tell someone you'll answer his or her question offline during a break or after the conference. Deal decisively with people who try to dominate your talk.

Technical bullies can be beaten with their own weapons: If you can, stump *them* with some bit of ephemera. Turn the tables by asking them questions, or you can even ask if they'd like to take your place and actually give the talk. And even if a technical bully is telling interesting stories, remember that the audience is there to see and hear *you*.

You can deal with a heckler to your and the audience's benefit by controlled displays of dominance. Address the heckler with direct eye contact, speak in short phrases, and quickly escalate to simple commands to stop interrupting and leave the room if necessary. This is a difficult technique for many presenters to master, and overdoing it is a costly mistake that leaves the presenter looking like a bully. You always have the power *in fact* to enforce control over the conversation in the room, and you need only exercise it in a matter-of-fact way when the occasion arises. Countering abuse with abuse communicates to the audience that you are uncomfortable in your role as presenter and must resort to rude behavior to maintain order. When dealing with hecklers, remember that your goal is not to punish them but to serve the rest of the audience. This should keep you from stepping over the line, harming the heckler, and turning off your audience.

Knowing your limitations goes a long way toward disarming most negative audience members. It's important to know what you don't know. You're far better off admitting you don't know the answer to a question than attempting to fool the audience. Rather than stammer your way through an explanation, jot the question down and follow up with an answer later. Though it may seem like the questioner is just trying to antagonize you, most people are genuinely curious and will accept "I don't know" or "I'll get back to you."

Related Patterns   The Know Your Audience pattern should decrease the likelihood of Hecklers or, barring that, at least reduce your surprise at their presence.

People are less likely to heckle you if you have a moat around you—one way in which the Bunker antipattern can be helpful.

The Display of High Value pattern might help deter hecklers.

Antipattern: Going Meta

Also Known As   Talking about the Talk

Contributed By   Ted Neward

Definition   To bore your audience (at best) and annoy it (at worst), talk *about* your presentation *within* the presentation.

Motivation   In programming, the *meta* prefix refers to a self-referential topic. For example, *meta*data is information *about* data; it's not the data itself. When you "go meta" in a presentation, you're succumbing (because of nervousness, exhaustion, insecurity, frustration, embarrassment, or any other all-too-human foible) to the temptation to mention any or all the following to the audience:

- The fact that you built the talk last night
- Misunderstanding your assigned talk-slot duration until five minutes ago
- Thinking you were going to give the talk to a different type of audience (technical/nontechnical/adult/collegiate/apprentice/master).
- Having had trouble with the projector, now that it is working fine

- Forgetting your remote-control clicker
- Not being fully prepared
- Not knowing anything about the culture of the audience you are speaking to
- In general, any last-minute stressor that has since been resolved, which the audience wouldn't even know about if you weren't talking about it

Applicability/ Consequences

Any talk suffers if you don't use your time with the audience in the most efficient manner. Talking about how short or long you are going to run—or any other meta aspect—eats away at that precious time without enlightening your audience. Let the talk and your delivery of it speak for themselves.

Mechanics

Use your limited time with the audience to maximum effect. Your talk should be well-structured, with a definitive Narrative Arc that helps audience members sense intuitively where they are on the journey. If you need to cut the talk a bit short, make that transparent to the audience by building the presentation with the Breathing Room pattern in mind.

Preparedness and having fallbacks are key to avoiding this antipattern:

- Prepare diligently for the presentation, well in advance. Embrace both the Carnegie Hall and Crucible patterns.
- If possible, do a practice run on the actual venue equipment.
- Implement the Know Your Audience pattern.
- Prepare two versions of your most dangerous diagrams (ones with complex colors or small sizes) and test-view them from the back of the room in advance of your talk so you'll know which versions work best.
- For any device that is critical to your talk, bring a backup if it's financially feasible to do so. At least bring backup batteries.
- Build Breathing Room into your talk.
- Practice the talk a sufficient number of times with a sample audience asking questions to give you a good feel for its *real duration*.

Known Uses

An example of this antipattern can be found in the opening moments of the Chris Chabris's *When Intuition Fails* talk[6] at Pop! Tech. He mentions that his clicker isn't working correctly, but scarcely anyone would have noticed if he hadn't mentioned it. Never go meta, Chris.

Related Patterns

One reason presenters Go Meta is nervousness, brought on by the fear of silence. Embrace the Breathing Room pattern to help find a proper way to deal with silence.

Developer Dave's Meta Moment

Developer Dave was asked to deliver a keynote at a major developer conference in Norway on a topic in which he has deep expertise. Dave has a killer hour-long presentation on just that subject. When he was invited, he mentally checked off that he had material.

When he arrived at the conference and looked at the agenda, he was surprised to see that the keynote slot was only 45 minutes. That's only 15 minutes less than the usual length of his talk, so he felt he could manage. At the beginning of the presentation, he warned the audience, "This is normally a 60-minute talk, but I'll try to get through it all in 45 minutes." And a funny thing happened. Having failed to take into account the reputation that some Scandinavian audiences have for remaining stoically quiet, he got none of the talk's normal feedback and finished in 40 minutes.

Because Dave told the attendees beforehand that he was compressing the talk, *nothing he did could make them happy.* Even though he finished early, many people suspected that he glossed over material he could have spent more time on, even though he didn't: He didn't follow the Know Your Audience pattern and didn't realize that you can expect less interaction in some parts of the world. He actually had plenty of time if he had accounted for the circumstances. By Going Meta, he set himself up to disappoint the audience. Instead of enjoying the topic, they felt cheated.

Developer Dave went meta, and it cost him. If he hadn't said anything at the outset about the presentation's length, his talk would have been well-received.

Antipattern: Backchannel

Also Known As   Chattering Classes, Magpies

Definition   The backchannel encompasses all the ways people can chat about your presentation while it's occurring, such as text-messaging during a business meeting or tweeting at a conference.

Motivation   Audiences have a finite amount of attention to give to your presentation, and the competition for it by no means ends once people are in their seats. Odds are that something to read, write, or play with is tempting them to turn away from your message. They might be jotting down notes, but don't be surprised if they're reading e-mail, checking stocks, or just surfing the web. Or they're engaged in a Backchannel conversation about your talk via Twitter, a chat room, or some other technology that enables people to connect.

You hope that as you deliver your well-crafted talk, people will be happily tweeting the ideas that are flowing forth and that their feedback will be full of glowing praise for your oratorical skills. Alas, this isn't Lake Wobegon; inevitably someone will post something less than positive. In some venues, that comment will reverberate, and you'll practically feel it in your bones.

Some conferences embrace the backchannel to the point of projecting real-time comments in hallways or even on the main stage. This has caused some controversy, with presenters confronting audience members' snide remarks directly during talks. When the backchannel is projected behind the speaker, suddenly you are faced with a conversation you can't engage in. As you might expect, some audience members use this as an excuse to play class clown. Mob mentality will lead to gobs of negative comments that add nothing to the conversation.

For presenters of all stripes, the Backchannel presents unique challenges. Attendees' tolerance for poor performance is at an all-time low, and many are quick to post an opinion online. Often people will say things there that they wouldn't say out loud in public. In some cases comments are little more than snarky noise, but unlike session evaluations that remain largely private, these public statements can sway people to walk out or avoid your talks altogether. Backchannel is yet another reason to be prepared with a meaningful message.

On the upside, the Backchannel can vastly increase the size of your audience via public formats like Twitter. Your message reaches not only the people sitting in front of you but also anyone who follows their posts. Even if only a small percentage of your audience engages in the backchannel conversation, your voice is greatly magnified. In many cases, the backchannel audience will debate your ideas, helping you to refine them.

Mechanics   Despite its potential drawbacks, the Backchannel represents an outstanding resource. Attendees are quick to post links and resources. At one conference, Nathaniel mentioned an article, which then appeared on Twitter within five minutes. Positive vibes on the backchannel can drive bigger crowds to your talks.

Odds are you'll get a fair amount of direct feedback—good or bad—on the backchannel as well. Just as you should review and react to session evaluations and attendee comments, check the conference or talk hashtag and respond appropriately. People will post questions on Twitter that they might not ask in public; take advantage of that feedback to hone your message. Harvest the crowd's work, adding any links or resources that your audience takes the time to mention.

You must deal with the inevitability of distraction. Like it or not, the Backchannel is here to stay. You can't avoid it, so learn how to use it to your advantage:

- While you're creating your slides, consider how your main message(s) would sound if condensed into a set of tweets. In other words, write the tweets that you'd like to see posted during your talk. What is the talk's central message? What is the *one thing* that you hope your attendees repeat to their friends and colleagues?
- Some authors include book and chapter summaries in their work, including a tweet-sized synopsis. How would you condense your talk into 140 characters or a couple of paragraphs? You might not include such a snapshot in your slides or on your website, but the process of creating a recap can help sharpen your message.
- Write down your central message and keep it in sight as you build your presentation. With each slide, ask yourself if you're helping or hindering that message.

Whether comments you get via the Backchannel are positive or negative, it's in your best interest as a speaker to read and reflect on them. Responding to an attendee is almost always a good idea. You'll have a chance to answer a question, correct a misunderstanding, or just thank people for their time and attention.

Related Patterns   The Backchannel is a great avenue for Seeding Satisfaction.

Consider having one of your Posse tweet a positive forward-looking remark such as "Join my colleague Danny in the Washington Room, where he's giving an excellent speech about Widgets, starting in 15 minutes." It primes the mood of the other audience members and can significantly increase attendance.

Antipattern: Laser Weapons

Also Known As   Lose the Laser Pointer

Definition   The laser pointer seems like such a useful device at first look because it gives you a way of highlighting, identifying, and harmlessly drawing on the presentation surface as you deliver your talk.

Motivation   The laser pointer is a means of tying the audio channel of the presenter's spoken words to the visual channel of the presented slides.

Applicability/   Use of a laser pointer often coincides with presentations that fail to leverage
Consequences   features in the presentation software that produce more effective highlighting. It's applicable at all only when the information on a slide is dense. (A slide implemented with the minimalist Takahashi pattern would scarcely

benefit from a laser pointer because so few elements appear on the screen, and all verbal references by the presenter are automatically *assumed* to be parallel to those few elements.)

Audience members and presenters alike have certainly heard or experienced the top three complaints about laser pointers: They give viewers motion sickness, people sitting toward the back of the room can't see the small laser point, and the highlight disappears as soon as the presenter releases the pointer's button.

Mechanics   Presenters use a laser pointer to point out elements *within* slides, not the slides themselves. A good presenter who reflects on this fact will think, "Why didn't I highlight that with some tool given to me in the presentation software?" Clearer, more reproducible, better animated, and printable means of accomplishing the same element-identifying effect are possible with the Traveling Highlights pattern.

Related Patterns   Use of a laser pointer isn't always bad. We cover good uses in the Lightsaber pattern.

A better alternative to this antipattern is the Traveling Highlights pattern, which builds emphasis into the talk rather than relying on the presenter for that purpose.

Analyst Alan's Blank Stares

Analyst Alan was accepted at the big finance conference to speak about his perspective on market forces. He guesses that most of the audience is pretty advanced, but he isn't sure.

Alan gets the first slot of the day, when everyone will be nice and fresh. Just to make sure that the context is correct, he starts the talk by asking, "Who here is *not* familiar with the CAP theorem? Raise your hands." No one raises a hand, which is comforting. When he prepared his talk, Alan was pretty sure that this audience would know the theorem pretty well; the talk is virtually impossible to follow if you don't.

So Alan plunges into the meat of his talk. As the presentation continues, the crowd never really engages, even though Alan tries several techniques, including Make It Rain.

When the talk is done, Alan asks a friend in the audience how it went. The friend tells him that no one around him had any idea what Alan was talking about—and that he himself didn't have enough background to follow the talk. But because it was the first talk of the day, and he was in an unsure social setting, the last thing he was going to do was raise his hand and admit that he might be the least knowledgeable person in the room. In fact, he represented the exact median of audience knowledge. Alan didn't realize he had stumbled into the Negative Ignorance antipattern.

Antipattern: Negative Ignorance

Contributed By   David Bock, CodeSherpas[7]

Definition   Try to gauge attendees' familiarity with an important concept by asking them if they are (un)familiar with it, typically by requesting a show of hands.

Motivation   One of the variables that you have little control over is your audience's experience level and existing knowledge, especially when you're speaking at a public event. Presenters always have the fear that the audience already knows much of the material, creating a tendency to fall into the Disowning Your Topic antipattern. One way to assuage your fear is to ask the audience up front what they already know or don't know. But you don't want to insult their intelligence, so you pose the question in a way that asks people to admit ignorance.

Applicability/ Consequences   People in an audience are unlikely to answer a question that makes them uncomfortable, especially if you ask them to admit ignorance in front of their peers. Turning it around to a positive question isn't much better. Audiences are fickle about admitting their knowledge level, so you can never trust that you're getting accurate feedback.

Don't ask rhetorical questions either; they make the audience uncomfortable as to whether or not an answer is expected.

Mechanics   It's best not to ask the question at all and to use other means (preferably well in advance of the talk) to ascertain the audience's knowledge level. If you still feel a need to ask, assume that some nontrivial part of your audience doesn't know the concept, some nontrivial part would like to stand up and give a Lightning Talk on it, and everyone else is someplace in the middle. Prepare a 30- to 60-second summary of the subject or—if it is particularly complex—a stand-alone Talklet that covers the important details the audience will need for the remainder of the presentation. The people who already know the subject will nod along and feel smart. Those with marginal knowledge will gain enough context to understand your next point, feel smart, and think of you as smart. The people who don't know the topic will get enough context that your talk doesn't bomb, and they'll have a foundation for researching the topic further later.

Related Patterns   This antipattern and the Disowning Your Topic antipattern have the same motivating fear: You aren't sure of your audience.

If you Know Your Audience beforehand, this antipattern won't affect you.

Antipattern: Dual-Headed Monster

Also Known As   Dual-Headed Class, Split Site, Killing Two Birds with One Deck, Remote Presenter

Definition   Deliver your presentation to two or more audiences simultaneously. One might be live and the rest watching "via satellite." Or the entire audience is "live via satellite"—with audience members either gathered in groups or watching by themselves—while you present remotely. (This antipattern sits on the edge of pattern-ness because it is an increasingly common occurrence and it *can* be done well, but the difficulties in doing so push it toward being an antipattern.)

Motivation   Many companies with more than one physical location try to save time and money by holding classes and presentations live in one site while some or all the audience attends virtually via video conference or similar technology.

Split sites are a fact of life in the modern corporation. Because of the increased costs and inconvenience of travel, videoconference, TelePresence, and web meetings are increasingly common. In a corporate setting, most presenters have a "day job," making it cost-prohibitive to have them deliver the same talk multiple times.

Remote presenting also enables "long-tail presenting." Some talks don't have a large audience in one geographical area, but when it is spread across (several states or countries), the audience might be much larger. A dispersed audience can make a talk that wouldn't ordinarily be cost-effective worth it for everyone involved.

Applicability/ Consequences   Technical difficulties connecting to the remote or virtual site are almost guaranteed. A bigger problem, though, is that the two audiences will experience the presentation differently. A talk can be compelling when delivered to either a live audience or to a remote one, but almost never when given to both at the same time. The remote audience will always have a significantly diminished experience of a Dual-Headed Monster, so you must take that into account.

Mechanics   When scheduling the meeting, verify that the remote room has the necessary equipment (phone, network connection, projector, etc.). Allow increased setup time and be sure to practice with the tools you will use to present to the remote site. Engage with your audiovisual people well in advance of the presentation to be certain everything is set up properly.

Allow increased setup time for all remote attendees too. Before getting started, check in with the remote audience to make sure it's connected and that everything sounds and looks good. If your presentation will be projected in a conference room at an alternate site, make sure someone is in charge of the remote setup.

If possible, engage with the remote participants *well in advance* of your talk. Provide alternative communication mechanisms (if possible) and have a plan B in case connections drop or the conference line is ineffective. Don't get flustered if technical difficulties occur; remote attendees aren't expecting perfection. When something happens (and it will), stay calm and carry on.

We don't yet live in a world with ubiquitous fast Internet connectivity. When presenting to remote participants, at least one attendee will likely have connection issues. If your talk relies heavily on streaming high-definition video content (or any bandwidth-hungry technology), consider scaling back or having an alternative for those with slower connections.

Be careful about platform issues such as Mac versus PC. If the remote video setup requires Windows and PowerPoint—and you have OS X and Keynote—you'll have a hectic situation just before your talk that will tempt you into Going Meta (which you shouldn't).

Related Patterns   When (not if) things break, Going Meta can be a temptation, but beyond a simple explanation of technical difficulties, don't bother to go into details.

Because the visual will be poor for remote participants, you might be pressured to create Slideuments for your talk so that those people can follow along on a printout. Before agreeing, take heed of the significant extra work required to create effective Slideuments.

CHAPTER 8
PERFORMANCE PATTERNS

REPEAT AFTER US: GIVING A TALK ISN'T ABOUT YOU; IT'S about your audience. Just because you're at the front of the room under the bright lights doesn't mean you're the focus. Now isn't the time to show off your amazing intellect or your snazzy stock photography. Your presentation is for the benefit of the people who have given up two of their most precious resources: time and attention. Yes, your audience is probably there to see you and to learn your slant on the topic of the day, but remember that you'd feel pretty silly talking to an empty room.

Losing sight of your audience nearly guarantees a poor presentation. No one likes to be talked down to or disrespected, and crowds are quick to show their displeasure. Some attendees will walk out, and others will leave you scathing reviews. Conversely, an audience can sense a considerate presenter and will often react positively.

This chapter covers some *patterns* for giving your presentation.

Pattern: Carnegie Hall

Definition

Dedicated practice of your presentation is important, but it does more than hone your message—it allows you to discover what the presentation is really about.

Motivation

First, a worn-out joke everyone has heard, attributed to Syd Fields:

> A New Yorker (in some versions, Arthur Rubinstein) is approached in the street near Carnegie Hall and asked, "Pardon me, sir, how do I get to Carnegie Hall?" He replies, "Practice, practice, practice."

Not surprisingly, this pattern is about practicing your presentation, gradually escalating the size and quality of your audience before you get to the real show. Start by presenting it to your cats, and don't be offended if they drift off to sleep. This may sound silly and counterproductive, but saying the words out loud changes the way you think they'll sound and their consequent meaning in the context of your presentation. Even experienced presenters notice that the same words come out different when you *speak* them rather than plan or type them. The sooner you start saying your talk aloud, the more you refine the real deliverable—the presentation (not just the slides).

The more you present the material, the more polished and refined it becomes. *Present* doesn't mean *thinking* about giving the presentation or even delivering it to yourself in front of a mirror. Actors know that performing for an audience differs from rehearsal.

Applicability/
Consequences

This pattern applies to all types of presentations; all will benefit greatly from practice.

As we mentioned in the first chapter, all the authors have been speakers for the No Fluff, Just Stuff conference series, whose best feature for presenters is the sheer number of sessions and presentations within each conference. If you can give a technical presentation at a conference two or three times, you feel that it's honed. Practice always makes it better. Practice is one of the secrets of the quality of the presentations at No Fluff, Just Stuff: Regular presenters on that tour can give the same presentation more than a dozen times. Neal has some talks he has presented more than 50 times. If you can't make it better with that much practice, you should just stop!

Finding opportunities to reuse material provides ancillary benefits. Because you know that you're going to use the material more than once, you'll tend to spend more time honing both the content and the presentation style, amortizing that effort over a large number of talks. It also makes it more reasonable to incur expenses such as more expensive stock photos, cartoons, and other assets.

Neal attended a progressive-rock festival every year and was struck by how much each band managed to "own" the stage, even though they were all forced to use the same lighting, sound system, and even drum kit, modified for each band. He realized that their comfort in this environment came from the sound check that happened away from the eyes of the audience. Between each act, they evacuated the auditorium to set up for the next band, and they did a sound check. They felt comfortable because they were able to use the real space and practice a bit before the crowd arrived.

Practice makes presenting easier when everything goes well, and it's crucial when things go badly. Neal gave a presentation in Brisbane, Australia, to a group of developers one summer, and the air conditioning was broken. Brisbane can become quite tropical in the summer! He fought through it, and because he had given the presentation dozens of times, the heat was distracting but not devastatingly so.

Another thing that can throw you off your game is stage lighting, which is very distracting if you aren't accustomed to it. Stage lighting makes it easier for the audience to see you but much harder for you to see it. Even if you have given the presentation several times before and become comfortable with the audience interaction, that comfort suddenly disappears when all you can see is a wall of light. Practice saves you in those situations because you have the experience of how the audience reacts to the presentation, when to pause, what parts elicit the biggest laughs, and so on.

Any presenter can tell you war stories of having to put the computer next to the projector at the back of the room because of a bad cable, and doing the presentation from memory with someone else advancing the slides. The more you've presented a certain set of material (either for real or simulated), the more easily you can handle even massive distractions.

Mechanics When you think you have the presentation done (or even a good draft), present it to a friendly crowd. Perhaps you can bribe some of your coworkers with lunch to sit through an early draft. Do a dry run and record it as video. You'll be shocked (and mortified) at how you look and how it sounds (and not just at how annoying your voice sounds). Pay attention to the Narrative Arc and try to chase away any Hiccup Words.

As the presentation gets better, schedule yourself for a local special interest group (if you are in a community, such as software, that supports numerous user groups) or local industry gathering.

You should plan to do four real rehearsals of your talk:

1. The first time helps you to pace the content, get the timing right, and realize how many things don't work well. You should try to focus on content for this run-through and not worry too much about presentation concerns.

2. Assuming that you've resolved the major problems from the first attempt, the second rehearsal should be about the presentation itself: pacing, delivery, and appropriateness of the content. Don't put off thinking about metapresentation issues too long; you should fix any such deficiencies as quickly as possible.

3. The third rehearsal serves two purposes. First, it gives you an opportunity to audition the content and presentation fixes generated by the first two passes. Second, it gives you a chance to go over the (ideally) more and more ingrained material, enabling you to hone the pace you established during the first time.

4. The fourth time through you should start to find the talk's groove. The content should be aligned with your goals, and you should be developing a good sense of which parts work well and which are weaker. After this fourth rehearsal, you should feel better about the material and the technical aspects of the presentation, and you should be more relaxed as you deliver it.

Setting a definite rehearsal schedule forces you to go through the exercise with full concentration rather than read slides to yourself as you sit at your desk. Having specific goals for each rehearsal gives you actionable targets. By giving the talk in a realistic setting, you can see how the material works in its presentation context, see the best way to deliver that material, and gain more confidence that you know the presentation well.

Related Patterns   This pattern and the Crucible pattern seem similar but are actually quite different. Carnegie Hall is about practicing your presentation with specific goals in mind. Crucible is about the *changes* that occur over time as you hone your material under the refining process of presenting it.

Pattern: Emotional State

Definition

Know your audience's general emotional state and the factors that influence it positively. Springboard from attendees' positive feelings to make a more lasting favorable impact on the audience.

Motivation

By gathering an impression of your audience's frame of mind, you can significantly amplify your talk's positive impact. Awareness of the general mood around the office or conference hall can help you modulate the tone of your talk, decide which jokes to try, and make other adjustments. Modifications you make to content, verbal delivery, and rhetoric—be they minor or dramatic—demonstrate that you care about mapping your topic to this audience's particular needs.

Applicability/
Consequences

It never hurts to ascertain the emotional state of a group of people before you stand in front of them.

Mechanics

The adjustments you make typically stem from your knowledge that the audience either has recently been through troubling times or is embarking upon a bright new era. Use all your social-networking skills to get the lay of the land. For important meetings, find coworkers or important stakeholders and learn what kind of day they are having. Conferences have distinct personalities, expressed via Twitter, conference blogs, and all the other innovative ways conferences project themselves into the world. Review presentations from previous events to see how other speakers have shaped their message. Don't be afraid to reach out to the organizer of the event; most will be more than happy to help you cater to their audience. Chat with your fellow speakers. Many events provide a speakers' room where you can get away from the crowds and work in peace. Ask the other speakers for input on the audience, but be respectful of their time; they might be busy preparing. If the event has a speakers' dinner, use that as an opportunity to gather more intelligence.

Related Patterns

You can determine some aspects of the Emotional State by utilizing the Social Media Advertising pattern.

Pattern: Breathing Room

Also Known As   Accordion, Padding

Definition   Don't fill every moment with sound. Sometimes a well-placed silence speaks volumes.

Motivation   Presenting in front of a group is nerve-wracking. One of the ways people deal with nerves is to speak more rapidly. A silent crowd amplifies your stress because it's hard to determine the root cause of the silence: boredom, rapt interest, uneasy social setting, and so on. As the center of attention, you feel compelled to fill all the time and space in the room. Even short pauses seem excruciatingly long—but only to the presenter. The natural tendency is to speed up and fall back on Hiccup Words to fill every moment with sound. The Breathing Room pattern suggests that you force yourself to slow down, planning short silences if necessary.

Applicability/
Consequences   Speaking too rapidly diminishes comprehension. When taken to the extreme, it hurts your credibility because it indicates nervousness, which suggests deviousness, which you probably don't want to project.

Mechanics   You have too many things on your mind already when performing a presentation to remember to slow your speech down. Plan some points in the talk to have slightly longer-than-normal pauses. Time is one of your most potent information channels during a presentation, and sometimes a lengthy silence emphasizes a point better than flashy graphics or some other device. Just as you plan Brain Breaks in your Narrative Arc, plan some places to encourage contemplation or extra emphasis.

   Neal has a special symbol he places as the first character of the speaker's notes as a cue to pause a bit to let something sink in. If you know you want to emphasize something with an extra pause, don't rely on remembering it during the presentation. Make yourself a note instead, freeing yourself to think about situational concerns.

Related Patterns   When you Know Your Audience, you are able to pace the materials according to their proficiencies, capabilities, and learning style.

   Forging the Narrative Arc is the opportunity to build in Breathing Room rather than hurry through too much material in a mere linear or haphazard form.

Pattern: Shoeless

Definition	Make yourself more relaxed while speaking via some small creature comfort such as taking off your shoes.
Motivation	Some surveys and research results indicate that fear of public speaking is second only to fear of death for many people. It's not surprising, then, that presenting is nerve-wracking work, even if you've been diligently following the Carnegie Hall and Crucible patterns. If you can find some small physical trick to calm your nerves, use it.
Applicability/ Consequences	You might get some odd looks.
Mechanics	Several of our professional speaking colleagues started removing their shoes before their presentations as a relaxer. When we tried it, we were surprised at how well it works. Your Shoeless implementation doesn't need to be anything that obvious: wearing a favorite undershirt or pair of sneakers might suffice.
Known Uses	Many well-known professional speakers have little quirks to help them relax, particularly in high-stress situations such as speaking at important meetings or before large audiences.
Related Patterns	Both this and the Breathing Room pattern are relaxation techniques.

Terry's Tipsy Talks

Neal has a speaker friend who often found himself in high-pressure, last-minute situations. Terry always had good intentions to have his conference presentation material ready well in advance, but it always seemed to come down to the last minute.

Terry was a master at the all-night preparation, so when the time came for the talk, he had all the materials at hand. But he was also plagued with nerves, brought on by a combination of last-minute fire drill and the general stress of delivering new (as in minutes-old) material. Still, he did a stellar job with the presentation. After the fact, Neal learned his secret: alcohol.

Before particularly stressful talks, Terry would drink a glass of wine or two—not enough to diminish his capacity noticeably but enough to relieve stress to let his natural speaking style come through. Although an extreme example of the Shoeless pattern, it was what Terry needed to relax and do his best.

Pattern: Mentor

Also Known As   Tutor, Knowledge Gifts, Gradual Revelations

Contributed By   Nancy Duarte, CEO, Duarte Design Inc.[1]

Definition   When you give a presentation, play the role of mentor, not the role of hero. The audience is the hero.

Motivation   Many familiar Hollywood tales have a hero and a mentor. The mentor's role is to impart knowledge and tools to help the hero solve problems. If the audience is the hero and you're the mentor, attendees will leave your presentation armed with a new skill and enlightened with wisdom. They gave you a significant chunk of their time and should leave with the feeling that spending that time with you was a wise choice.

Applicability/ Consequences   This pattern applies to any presentation whose objective is to convince, instruct, or inform.

If you develop your presentation from the humble perspective of helper rather than star, you will endear yourself to your audience. The audience's sense that you *care* how people use their time with you is a reaction that you should crave.

This pattern can sometimes lead you to reconsider the order of your presentation material. For example, you might have a presentation that shows off your expertise by progressing from the lowest-level details to the highest abstractions. However, you decide to reverse the order when you realize that most attendees will benefit more if they get the higher-level information first.

Mechanics   Before building your presentation, analyze your audience's knowledge level to the extent possible, and think through what you want people to gain from the talk. Make sure all your content supports that end.

The challenge to subject-matter experts of following this pattern is the *curse of knowledge*. You can't unlearn the deep knowledge you hold on your topic. But you need to try to simulate a state of ignorance about the topic in order to empathize with your audience.

When you research a new topic well in advance of preparing a talk on it, note the order in which you achieve epiphanies and break through mental barriers to comprehend the topic fully. Later, you'll be able to help your audience as it struggles with the same issues, albeit in the compressed timeframe of a presentation.

Known Uses   Many of the best product and process trainers have discovered this pattern.

Related Patterns You must have a firm Narrative Arc to support the correct role you want to take with your audience.

This pattern nicely complements the Display of High Value pattern, as both encourage empathic interactions with your audience.

Nathaniel's Nearly Nano New Presentation

Several years ago, Nathaniel gave a new talk at a local single-track conference. The speaker who preceded him ran a little long, and Nathaniel decided to do the organizer a favor and "speed up" to get back on track. Luckily for Nathaniel, he was using the heads-up display (for the first time, as it happens), so he *knew* how long he'd been talking and how many slides he had left. Unfortunately, ten minutes into his talk, Nathaniel realized that he had set a blazing pace and was more than a third of the way through his slides. Needless to say, that wasn't part of the plan.

Realizing that he needed to slow down, Nathaniel expanded on much of the remaining material. When it was all said and done, he finished a few minutes early. He learned an incredibly valuable lesson: Pay attention to the clock. Did the attendees notice the difference in tempo? Nathaniel hopes not, and he avoided Going Meta by not mentioning it. Without the timer and the heads-up display, the talk could have been a disaster; with them (and some improvisation), Nathaniel delivered a well-received talk that is a staple of his rotation to this day.

Pattern: Weatherman

Definition Speak directly to the audience, even when gesturing about things on the screen.

Motivation When you show your back to the audience to read things off the projected slides, you subject your audience to a special form of torture. TV weather reporters incorporate technology (green screens and teleprompters) seamlessly into their presentations so that they can face the camera continuously. Similar techniques enable you to deliver more polished presentations.

Applicability/ Consequences By learning to use the tools that help you interact with your audience, you'll make the technical parts of your presentation blend into the overall experience.

Mechanics Presentation tools like Keynote and PowerPoint allow you to project one image onto the projector (the current slide) while showing something different on the laptop screen (the *heads-up* display). Different laptops use different terms for mirroring displays, so for clarity we'll use the following terms:

- *Display* refers to what is displayed from the presentation tool, regardless of the source.
- *Laptop* refers to the monitor that is part of your laptop.
- *External* refers to an external display device, either a projector or separate monitor.
- *Mirrored* indicates that both displays (the laptop and external) show the same image.
- *Unmirrored* indicates that the laptop display and external displays show different things. Generally, you do this to extend your desktop across two monitors.

Traditionally, when you present from a laptop, the display is mirrored; you see exactly what the audience sees. However, modern presentation tools allow you to unmirror your display, showing the full screen slides on the external display and a special "heads-up" display on the laptop. For example, Keynote allows you to customize the heads-up display by rearranging the elements to your liking. Figure 8.1 shows Neal's setup.

In Figure 8.1, the current slide appears on the left, the next transition appears on the right, the time of day and a countdown timer appear in the upper-right corner, and the speaker's notes appear at the bottom.

True to its name, the Weatherman pattern suggests that you should interact with the screen. Traditionally, the presenter and the screen are distinct and separate. Occasionally, in movies and TV shows, actors turn to address the camera, called "breaking the fourth wall," which has a profound effect because the audience isn't expecting it. You can do the same in presentations by interacting, either subtly or overtly, with your onscreen presentation.

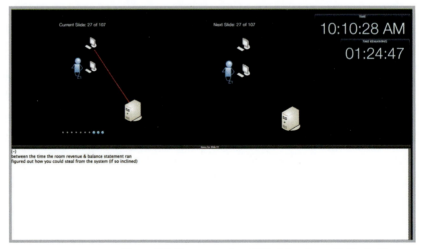

Figure 8.1 Representation of Neal's heads-up display in Keynote

Some animations work particularly well for this pattern. For example, Neal uses the *confetti* animation in Keynote to suggest something being broken up. In his *Test-Driven Design* presentations, he walks over to the screen (when possible) and taps the screen at the same time he clicks the mouse to trigger the *confetti* animation. It looks like he's tapped the screen and caused the words to fall apart.

One shortcoming of the heads-up view in Keynote is the lack of live animation for transitions. You see the starting and ending state but not the changes as they occur. However, you have the option of turning on the transition indicator at the top of the heads-up display (the bar at the top, either red or green, as shown in Figure 8.1). This bar is red while a transition or animation occurs on the projected screen, and it turns green when the animation is complete. The heads-up view doesn't show you the next slide, but it does show the outcome of the next animation, which is exactly what you need when using patterns like Soft Transitions.

Another connection between weather reporters and presentations solves the problem of the lack of live animations in the heads-up display. Many modern laptops have glossy displays. When possible, set up your laptop so that you can see a reflection of the screen behind you in the display. Once you get used to seeing this view of the world, you can look at your notes and, by shifting the focus by your eyes, see a reflection of what's happening on the screen, including animations and other special effects. Using the reflection enables you to face your audience and still interact with things happening on the screen, much like an experienced weather reporter.

Using the heads-up display makes it harder for you to do live demonstrations or otherwise interact with your computer during the presentation. Because you essentially have two displays attached to your laptop, if you need to do something that everyone should see, you must drag it to the alternate display. But that means you no longer see it on your laptop screen. We have seen many contortions and other unnatural acts by people craning their necks around while using the mouse, trying to use the wall screen as a monitor. Try to avoid this eventuality, either by using some of our demonstration patterns (such as Lipsync) or by switching back to mirrored mode for the duration of the demonstration. But be aware that the transition from one mode to the other is frequently harsh because it operates at the hardware level, making it virtually impossible to make the change suavely.

Even though some things become more difficult, the time it takes to get accustomed to the heads-up display is time well spent.

Related Patterns   Similar not only in name, the Make It Rain pattern also suggests breaking the fourth wall and interacting with your audience in innovative ways.

Pairing with Yourself

In a pinch, you can be your own Greek Chorus. How? Embrace the power of video. In one of the most memorable presentations Nathaniel has ever seen, one of his students "pair presented" with his celluloid alter ego to demo a tool to the class. Not sure what that looks like? Watch the movie *Jurassic Park*. In an early scene, the park owner engages in a dialog with his prerecorded self to explain to the skeptical guests how his company brought dinosaurs back from extinction.

Nathaniel's student followed a similar path and nailed the presentation. He recorded himself interacting with the tool, using his recorded self as a foil to his talk. On multiple occasions, he ping-ponged between his live and Live on Tape words. His approach embraced Lipsync as well as Entertainment, and it blew the class away. Not surprisingly, the student aced the class.

Pattern: Seeding the First Question

Also Known As	Warming Up the Audience, Breaking the Ice, Kickstarting
Definition	Subtly raise an obvious question or small doubt early in your presentation as a way to encourage question-and-answer activity.
Motivation	People hate to look ignorant or foolish, and it's surpassingly difficult to get some audiences to start asking questions at the end of the presentation. This pattern's purpose is to bait your audience into asking a question early on so that question-and-answer activity increases throughout the talk. After someone breaks the ice with the first question, others will relax and interact more freely. Seeding the First Question is a nonthreatening way to get someone to start the process. The audience then warms up, and questions flow.
Applicability/ Consequences	This pattern applies when you anticipate a shy audience or want to encourage immediate interaction.
	This ploy is usually obvious, but that doesn't lessen its effectiveness. Any trick you use to diffuse social barriers and other impediments to understanding are effective even if they are obvious.
Mechanics	You can place the "seed" anywhere in the talk, depending on how much anticipation you want to build for the answer. Neal used this successfully in a talk about presentations. His opening slide used the Preroll pattern, which no one in the audience had ever seen. At the start of the talk, he said that at the end he'd show how to create that effect. When the talk was over, just like clockwork, the first question was about how to implement Preroll. After that, the questions flowed freely.

Related Patterns   A Preroll is a good place to Seed the First Question if it's a question you suspect the audience already has about your topic. This illustrates adherence to the Know Your Audience and Display of High Value patterns.

You can combine Seeing the First Question with Greek Chorus, allowing the chorus act as questioner or answer source.

Pattern: Make It Rain

Definition   Move chairs, throw paper airplanes, lob candy, and other props and devices to add flair to your presentation and help encourage interaction in preternaturally shy groups.

Motivation   A presentation is an odd social setting, especially if it's at a public gathering. Using props and other unusual activities can help the audience come out of its shell.

Applicability/Consequences   This pattern is effective in educational settings, especially at the common intersection of difficult, nuanced subject matter and a strong desire on the presenter's part to encourage interaction. It works particularly well with children, who love to receive little treats and favors.

Be careful you don't put someone's eye out throwing candy!

Mechanics   The mechanics of this pattern require either careful preparation or clever improvisation. As you build your talk, think about props you could use to drive the point home more forcefully. If you think you might have a shy group, pack a bag of candy along with your laptop. When you see where you'll be doing your presentation, scout for props that you can subsume into your talk.

Setting up a reward system for questions works well. Keep that bag of candy with you, and reward good answers (and questions!) with a treat. This helps you plug into the competitive instincts of your audience; even people who don't want candy will put in more effort to win the competition.

Don't discount improvisation in the moment. If you are in the middle of a presentation and you're having a hard time conveying a message, is there something physical in the room you can co-opt and put to use?

Known Uses   As you can well imagine, this pattern is very common in the technical-training community. Bruce Tate, a well-known technical speaker, used to do a talk about concurrency in web applications (i.e., what happens when multiple people try to interact with an application simultaneously). This is a difficult subject, so he used chairs and queues of people to illustrate his points and concretize some concepts. And getting the audience out of their chairs and walking around made it a more entertaining talk.

Related Patterns   This pattern is a specific implementation of the Entertainment pattern.

Neal and Joe's Riotous Ruby Class

Neal and his colleague Joe O'Brien volunteered to do a short training class on the Ruby programming language at the big company gathering of techies. But the company they work for is notorious for hiring advanced developers, who are in turn notorious for not paying close attention in traditional training settings because the pace is too slow for them. The challenge Joe and Neal face is how to do the class and convey a lot of information yet keep everyone thoroughly entertained.

They ended up doing a variation of a Live Demo, in which the speaker types source code while talking about it. But in this group, a single person typing source code would never keep everyone entertained. So they created a variation of Live Demo. Instead of a single speaker, computer, projector, and screen, they put two of each at the front of the room, on either side. Each of the laptops was hooked to its own projector, enabling Neal and Joe to do two talks side by side.

During the presentation, one of the presenters would talk, using slides. While he was talking, the other presenter was furiously typing, implementing what the speaker was talking about in close to real time. As they switched topics, they switched roles; at any given time, one was talking and the other was coding like mad.

The colleague most notorious for losing attention easily came up afterward to say that he was thoroughly entertained and that his attention waned for only 10 or 15 seconds. He suggested that the only way to make the talk better would be to hire a juggler to walk around the room; the juggling would consume his remaining 15 seconds of wandering attention.

Pattern: Entertainment

Definition   Use humor, stories, and analogies to hook your audience and help convey your message.

Motivation   Presentations are a continuation of the millennia-old tradition of sharing information orally. To truly engage an audience, you need to do more than just read a bunch of bullet points. Effective presentations include analogies and stories to help your audience integrate the material. Anyone can simply spew facts, but a compelling narrative is something people will remember. People respond to stories, and audiences engage when you share a personal tidbit or an amusing anecdote. Though perhaps not as compelling as a great movie or a concert, presentations can and should be entertainment.

Applicability/ Consequences

Humor delivered in moderation works for nearly any talk. Stories are vital to how people learn and remember; they, too, should be used in nearly every presentation.

Humor is an effective element of any good presentation; witty banter can put you at ease and also warm up your audience. But like any tool, humor can become a golden hammer. Resist overusing it, otherwise your audience won't know when to take you seriously and your message will be lost in the laughs.

In an effort to generate some buzz or even shock an audience, some speakers resort to jokes and language that you wouldn't hear on prime-time broadcast television. No matter how funny you think a joke is, if you're going to use it during a presentation, keep it clean. The fact that you don't consider a particular joke offensive doesn't mean your audience will agree. If you'd feel uncomfortable telling that joke at work or in front of your children, it doesn't belong in your talk. Humor can all too easily degrade into an Alienating Artifact.

Mechanics

Telling a good story is similar to creating a good movie. Introduce your story and lay the foundation for what you want it to convey by presenting the characters and whatever situation they're in (the *hook*). All good stories have a climax, a plot twist, or something else unexpected that resolves the story's central question. Wrap up your story by revealing the resolution and then recap by restating your point in different words.

Most stories should be short and leave little doubt as to how their message fits into your talk's Narrative Arc. That tale you heard in Vegas might be entertaining, but if it doesn't relate to your presentation, leave it for the breaks.

Keep a few stories in your metaphorical back pocket and bring them out when attention wanes or if your timing happens to be off one day.

Use humor somewhere toward the middle of your talk and then again at the end. This timing will help reengage the audience. Starting with a joke can also help launch things on the right track. Use the Brain Breaks pattern to strategically leverage Entertainment elements.

Make sure that the humor you use is aligned with your talk. A spate of one-liners won't turn an average talk into a winner, but humor that fits your talk will help elevate it. Tasteful, lighthearted self-deprecating humor helps humanize you to your audience and shows that you don't place yourself above them. Always exercise caution: Things that you find hilarious might be offensive to your attendees, and comedy can be very culture-dependent. Some cultures are more reserved, so lines that draw huge laughs in one country (or even one city) can fall flat elsewhere. Before heading to a new location, do your research (see Know Your Audience)! When in doubt, leave the jokes out.

It can take a surprising amount of effort to generate just a few bits of humor; if you don't believe us, watch the Jerry Seinfeld documentary *Comedian*.

Related Patterns

It's easier to set the right tone for jokes, inside humor, and anecdotes if you Know Your Audience.

If you get the opportunity to deliver a presentation multiple times, apply the Crucible pattern and remember the shtick that worked well so you can reuse it in subsequent performances.

Pattern: The Stakeout

Definition

Get to your presentation venue early.

Motivation

The last thing you need is a traffic problem—or anything else that delays the start of your presentation—turning your carefully prepared talk into a sketch worthy of a sitcom.

Applicability/ Consequences

This pattern applies *always*—no excuses.

Arriving early is *never* a bad plan. At worst, you'll have some time to collect your thoughts and chat with attendees to Seed Satisfaction. If you're late for your talk, you make the audience sad and annoyed, which is the opposite of Seeding Satisfaction.

Mechanics

Repeat after us: Arrive early at your room. If you have to commute to the venue, leave plenty of time for traffic and parking snafus. Murphy was right: If something can go wrong, it will. When you arrive, get your bearings. Are the rooms near one another or spread out over a corporate campus? Where are the restrooms? Is there a speaker room? If you need help, where can you find the organizer, facilities people, or AV staff? Neal once spoke at a conference in Las Vegas where the hotel room was one-quarter of a mile from the conference room . . . all indoors.

After you find your room, take a few minutes to explore. Will you present from a lectern or a table? Will you be on a stage or at the same level as your audience? How do you adjust the lights? Double-check the projector and audio connections. If you have questions or concerns, don't assume it'll all work out; instead, track down an AV person to help. If you can, attend the talk preceding yours, note any issues the presenter has, and make plans to correct them.

Don't assume that every room at a conference center or hotel is the same. Room sizes vary from intimate breakout-sized rooms that comfortably fit a couple of dozen people to huge halls that can easily seat thousands. Some rooms are amphitheaters where much of your audience will be above you in stadium seating. Stages are challenging implementations of the Bunker antipattern, especially if you like to wander around while talking. As silly as it sounds, make sure you know where the edges are! Falling off a stage makes for a memorable talk, but it can also lead to embarrassing (and painful) injuries.

Stages typically force you to present from a lectern and, depending on the room size, you may need a microphone. Well-equipped conference centers have lavalier microphones (lavs, or lapel mics), which allow you more freedom while you present. Lavs are convenient but not without drawbacks. Be sure you know how to mute or turn them off. *Always* assume a microphone is active even if it isn't projecting into the room. Don't say anything near a microphone you don't want to share with the entire conference. And make sure you turn the microphone off when you're not using it; nothing is quite as embarrassing as a trip to the restroom broadcast to a few hundred people.

Related Patterns   You can't very well be Seeding Satisfaction if you are late or even noticeably harried during setup.

An important aspect of this pattern is the ability to explore the room before you must present, allowing you to identify a Bunker that might interfere with your ability to perform well.

Pattern: Lightsaber

Also Known As   Correct Use of a Laser Pointer

Definition   Yield your laser pointer with the grace of a Jedi knight. Unless you are indeed a rock star, your laser pointer is not meant to be a stage effect.

Motivation   Have you seen a cat playing with a laser dot? Just like our feline friends, people instinctively follow motion, and using a laser pointer can direct the audience's attention to visual elements in your presentation. It's no substitute for a compelling message, but in small doses at the proper moment, it can reengage a crowd.

Used *sparingly*, a laser pointer helps you to make extemporaneous comments. The Traveling Highlights pattern works well when you know during slide construction what you want to emphasize. But some highlights occur organically during a presentation, sparked by a question from the audience or the flow of the talk. A laser pointer gives you some freedom to highlight on the fly.

Applicability/
Consequences

Lightsaber is applicable in nearly all presentation settings.

Judicious use of the laser pointer can grab an audience's attention; using it when attention wanes can bring attention back.

The single biggest Lightsaber mistake is overuse. People will quickly start ignoring a laser if you use it to illuminate every slide. Overuse also disenfranchises people with bad vision or color blindness. A laser pointer is not a crutch. Any time your presentation starts to resemble a rock concert, you've gone too far. Err on the side of underuse.

Pay attention to what you highlight *during* a talk; if you highlight the same things in multiple talks, add Traveling Highlights.

Mechanics

In the *Star Wars* franchise, the bad guys use red lightsabers and the good guys wield green ones. Be a good guy and use green. Color-blind people can pick up the green laser but can rarely see the red. As one color-blind attendee described it, "With most laser pointers, I just try to guess where their arm is aimed."

A handheld remote-control slide advancer (a "clicker") is a must for any presenter, and many include built-in laser pointers. Opt for one that includes a green laser. Built-in laser pointers are convenient (less to carry, fewer batteries to manage), but they are rarely as powerful as the stand-alone units. For large audiences and bright rooms, consider getting the more powerful and expensive green laser pointers.

When you do highlight an element with a laser pointer, don't try to "underline" it by swiveling your wrist madly back and forth. Laser shows can do this because they have machines designed for that motion; you're just making everyone ill. If you need to highlight something, put the dot on it and leave it there.

Related Patterns

The overuse of the Lightsaber leads to the Laser Weapons antipattern.

A good alternative to using a Lightsaber is the Traveling Highlights pattern.

Pattern: Echo Chamber

Also Known As	Repeat the Question!

Definition When someone in the audience asks a question, repeat and paraphrase the question before answering it.

Motivation Echo Chamber encapsulates one of the most common pieces of advice given to speakers. It's frequently given live by a frustrated audience member, as in, "What was the question?!?"

If you answer a question that the entire audience hasn't heard, your answer is out of context and meaningless to anyone who didn't hear it. Everyone in the audience needs to hear all questions and answers because they likely have some of the same questions.

Applicability/ Consequences Repeating every question shows consideration for the audience and eliminates duplicate questions. It also gives you time to construct your answer. By paraphrasing questions, you show that you understand them. Some questioners tend to ramble on a bit (perhaps because they are unaccustomed to speaking succinctly, or, less charitably, it may be the questioner's only time in the spotlight), so paraphrasing helps to summarize and contextualize.

Mechanics Get in the habit of always repeating and paraphrasing audience questions as soon as they're asked.

Related Patterns Learning to think while paraphrasing a question is a practicable skill. When you apply Carnegie Hall, get your rehearsal audiences to ask topical questions, and practice repeating and paraphrasing them.

When applying the Crucible pattern, remember well-received questions asked at your live talks and incorporate them into future versions of the presentation.

Pattern: Red, Yellow, Green

Also Known As	Quick Vote, Straw Poll

Definition

Some conferences use a quick and easy voting system to assess a talk's quality, placing stacks of red, yellow, and green index cards (indicating bad, fair, or good, respectively) near the exits. Audience members choose a card and drop it into a bucket, and a room coordinator tallies up the scores.

In a similar vein, some shows use green/thumbs-up or red/thumbs-down during panel discussions to decide whether to continue the conversation or to move on to another question.

Motivation

Getting feedback of any kind is good. The relative coarseness of just three options—good, bad, or fair—forces people off the fence about a talk. Many attendees are less inclined to fill out a full feedback form. Participation rates with Red, Yellow, Green pattern are significantly higher because it involves minimal effort by attendees.

Depending on the corporate culture at your employer, it can be hard to solicit feedback on meetings and other intracompany presentations—making it doubly hard to apply patterns like Crucible to improve them. Even in rigid companies, you might start a simple Red, Yellow, Green voting system to gather an overall evaluation of the quality of time spent.

Applicability/ Consequences

This pattern is especially useful if the event has a record of little to no feedback for speakers. Statistically, this approach is more meaningful with larger audiences.

Because attendees will actually provide feedback, you'll get a pretty decent idea if your talk resonated. But though you'll have a general feeling about how the talk was received, Red, Yellow, Green leaves you with little actionable content. The talk may have done very well (or poorly), but you have no real notion why. Because the colored cards don't offer space for comment, you're left to guess what worked and what didn't.

Some attendees might "green shift" their votes because, in most cases, the presenter can *see* which card they are choosing. Attendees might also be swayed by how they see that others are voting.

The voting can slow down the exit process. That can lead to delays as people try to move from room to room, which is especially problematic if breaks are short (15 minutes or less).

Mechanics

At the end of the talk, the speaker or room monitor explains the process to the attendees. Each room needs stacks of red, yellow, and green cards plus a bin or box for people to deposit their votes. As attendees file out of the room, they pick the color representing their feeling about the talk and place it in the box. After all the attendees have left, the room monitor tallies the results and records them.

Because voting while departing can dramatically slow down room egress, pay attention to room layout and table placement. Position a table in a way that lets people easily grab the card of choice (multiple stacks can facilitate this) and deposit it. If the room has multiple exits, set up the voting at each exit. Be sure to have ample supplies of all three colors; you don't want to run out of one color and see people grab the next-closest one! Be sure your room monitor(s) have enough time to tally the votes and that they understand the procedure.

Known Uses   Øredev, an international developers conference in Malmo, Sweden, and QCon, a series of technical conferences in major international cities, both deploy Red, Yellow, Green.

Related Patterns   You're more likely to get favorable scores if you spend some time Seeding Satisfaction before the presentation.

CONCLUSION

We've spent the entire book so far showing you patterns and antipatterns for your presentations. In this chapter, we put the onus on you to use our work as a starting point for your own patterns, antipatterns, and *recipes*. We discuss why our use of patterns is slightly different from their use in the software world, give you some advice on creating your own patterns, and finally offer some guidance for creating your own recipes.

Patterns Redux

In the first chapter, we introduced the patterns concept and described how we borrowed the idea from the software engineering world, where pattern names are meant to be descriptive, first and foremost. In fact, many patterns in other books have an extensive "Also Known As" section to delineate the history of names that a pattern has held over the course of its development. For software engineers, the pattern name has become *nomenclature*—an officially recognized term that encapsulates all the aspects of the pattern. This building of a technical vocabulary was one of the most beneficial aspects of the pattern movement.

We use presentation pattern names slightly differently. As with software patterns, some of our names are intended to become nomenclature. For example, we would love to overhear a conversation like this: "We've decided that the Narrative Arc is going to follow three acts. I have a Talklet for each of the parts, and the Unifying Visual Theme will be last year's World Series." However, we also use pattern names as advice, such as Seeding Satisfaction or Defy Defaults. This is particularly true with the antipatterns, which are almost all advisory; that is, the antipattern name indicates something or someone that we advise you to avoid doing, creating, encountering, or becoming.

Build Your Own . . .

. . . Patterns (and
Antipatterns)

We don't believe that we have a monopoly on the ability to find patterns and antipatterns in presentations. In fact, now that we've shown you how, our guess is that you can't *stop* doing it! You capture patterns for any good (or bad) thing so common that it's useful to attach a name to it. The name you attach might invoke some imagery evocative of the meaning. For example, Charred Trail doesn't really mean anything by itself and won't mean anything to you until you've seen the pattern, but after that it's an excellent name because of the memorable imagery.

Alternatively, the name you attach might be advisory. For example, perhaps in your company it's considered a nice touch to include team names in retrospectives, so you might create a *Remember the Team* pattern that's included in any retrospective presentation recipes you build.

Don't get caught up in the formality of the original *pattern* concept. Presentation patterns don't need the same level of rigor. We've bent the rules to make it fit this space better and we suggest you do the same.

. . . Recipes

We suggest that organizations create *recipes* for common presentation types, expressed using pattern names. We use *patterns* as a way of identifying presentation behavior at a higher level of abstraction than individual presentation tool features but at a lower level than *recipes*. A recipe can be written as a collection of patterns. This relationship is shown in Figure 9.1.

In Figure 9.1, presentation tool features—facilities such as animations and transitions—reside at the lowest level. The tool features in many ways determine the vocabulary of your patterns, except in special cases such as Composite Animation. *Patterns* exist at the next higher level of abstraction, combining tool features and conventions to create a named vocabulary of nicely encapsulated techniques. *Recipes* exist at the highest level, combining a collection of patterns to make an actual presentation.

Companies have standard types of presentations: marketing reports, project status, retrospectives, financials, board meetings, and so on. Yet it is unfortunately not common to create reusable assets to make it easy to create consistent versions of these presentations. In many places, the starting point for the next retrospective is to copy the old presentation file, reopen it, and start making changes. Useful material and behavior accrue over time within that copy/paste template, but not in a formal way.

In the first chapter, we suggested that *building* recipes is one excellent use of patterns but didn't carry the conversation further because you didn't have extensive experience with patterns yet. But now you do. Rather than collect Floodmarks in a master slide template and force it on each

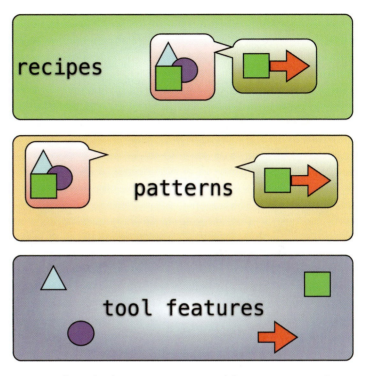

Figure 9.1 Relationship between presentation tool features, patterns, and recipes

employee, you can build recipes, using our patterns and the ones you'll create along the way.

Here is an example recipe:

- The following are antipatterns to avoid:
  - Bullet-Riddled Corpse
  - Cookie Cutter
  - Floodmarks
  - Alienating Artifact
  - We have a company policy against Vacation Photos–style presentations.
- The company provides a default slide template but we encourage you to Defy Defaults when you feel it will make the presentation better.
- When preparing presentations for both teams and management, take the extra time to use the Á la Carte Content pattern to allow for extra details.
- Build product feature presentations with Expansion Joints to allow for detailed questions.
- Be sure you use Fourthought for your ideas; we spend a lot of money on meetings!
- Use Lipsync for all presentations about products or projected features, but use Live Demo for all showcases.

Summary

We set out to create a new vocabulary for building presentations, borrowing a concept from another world. We think we've succeeded, but your success in applying these techniques will be the ultimate test.

Glossary of Patterns

A

Abstract Attorney (Antipattern)

An abstract attorney is someone who takes the description of the presentation from the formal conference brochure way too seriously. They'll often comment (negatively) on any and all deviations from the abstract either during the talk (in the form of an often condescending question) or afterward on session evaluations or on social media.

Á la Carte Content

Creating a presentation "on the fly" using the interest of the crowd to guide the presentation. Typically, this approach begins with a set of related slides (often structured as a Talklet series) that can be alternatively arranged. This technique works well if you have more content than the time slot allows or the talk naturally breaks along several subtopic lines.

Alienating Artifact (Antipattern)

An alienating artifact is something that disenfranchises an audience member or audience members from the topic at hand. This can take the form of an image, a quote, or offensive language.

Analog Noise

Computers make it possible to create visually flawless imagery and text. However, in sci-fi movies, even apparently digital communication has jitter, breakups, blockiness, and noise. The imperfection is a cue that the communications are happening over a long distance. "Analog noise" can be an endearing quality that makes the situation more believable for the audience. Such noise can be intentionally introduced via handwritten fonts, film grain, uneven lines, monochrome colors, and "amateur" photograph errors. Adding some noise to your slides adds visual interest and garners greater attention.

Ant Fonts (Antipattern)

Don't use tiny fonts in a desire to cram more information on a slide. Slide size is completely arbitrary and has no relationship to the proper size of the content. If you ever think (or worse, say) "You probably can't read this in the back," you've failed your audience. Slides with unreadable fonts often result from "helpful" software that modifies font size as you add more content. You don't get bonus points for using fewer slides.

B

Backchannel (Antipattern)

The backchannel encompasses all the ways people can chat about your presentation while it's occurring, either via text messages during a business meeting or tweeting during an event.

Backtracking

Backtracking is the intentional repetition of material for the purpose of reestablishing context. This helps the audience regain their conceptual footing as the narrative moves forward.

Big Why

You should be clear with yourself and to your audience as to why you're giving this talk. It is a critical foundation for the vector you are using to address this talk's topic. Clarifying your motivation does not rule out giving a talk for money, as advertising, to educate, or just to inspire.

Bookends

Use distinct slides throughout the presentation to supply agenda context. Often visually distinct from the standard slides, they provide a sense of progress as well. Bookend slides indicate the end of one section and the start of a new one.

Borrowed Shoes (Antipattern)

From time to time, you may be called upon to deliver someone else's presentation. You are speaking about something that you're not sincere about, that doesn't quite fit you, and that smells funny the entire time you're delivering it. While it can be done in a pinch, the results are rarely awe-inspiring.

Brain Breaks

Research suggests that the average adult attention span is about 20 minutes. Plan something that breaks the concentration coma: humor, a story, something titillating, audience participation, and so on roughly every 10 to 20 minutes. Reengage your audience or lose them to their smartphones.

Breadcrumbs

Create an agenda trail throughout your presentation to provide context on progress. In addition to providing context, this gives the audience a familiar element to ground them.

Breathing Room

Talking too fast and not leaving enough time for the audience to fully understand the deeper implications of the talk is a common antipattern many many presenters exhibit. While difficult, breathing room is the purposeful insertion of quiet to allow important concepts time to settle and germinate.

While dead air might be a cardinal sin in radio, moments of pause allow your audience to integrate your message.

Bullet-Riddled Corpse (Antipattern)

A Bullet-Riddled Corpse is a presentation where every slide is a long series of dull bullet points. Typically, these slides will then be read to the audience insinuating they can't read.

Bunker (Antipattern)

Hiding behind something doesn't engender trust with your audience. You speak to a group of people; making a more personal connection with them adds nuance and extra meaning to your presentation. Avoid podiums; walk around and engage with your audience. Stationary presenters often give very static presentations.

C

Carnegie Hall

The only true preparation for unusual occurrences is practice. This pattern defines the types and number of practice sessions you need.

Cave Painting

Use a huge sectioned canvas with your presentation laid out linearly, zooming in on the constituent sections as you proceed through your presentation.

Celery (Antipattern)

Just like the vegetable, a celery talk is one that expends more effort chewing (processing) on the part of the audience member than they get back in calories or value and new materials learned.

Charred Trail

The slide shows out-of-date content by graying it out as the presenter progresses through the slide. This prevents the audience from reading ahead and results in a more printable artifact.

Coda

The coda is the concluding piece of a slide deck. It provides a partitioned place to put topic-relevant material that isn't delivered in the spoken portion of the presentation.

Composite Animation

A composite animation is when more than one simple animation provided by the presentation tool is applied to an object for a more impressive and educationally helpful combinatory effect.

Concurrent Creation

Presentation materials don't need to be created in the same order as they are found in the presentation. Craft the material in the order that fits; no one will know you did things out of sequence.

Context Keeper

An organizational device within a presentation that reveals the structure of the talk, either temporally, by subject matter, or by some other contextually meaningful manner.

Cookie Cutter (Antipattern)

Ideas don't have a predetermined word count and accordingly you shouldn't artificially pad content to make it appear to fill a slide. No law says that everything worth having will fit on a single slide, so stop trying.

Crawling Code

Code is difficult to display inside a presentation. Simply pasting monochrome text onto a slide is not only ugly, but it often doesn't fit on one screen. Crawling code is a means of showing just a portion of the code at a time while offering context of the other previous and upcoming lines. The out-of-attention lines are shaded to focus attention on the lines being discussed.

Crawling Credits

As pioneered by the movie *Star Wars* (with the later addition to the title *Episode IV: A New Hope*) in 1977, credits can be calmly and progressively shown in a seemingly infinite bottom-to-top slide. This gives each name, company, or URL equal but limited screen time without seeming hurried.

Crucible

The act of *constructing* the presentation differs from *presenting* the presentation. The presentation will change (sometimes drastically) under the pressure of presenting it.

D

Dead Demo (Antipattern)

This antipattern uses a live demonstration as a time filler when the presenter is short on expositional content.

Defy Defaults

Don't settle for the defaults or stock templates from any tool. If you do use a stock template, at least customize it so that it's as unique as a signature.

Disowning Your Topic (Antipattern)

If you think a topic is rudimentary, expect it is for your audience as well. Accelerate if you think the audience is already familiar with the topic. Don't treat your topic as if it was the most interesting thing in the world—it's not. Assume you're speaking to a group of smart people who are terribly bored of hearing about your topic; ad-lib and go off the prepared path at will.

Display of High Value

As a presenter, you should demonstrate to the audience that there is a difference between the speaker and audience members; the speaker is bringing new knowledge and discoveries and the audience is there to absorb, question, and clarify these new points.

Dual-Headed Monster (Antipattern)

This antipattern delivers a presentation to both a live and a remote audience via some desktop sharing or video streaming tool. It reduces the value and richness of the presentation by trying to serve two audiences, each with disparate and competing format and delivery requirements.

E

Echo Chamber

When an attendee asks a question, *always* repeat the question before answering. Restating the question assures you've heard the query and gives you time to formulate a response.

Emergence

Emergence suggests that the big thing you're ultimately going to show (tool, giant diagram, source code, etc.) isn't a static display. Use motion, transitions, highlights, and other presentation effects to gradually reveal pieces or details.

Emotional State

Presenters should be attuned to the condition and situation of their audience. Adapt the talk to fit the mood and needs of the audience.

Entertainment

Entertaining the audience is an important device to capture the attention but should not be used to excess. Like any seasoning, a little bit goes a long way; don't confuse your message with your method.

Expansion Joints

Building a presentation for one (and only one) length is a missed opportunity. Crafting short-, medium-, and full-length versions of your talk provides additional opportunities for delivery and simplifies adapting to shorter windows if the promised time slot is cut short.

Exuberant Title Top

A technique that allows you to place a core idea on the center of the slide and then add supporting elements underneath as the main idea migrates to the top of the slide. The Slideuments pattern allows you to use fewer slides yet separate important points.

F

Floodmarks (Antipattern)

Floodmarks are marketing and branding headers, footers, and watermarks that invade the content area of the slide. Your audience won't forget who you work for or the name of the conference during the course of your talk. Egregious instances of this antipattern lead to several other antipatterns by occupying valuable real estate.

Fontaholic (Antipattern)

A Fontaholic is someone who believes using a cacophony of fonts will "jazz up" a presentation. Disharmonic fonts are jarring. They make presentations gruesome and more difficult to read.

Foreshadowing

Like foreshadowing in literature, this pattern adds elements early in a talk to seed an idea that will be resolved (hopefully with more resonance) later.

Fourthought

Don't rush to use a presentation tool when building a presentation. The four stages of creating a presentation are *ideation*, *capture*, *organize*, and *design*.

G

Going Meta (Antipattern)

Never talk about the talk itself. The audience isn't interested in mechanics; they came to hear about the interesting topic that you are uniquely equipped to expound upon. This would be akin to a theatrical (not a director's cut) release of *Star Wars Episode IV: A New Hope* spending time discussing how George Lucas used a certain kind of lens, the temperature of lighting on the set, and the brand of makeup on the actors.

Gradual Consistency

Reveal content bit by bit, only showing the full connection between all the ideas as the conclusion of segments or modules.

Greek Chorus

Ancient Greek plays often featured a *chorus*, a group of players who stood aside from the action, making occasional comments and interludes during the play. Adding a Greek Chorus means you seed the audience with some partisans to interject comments, enthusiasm, or to help defend your case if you are outnumbered.

H

Hecklers (Antipattern)

An audience of any substantial size will have individuals that aim to gain recognition through attacks on the presenter's premise, approach, or discoveries. Coping with them requires preparation, a cool head, and decisive action. Dealing decisively with hecklers keeps the presentation on track and protects the congenial members of the audience.

Hiccup Words (Antipattern)

Hiccup Words are involuntary exclamations ("Ummm," "Ahhh," etc.) that distract and detract from the presentation. Dead air isn't a cardinal sin, and it's unlikely anyone in your audience will break into a presentation just because you paused.

I

Infodeck

Infodeck is an emerging form of presentation intended to be consumed in solitude rather than to be presented to an audience. It is an instance of the Slideuments antipattern that actually works for its intended purpose.

Intermezzi

Presentations should be made up of logical parts in the form of a Triad or Narrative Arc shape. Sometimes, these sections necessitate a color change, thematic shift, or outline introduction to clearly signal the beginning or ending of an act. This pattern is an implementation of the Context Keeper pattern and is similar to Bookends but is used during the course of the presentation to wrap sections, as opposed to wrapping the entire presentation.

Injured Outlines (Antipattern)

Outlines should never have a single point at an indent level; don't create bullet points that have only one sub-bullet. Bullets in presentations mimic outlines and it "looks" grammatically incorrect to have orphan bullets.

Invisibility

This pattern uses invisible elements that don't appear on printed versions of the slides but are revealed throughout your talk. This preserves a sense of surprise when you are forced to provide handouts (Slideuments?) in advance of your talk.

K

Know Your Audience

Preparing a great presentation is lost if you present it to the "wrong" audience. Seek data on your attendees; their occupations, relative ages, comfort level with the material, and general background. Tune your material to match as many of the attending demographics as possible.

L

Laser Weapons (Antipattern)

Laser pointers are generally a crutch for identifying content elements on a slide that could otherwise be emphasized by Traveling Highlights or as an attempt to explain a slide that "you probably can't read in the back."

Leet Grammars

Leet Grammars refers to correctly using appropriate slang, jargon, and other "insider" colloquialisms in your presentation to bond with your audience.

Lightning Talk

Lightning Talk is a timed presentation, usually five minutes long and optionally constrained by aspecific number of slides. In many formats, the slides advance automatically.

Lightsaber

When used minimally in the hands of a thoughtful presenter, a laser pointer can be a useful on-demand teaching tool.

Lipstick on a Pig (Antipattern)

This antipattern are talks with pointless or weak content dressed up with special effects. Contrary to the wishful practitioner's hopes and dreams, audience members will see through the decorative facade to the fundamental lack of useful material or insight.

Lipsync

Rather than giving a live demonstration, record the interaction with the tool and play it back as part of the presentation. This approach reduces stress, prevents errors, and allows you to use the heads-up display to see slide metadata. You can also make additional points while the demonstration is playing.

Live Demo

Live Demo is running the product live in front of the audience. Thought of as a way to gain credibility and actively promote the product, this approach carries the significant risk of a failing demo. The return on investment is rarely worth the risk.

Live on Tape

This term refers to a recorded version of your entire presentation provided electronically. More effective and interactive than the standard "saving your presentation as a PDF."

M

Make It Rain

Use props like chairs, paper airplanes, candy (typically thrown at/to audience members), and other devices to add flair to your presentation and encourage interaction, especially with preternaturally shy groups.

Mentor

The audience wants to be led but not by the nose. Take on the role of guide and, via the presentation, provide your audience with new skills, ideas, and techniques as if you were their private tutor in your field.

N

Narrative Arc

Presentations are a form of storytelling; don't ignore a few thousand years of oratory history. A Narrative Arc is a common trope; organizing your presentation in a similar way leverages your audience's lifetime of story listening experience.

Negative Ignorance (Antipattern)

Never pose a question to the audience in the form of "Who here is *not* familiar with X?" People dislike admitting ignorance, especially in a circle of their peers. And turning it to a positive question isn't much better.

P

Peer Review

Your first draft of a presentation won't be your best, nor should it be your last. Find a well-informed colleague who knows the topic and have them critique your first draft.

Photomaniac (Antipattern)

A Photomaniac picks up random pieces of clipart, stock photography, and other tchotchkes, littering them about a presentation, filling any and all empty spaces.

Posse

Having team members or friends in the audience not only provides a visual focal point of some likely-to-be-smiling faces but also can act as assistants in times of need. They can also be seeded with useful questions and they can clap and nod at appropriate times; the audience symbiotically follows suit and has a more positive impression of the talk and you as the presenter. Friendly faces reduce stress and put you more at ease.

Preparation
Murphy's Law applies to presentations; nothing trumps being prepared. Plan for as many eventualities of as possible, be it a hardware failure, a room change, or an unruly crowd. It may seem prosaic, but consider a checklist: supported projector resolutions, techniques to manage the audience, display dongles, presenter remotes, notes on your topic, a bottle of water, and other needed items reduce the risk of common mistakes that less prepared presenters might make.

Preroll
Prior to the start time of your talk, displaying the topic and presenter on screen can be informative and clarifying. If the information cannot comfortably fit on one slide, a series of slides can be recorded as a video and then embedded into the actual presentation and set to loop. When the presenter is ready to give the talk, he or she clicks the remote to advance past the animation to the first content slide.

Proposed
Most presenters are required to submit a talk title, abstract, topic outline, and perhaps even samples of past work in video or PDF form. The most common ways to get into a conference—paying attention to the details and presenting a polished proposal—increase your odds your talk will be accepted.

R

Red, Yellow, Green
Several conferences, in order to simplify the voting process and increase participation, put red, yellow, and green cards near the entrance to the room. Upon exit, attendees drop a card into the voting bucket indicating their opinion of the talk. The scores can be tallied immediately.

Required
A command performance presents unique challenges and added stress. Unless the topic is near and dear to your heart, you may have to manufacture motivation and interest.

S

Seeding Satisfaction
Even the friendliest of audiences benefits from some warm-up. Simple greetings, handshakes, and sincere questions, prior to the start of your presentation, break the ice and prime your audience to be more receptive to your message.

Seeding the First Question
Purposely placing an obvious question for your audience to ask somewhere in the presentation as a way to break the ice for question-and-answer sessions.

Shoeless

Presenter creature comforts, while possibly perceived as odd or eccentric, can put the speaker at ease, enhancing the delivery. Such comforts include the removal of shoes, certain placement of the laptop, comfortable clothes, a favorite beverage, or stepping away from the lectern to mingle among the audience.

Shortchanged (Antipattern)

Dealing with a last-minute reduction in presentation time is unfortunately one of the skills frequent presenters have to hone. Coping well with the situation leaves the audience none the wiser. Managing this situation poorly leaves you rushing, cutting important material, and delivering a less meaningful presentation.

Slideuments (Antipattern)

A Slideument is a presentation that is trying to be both a presentation aide and an attractive printed version of the presentation. An entire chapter is devoted to dealing with the issues raised by this commonly required antipattern.

Social Media Advertising

Our current digital age has shifted the focus of marketing presentations from printed flyers and bulletin boards to Twitter, Facebook, blog posts, and e-mails. Presenters should aggressively utilize free and low-cost avenues to advertise their talk in an effort to increase attendance, ticket sales, or just general awareness, all of which can manifest as greater credibility for the presenter.

Soft Transitions

When you have stale content, one way to subtly transition away from it uses an almost-imperceptible fade transition for either the slide or elements on the slide. It should happen so gradually that the audience doesn't even realize it's happening. Add both slide and element transitions to soften the transition between slides.

Stakeout

Arriving on time for your talk seems too simple to even mention. However, chaos is conspiring to prevent you from doing just that. If the venue isn't amenable to corporate camping, locate a nearby coffee shop or other work-conducive location. You can arrive at this staging area with ample time to spare but still have the opportunity to use your cushion productively should mayhem take a holiday. It also avoids aimlessly wandering the venue hallways.

T

Takahashi

Takahashi is a stylized talk format originated by Masoyoshi Takahashi (and popularized in the West by Laurence Lessig) that uses one or two words per slide but transitions through them very quickly.

Talklet

Instead of doing an hour-long presentation, do three semirelated 20-minute talks. This allows great flexibility for time, content, and narrative flow.

Tower of Babble (Antipattern)

Presenters are inclined to use arcane jargon irrespective of the skill level of their audience. Follow that inclination and use three-letter acronyms and technospeak at liberty. Feel confident your audience understands those phrases even if they are giving you puzzled looks.

Traveling Highlights

Use highlighting (either intrinsic in the tool or a third-party add-on like OmniDazzle) to draw attention to something on the slide such as a picture or screenshot of another tool or application. Traveling Highlights implies that you use transitions to highlight different parts of the slide as you walk through the details.

Triad

Your audience can only absorb a certain amount of material in a short time. If you limit your presentation to three main talking points, it allows you to cover them thoroughly without overwhelming your audience.

U

Unifying Visual Theme

Use a common, repeating visual element to tie together the disparate parts of your presentation.

V

Vacation Photos

A picture is worth a thousand words, but does that translate into an effective presentation? Carefully selected images can stand in place of wordy slides. With this approach, the presenter becomes a greater focus of attention, supplying the full verbal channel and allowing the well-chosen images to amplify the spoken words.

W

Weatherman

TV weathermen use green screens and monitors to see and gesture toward map details. Never turn your back on the audience. If you need to point to something on the screen, do it like a weatherman: Stand off to the side so that you can see both the screen and the audience as you gesture.

RESOURCES

We've mentioned many software tools, reading materials, and useful websites throughout the course of this book. To make all those resources more navigable and reference-able after you've read it cover to cover, we've collected and grouped them by category.

Presenting Books
- *Resonate: Present Visual Stories that Transform Audiences*[1]
- *Slide:ology: The Art and Science of Creating Great Presentations*[2]
- *Presentation Zen: Simple Ideas on Presentation Design and Delivery*[3]
- *Presentation Zen Design: Simple Design Principles and Techniques to Enhance Your Presentations*[4]
- *The Non-Designer's Presentation Book*[5]
- *Confessions of a Public Speaker*[6]
- *Advanced Presentations by Design: Creating Communication that Drives Action*[7]

Presenting Blogs
- *Presentation Zen*[8]
- *Slide:ology*[9]
- *Duarte Design Team Blog*[10]
- *Burt Decker's Blog*[11]
- *Six Minutes by D. Lugan*[12]
- *Speaking about Presenting by Olivia Mitchell*[13]
- *Recent Presenting Blog Bookmarks by Matthew McCullough*[14]

Presenting Websites
- *Presentation Patterns Site*[15]
- *Presentation Patterns Twitter Page*[16]
- *Matthew's Presenting Bookmarks*[17]
- *Matthew's Presentation Patterns Bookmarks*[18]
- *Extreme Presentation Method*[19]
- *Pop! Tech Presentations*[20]
- *TED Presentations*[21]

Presenting Tools

- *Apple Keynote*[22]
- *Microsoft PowerPoint*[23]
- *LibreOffice Impress*[24]
- *Prezi*[25]
- *SlideRocket*[26]
- *SpeakerDeck*[27]
- *Slideshare*[28]

CREDITS

Contributor Acknowledgments

The authors would like to thank the pattern inventors and idea contributors who made this book what it is today. In surname order, they are the following:

- Peter Bell
- Tim Berglund
- David Bock
- Scott Davis
- Nancy Duarte
- Martin Fowler
- Brian Goetz
- Stu Halloway
- Gregor Hohpe
- Jordan McCullough
- Ted Neward
- Mark Richards
- Ken Sipe
- Brian Sletten
- Venkat Subramaniam
- Billy Williams

The authors would further like to thank the idea and manuscript reviewers who offered fresh perspectives and polish to the material. In surname order, they are the following:

- Eileen Cohen
- Bradley Davidson
- Andy Ennamorato
- Justin Ghetland
- Kevlin Henney
- Mitch Hiveley

- Alex Miller
- Mike Noce
- Greg Ostravich
- Claire Pitchford
- Michael Plöd

Symbol Credits

This section constitutes a continuation of the copyright page.

The symbols that appear on the front cover are all from The Noun Project collection (www.thenounproject.com) and are either in the Public Domain or are covered by a Creative Commons licensed as noted below. The name of the designer of each symbol is identified if known.

Front cover symbols (in order from left to right)

Row 1
"3D Glasses" symbol by NDSTR, "Ambulance" symbol (Public Domain), "Booklet" symbol by Dara Ullrich, "Neurology" symbol (Public Domain), "Erlenmeyer Flask" symbol (CC BY 3.0).

Row 2
"Lungs" symbol (Public Domain), "Sheriff Hat" symbol by Camila Bertoco, "Teddy Bear" symbol (Public Domain), "Theater" symbol by Karl Turner, "Traffic Light" symbol (CC BY 3.0), "Notes" symbol (CC0).

Row 3
"Octopus" symbol by Carolina Costa, "Puzzle" symbol by John O'Shea, "Fallout Shelter" symbol (Public Domain) , "Tuxedo" symbol by Matthew Miller, "Weightlifting" symbol by Scott Lewis, "Eye" symbol by The Honest Ape.

Row 4
"Bread" symbol (CC BY 3.0), "Memory" symbol by Anne Marie Nguyen, "Binoculars" symbol (Public Domain), "Ant" symbol by Jacob Eckert, "Measuring Spoons" symbol (CC0), "Feather" symbol (CC0).

Row 5
"Handcuffs" symbol by Matt Crum, "Idea" symbol (CC BY 3.0), "Ticket" symbol by Plinio Fernandes, "Waiter" symbol by Scott Lewis, "Mute" symbol (CC BY 3.0), "Restaurant" symbol (Public Domain).

Row 6
"Roll Film" symbol by Scott Lewis, "Fitness" symbol (CC BY 3.0), "Dress Shoe" symbol by Proletkult Graphik, "Cleaver" symbol by Samuel Eidam, "Camera" symbol by Stanislav Levin, "Genetics" symbol (Public Domain).

Text Symbol
Credits The symbols associated with each pattern name are all from The Noun Project collection (www.thenounproject.com) and are either in the Public Domain or are covered by a Creative Commons license as noted below. The pattern names and symbols are listed below in the order in which they appear in the book. The name of the designer of each symbol is identified if known.

Know Your Audience ("Ranger Station"); Social Media Advertising ("Genetics"); Required ("Brass Knuckle," mathies janssen); The Big Why ("Information"); Proposed ("Ticket," CC0); Abstract Attorney ("Handcuffs," Matt Crum); Narrative Arc ("Waiting Room"); Fourthought ("Neurology"); Crucible ("Erlenmeyer Flask," CC BY 3.0); Concurrent Creation ("Fitness," CC BY 3.0); Triad ("Chain," Plinio Fernandes); Expansion Joints ("Measuring Spoons," CC0); Talklet ("Child Safety Seat," Sylvain Amatoury); Unifying Visual Theme ("Eye," The Honest Ape); Brain Breaks ("Memory," Anne Marie Nguyen); Alienating Artifact ("Octopus," Carolina Costa); Celery ("Restaurant," Sylvain Amatoury); Leet Grammars ("Tuxedo," Matthew Miller); Lightning Talk ("Thunderstorm," CC BY 3.0); Takahashi ("Noodles," Robb Whiteman, Patrick Fenn, and Jack Kent); Cave Painting ("Paintroller," CC BY 3.0); Cookie Cutter ("Gingerbread Man," Simon Child); Coda ("Music," CC0); Injured Outlines ("Ambulance,"); Peer Review ("Care Staff Area"); Foreshadowing ("Idea," CC BY 3.0); Bullet-Riddled Corpse ("Gun Chamber," CC0); Greek Chorus ("Museum"); Ant Fonts ("Ant," Jacob Eckert); Fontaholic ("Bar"); Floodmarks ("Water," CC BY 3.0); Photomaniac ("Camera," Stanislav Levin); Composite Animation ("Puzzle," John O'Shea); Á la Carte Content ("Waiter," Scott Lewis); Analog Noise ("Radio," SZ); Vacation Photos ('Seesaw'); Defy Defaults ("Public Domain"); Borrowed Shoes ("Shoe," CC0); Slideuments ("Skull," Matthew Hock); Infodeck ("Information," Sven Hofmann); Gradual Consistency ("Upload," CC BY 3.0); Charred Trail ("Fire Extinguisher"); Exhuberant Title Top ("Hat," Adhara Garcia); Invisibility ("X-Ray"); Context Keeper ("Book," CC0); Breadcrumbs ("Bread," CC BY 3.0); Bookends ("Booklet," Dara Ullrich); Soft Transitions ("Feather," CC0); Intermezzi ("Cinema," CC BY 3.0); Backtracking ("Repeat," CC0); Preroll ("Roll Film," Scott Lewis); Crawling Credits ("3D Glasses," NDSTR); Live Demo ("Health Education"); Dead Demo ("Skull," Matthew Hock); Lipsync ("Lips," CC0); Traveling Highlights ("Airplane"); Crawling Code ("Bug"); Emergence ("Sloth"); Live on Tape ("Cassette," mathies janssen); Preparation ("Weight Lifting," Scott Lewis); Posse ("Sheriff Hat," Camila Bertoco); Seeding Satisfaction ("Handshake," Jake Nelsen); Display of High Value ("Money," CC0); Shortchanged ("Cleaver," Samuel Eidam); Hiccup Words ("Drinking Water"); Disowning Your Topic ("Mute," CC BY 3.0); Lipstick on a Pig

("Piggy Bank," Thibault Geffroy); Tower of Babble ("Eiffel Tower," Camila Bertoco); Bunker ("Fallout Shelter"); Hecklers ("Announcement," Olivier Guin); Going Meta ("Russian Doll," Simon Child); Backchannel ("Television," CC BY 3.0); Laser Weapons ("Sword," Christopher T. Howlett); Negative Ignorance ("Opinion," Plinio Fernandes); Dual-Headed Monster ("Theater," Karl Turner); Carnegie Hall ("Ticket," Plinio Fernandes); Emotional State ("Teddy Bear"); Breathing Room ("Lungs"); Shoeless ("Shoe," Proletkult Graphik); Mentor ("Lecturer," CC0); Weatherman ("Rain," CC BY 3.0); Seeding the First Question ("Rain," CC BY 3.0); Make It Rain ("Falling Rocks"); Entertainment ("Magic Wand," John O'Shea); The Stakeout ("Binoculars"); Lightsaber ("Flashlight," Reinaldo Weber); Echo Chamber ("Bullhorn," Jeremy Bristol); Red, Yellow, Green ("Traffic Light," CC BY 3.0).

Personal Acknowledgments

Neal's Acknowledgments

I want to thank my incredible professional support network, especially ThoughtWorks and Roy Singham, the genius/madman who created it, and the many conference organizers and attendees I see over the course of a year—especially the No Fluff, Just Stuff conference, which ultimately enabled this book.

I would also like to acknowledge the support and foundation provided by my family and friends who now span the entire globe, especially the neighborhood Cocktail Club group and John Drescher. One of the great benefits of my life is the ability to meet and befriend people from all over the world, which is the true payoff for the many attendant inconveniences that accompany my lifestyle. My friends and especially my wonderfully understanding wife, Candy, bear the brunt of many inconveniences and absences during a project like this that eats a huge portion of already sparse time; thank you for your understanding—you hold the results in your hands.

Matthew's Acknowledgments

My audiences of the last 12 years have been kind; they have endured the early learning that accompanies a lifelong walk in the direction of becoming a better presenter. The Denver Open Source Users Group and No Fluff, Just Stuff conference series made sincerely appreciated investments in me that allow me to continually grow in my unique educator flavor of a technical career. That line of work led to what became the authors' conversational seeds of this book in 2008, unbelievably, almost four years ago. The subsequent three years of writing this book with my coauthors has been a treasured honing experience, both in my presentation patterns, my storytelling, my talk-assembly techniques, and my IT capabilities.

Having a great network of friends from all walks of life—scientists, attorneys, physicians, programmers, accountants, and chemists—has been a blessing. It has allowed me to capture valuable elements of their views on the educational and presenting world. To my friends and extended family who have endured the Presentation Patterns talk, honed the ideas, contributed thoughts, and helpfully criticized, thank you.

I continue to be amazed by the creativity, helpfulness, contributions, and counsel that my family provided during the formation of this book. Thank you Dad, Mom, and Jordan. And most of all, I thank my brilliant wife, Madelaine, for her medically attuned reviews and contributions, in addition to her willingness to shoulder many of my tasks. Those tasks included spending time with our treasured daughters, Scarlette and Violette, and in large part enabled me to help bring this book to completion.

Nathaniel's Acknowledgments

First and foremost, I want to thank my coauthors Neal and Matthew; their passion and dedication to the craft have made me a better presenter in ways too numerous to list. I'd also like to thank Jay Zimmerman for giving me the opportunity to hone my voice on the No Fluff, Just Stuff tour; the crucible of presenting week in and week out is invaluable. No mention of No Fluff, Just Stuff would be complete without a heartfelt "to evil" for my peers past and present: Stuart Halloway, Justin Gehtland, Venkat Subramaniam, Brian Sletten, Ken Sipe, Mark Richards, Tim Berglund, Peter Bell, Jeff Brown, Brian Sam-Bodden, Kenneth Kousen, Dave Klein, David Hussman, David Bock, Ted Neward, Brian Goetz, and Scott Davis. I cannot thank this group of men enough for the mentoring and inspiration they've given me over the years. I'd also like to thank my colleagues at the University of Minnesota, especially John Carlis, who taught me that lectures don't have to be dry, boring affairs. Last and certainly not least, I want to thank my wife, Christine, and my son, Everett; without their love and support, I wouldn't be where I am today. Everything I do, I do for them.

About the Authors

About Neal Ford

Neal is director, software architect, and meme wrangler at ThoughtWorks, a global IT consultancy with an exclusive focus on end-to-end software development and delivery. Before joining ThoughtWorks, Neal was the chief technology officer at the DSW Group Ltd., a nationally recognized training and development firm. Neal has a degree in computer science from Georgia State University specializing in languages and compilers and a minor in mathematics specializing in statistical analysis. He is also the designer and developer of applications, instructional materials, magazine articles, video presentations, and author of six books. His primary consulting focus is the architecture, design, and construction of large-scale enterprise applications. Neal is also an internationally acclaimed speaker, having spoken at over 500 developer conferences worldwide, delivering more than 2,000 talks. If you have an insatiable curiosity about Neal, visit his website at nealford.com. He welcomes feedback and can be reached at nford@thoughtworks.com, and you can follow him on Twitter at @neal4d.

About Matthew McCullough

Matthew McCullough is a 15-year veteran of enterprise software development and currently enjoys the role of vice president of Training at GitHub Inc. He is honored to be part of such an energetic team that is helping advance the software industry to a more collaborative and creative mode of working. Matthew's past as a cofounder of a US consultancy allowed him to have the job freedom to become a world-traveling open-source educator, with the support of many businesses, conference organizers, and friends making it viable. Matthew is a contributing author to the Gradle, Jenkins, and O'Reilly Git books, creator of the Git Master Class series for O'Reilly, speaker on the No Fluff, Just Stuff conference tour, author of three of the top ten DZone RefCards, and volunteer president of the Denver Open Source Users Group. He can be reached via e-mail at matthewm@ambientideas.com or on Twitter at @matthewmccull.

About Nathaniel Schutta

Nathaniel Schutta is a senior software engineer in the Twin Cities area of Minnesota with extensive experience developing Java Enterprise Edition based web applications. He graduated from St. John's University (MN) with a degree in computer science and has a master of science degree in software engineering from the University of Minnesota. For the last several years, he has focused on user interface design. Nathaniel has contributed to corporate interface guidelines and consulted on a variety of web-based applications. A longtime member of the Association for Computing Machinery's Computer-Human Interaction Special Interest Group and a Sun-certified web component developer, Nathaniel believes that if the user can't figure out your application, then you've done something wrong. Along with his user interface work, Nathaniel is the cocreator of the open-source Taconite framework, has contributed to two corporate Java frameworks, has developed training material, and has led several study groups. During the brief moments of warm weather found in his home state of Minnesota, he spends as much time on the golf course as his wife will tolerate. He's currently exploring Ruby, Rails, and (after recently making the switch) Mac

OS X. Nathaniel is the coauthor of the bestselling book, *Foundations of Ajax*. Nathaniel can be reached via e-mail at ntschutta@gmail.com and on Twitter at @ntschutta.

Contact

Feedback

Feedback about the book can be simultaneously directed to all three authors at info@presentationpatterns.com or on Twitter at http://twitter .com/ppatterns.

Digital Resources

The book's corresponding website with sample slide decks, supplementary blog posts, and extended author discussions is available at http://presentationpatterns.com.

Speaking Events

The book's authors frequently give private workshops that help emerging presenters tune up technical presentation decks to have maximum informative impact. Contact the authors at info@presentationpatterns.com for further information on pricing and availability.

Notes

Introduction

1. Alexander, Christopher. 1977. *A Pattern Language: Towns, Buildings, Construction.* New York: Oxford University Press.
2. Gamma, Erich, et al. 1995. *Design Patterns: Elements of Reusable Object-Oriented Software.* Reading, MA: Addison-Wesley.
3. This is one of the sample patterns from the book, available online at www.patternlanguage.com/apl/aplsample/aplsample.htm
4. Reynolds, Garr. 2008. *Presentation Zen: Simple Ideas on Presentation Design and Delivery.* Berkeley, CA: New Riders Pub.

Chapter 1

1. http://nofluffjuststuff.com
2. http://jazoon.com
3. http://devoxx.com
4. www.oracle.com/us/javaonedevelop/index.html
5. www.aapa.org/events/annual_conference.aspx
6. www.aaos.org/education/anmeet/anmeet.asp
7. www.aiche.org/Conferences/AnnualMeeting/index.aspx

Chapter 2

1. Martin's biography page on the ThoughtWorks corporate website, http://martinfowler.com
2. Information about *Dilbert* licensing is at http://thedilbertstore.com/pages/2481-about_licensing
3. Examples of United Colors of Benetton's shock-factor advertisements, http://linda03.wordpress.com/2008/01/08/united-colors-of-benetton-and-its-crazy-adverts
4. Definition of shock advertising, http://en.wikipedia.org/wiki/Shock_advertising
5. The official Ignite website is hosted at http://igniteshow.com

Chapter 3

1. Friedman, Daniel P. 2008. *The Little LISPer.* Cambridge, MA: MIT Press.

2. Prevalence of Age-Related Macular Degeneration in the United States, www.nei.nih.gov/eyedata/pbd4.asp

3. OK, we'll tell you, but only if you promise to use it for good, not evil. When you get the little "+" at the bottom of the text box, you can double-click it, and it will turn the text in the text box into autosizing text. Remember: With great power comes great responsibility.

4. Martin describes this strategy in his blog at http://martinfowler.com/bliki/HalfSizeComposition.html

5. http://channel9.msdn.com/Blogs/TheChannel9Team/Don-Box-What -goes-into-a-great-technical-presentation

6. http://levien.com/type/myfonts/inconsolata.html

7. FHWA Series Fonts Wikipedia article, http://en.wikipedia.org/wiki/FHWA_Series_fonts

8. Martin's biography page on the ThoughtWorks corporate website, http://martinfowler.com

9. ShutterStock homepage, www.shutterstock.com

10. iStockPhoto homepage, www.istockphoto.com

11. Flickr homepage, http://flickr.com

12. Corbis homepage, www.corbisimages.com

13. Venkat Subramaniam blogs at his Agile Developer homepage, http://agiledeveloper.com

14. http://hbr.org/2012/03/hard-to-read-fonts-promote-better-recall/ar/1

Chapter 4

1. www.youtube.com/watch?v=uOgHE5nEq04

2. Martin's biography page on the ThoughtWorks corporate website, http://martinfowler.com

3. The Backchannel: *How Audiences are Using Twitter and Social Media and Changing Presentations Forever* by Cliff Atkinson, http://amzn.com/0321659511

4. SpeakerRate audience feedback web application homepage, http://SpeakerRate.com

5. GitHub Git Workshop homepage, http://github.com/training

6. Martin's biography page on the ThoughtWorks corporate website, http://martinfowler.com

7. As of this writing, the common, safe, go-to resolution supported gracefully by all projectors is 1024 × 768

8. Nancy Duarte's biography page on the Duarte Design company website, www.duarte.com/team/nancy

Chapter 5

1. http://youtu.be/d0DnEoqm-wc

2. www.youtube.com/watch?v=UjZQGRATlwA

3. Milli Vanilli was a pop group that became (in)famous in the early 1990s when it was revealed that the "singers" were lipsyncing in

ostensibly live performances. Worse, it was revealed that the nominal singers were dancers only; the album producer had used other, uncredited singers on the hit album. After that, the group's popularity plummeted.

4. Nancy Duarte's biography page on the Duarte Design company website, www.duarte.com/team/nancy
5. www.apple.com/apple-events

Chapter 6

1. www.augusttechgroup.com
2. www.infoq.com/presentations/Simple-Made-Easy
3. http://martinfowler.com/tags/talk%20videos.html
4. http://vimeo.com/33530096
5. http://en.wikipedia.org/wiki/Larry_Lessig
6. www.ted.com/talks/hans_rosling_reveals_new_insights_on_poverty.html
7. www.ted.com/talks/stephen_wolfram_computing_a_theory_of_everything.html
8. www.ted.com/talks/ken_robinson_says_schools_kill_creativity.html

Chapter 7

1. www.inc.com/articles/201111/4-ways-to-avoid-rick-perry-presentation -meltdown.html
2. For more information about Railsconf, go to http://railsconf.com
3. Reynolds, Garr. 2008. *Presentation Zen: Simple Ideas on Presentation Design and Delivery.* Berkeley, CA: New Riders Pub.
4. Duarte, Nancy. 2008. *Slide:ology: The Art and Science of Creating Great Presentations.* Sebastopol, CA: O'Reilly Media.
5. Nancy Duarte's biography page on the Duarte Design company website, www.duarte.com/team/nancy
6. Pop! Tech presentation video of "When Intuition Fails," http:// poptech.org/popcasts/chris_chabris_when_intuition_fails
7. CodeSherpas company website, http://codesherpas.com

Chapter 8

1. Nancy Duarte's biography page on the Duarte Design company website, www.duarte.com/team/nancy

Resources

1. http://amzn.com/0470632011
2. http://amzn.com/0596522347
3. http://amzn.com/0321525655
4. http://amzn.com/0321668790
5. http://amzn.com/0321656210
6. http://amzn.com/0596801998
7. http://amzn.com/0787996599

8. www.presentationzen.com
9. http://blog.duarte.com/book
10. http://blog.duarte.com
11. http://decker.com/blog
12. http://sixminutes.dlugan.com
13. www.speakingaboutpresenting.com
14. http://delicious.com/matthew.mccullough/presenting+blog
15. http://presentationpatterns.com
16. http://twitter.com/ppatterns
17. http://delicious.com/matthew.mccullough/presenting
18. http://delicious.com/matthew.mccullough/tag_bundle/presentationpatterns
19. www.ExtremePresentation.com
20. www.ExtremePresentation.com
21. www.ted.com
22. www.apple.com/iwork/keynote
23. http://office.microsoft.com/en-us/PowerPoint
24. www.libreoffice.org/features/impress
25. www.prezi.com
26. www.sliderocket.com
27. www.speakerdeck.com
28. www.slideshare.com

INDEX

Note: Blue and red entries refer to patterns and antipatterns, respectively. **Bold** numbers indicate a pattern's (or an antipattern's) main entry, while other numbers indicate where the pattern or antipattern may have been mentioned or cross-referenced. The letter *f* indicates that the entry refers to a figure.

A

Abstract Attorney, **26–28**, 229
abstracts, 20, 24, 25, 26–28, 135, 176, 229, 237
after transitions, 160
À la Carte Content, 47, 67, **95–99**, 97*f*, 227, 229
Alexander, Christopher, 3, 7
Alienating Artifacts, 10, 29, 52, **53–55**, 179, 217, 227, 229
allotted time, 45, 94–95, 96, 151, 181
American Academy of Orthopaedic Surgeons Annual Meeting, 26
American Academy of Physician Assistants Annual Conference, 26
American Institute of Chemical Engineers Annual Meeting, 26
Analog Noise, 58, 60, 67, **99–103**, 100*f*, 101*f*, 102*f*, 103*f*, 119, 159–60, 229
Ancient Philosophers & Blowhard Jamborees keynote (Ford), 43–44
"Angel of Death" keynote speeches, 44
animations, 6, 9, 38, 57, 63, 68, 70, 92–94, 226
   animation pane, 121–22, 126
   appearance, 69, 93, 94, 129, 162

bottom to top, 144, 232
Breadcrumbs and, 134
build in, 69, 93, 122, 124–26, 130, 131
Cave Painting and, 63, 63*f*
Celery and, 57
Charred Trail and, 121
click triggers, 118, 125, 126, 213, 237
complementary, 93
Composite Animation and, **92–94**, 93*f*, 94*f*, 119, 226, 231
confetti, 213
Context Keeper and, 131–32
Cookie Cutter and, 68
Crawling Code and, 163
Crawling Credits and, 143
Defy Defaults and, 106
dissolve entrance, 134, 159
effect options, 121–22, 121*f*, 132
Emergence and, 164
emphasis, 162
entrance, 68, 93, 121, 126, 127, 130, 131, 132, 161, 164
exit, 130, 132
Exuberant Title Top and, 123–27, 123*f*, 125*f*, 126*f*
first slides with, 70, 131

animations (*continued*)
> Gradual Consistency and, 117–19, 117*f*, 118*f*, 119*f*
> hidden, 129
> Infodeck patterns and, 6, 115
> Invisibility patterns and, 127–30, 129*f*
> Keynote, 93, 122
> layering, 92, 130
> Lipsync and, 155, 156
> *magic move*, 63, 131–32, 132*f*, 165
> *motion path*, 127, 161
> *move*, 124, 126
> opacity and, 128–30, 130*f*, 132, 134, 160, 160*f*, 161*f*, 164
> PowerPoint, 93, 121–22, 128
> Preroll and, 142, 237
> *reveal*, 78
> Soft Transitions and, 137, 138
> surprise, 127
> Traveling Highlights and, 157–62
> Weatherman and, 213

Ant Fonts, 67, 79, **81–83**, 83*f*, 133, 229
antipatterns, 1, 3–8, 10, 11, 65
> origins of, 3, 7
> patterns versus, 3
> Performance Antipatterns, 10, 169, 183–201
> software, 7, 94–95

"antirecipes," 7
asides, 52
audiences, 1–2, 5, 8–10, 12–13, 39
> artificial personas, 17
> attention span of, 43, 47, 51
> boredom and, 9, 95, 151, 208
> composition of, 16
> dispersed, 200
> empathy with, 23, 32
> event organizers and, 17
> feedback from, 17–18, 21, 22–23, 26–27
> interactions with, 17, 45, 205
> knowledge/skill level of, 16, 199, 210
> Know Your Audience, 16–17, 25
> participation of, 45, 230
> polling, 95
> providing value to, 27, 32
> questions from, 70, 79–80, 135–36, 139–40, 149, 163, 169, 176, 178, 180–82, 191–92, 194, 196, 199, 214–15, 218, 221, 227, 237
> reactions from, 22
> remote, 200, 233
> requests from, 45, 149, 155
> shocking, 53–55, 152, 217
> skeptical, 80
> technical bullies, 191, 192
> warming up, 175

August Technology Group, 177
AVI file format, 143

B

Backchannel, 18, 19, **195–97**, 230
Backchannel, The (Atkinson), 136
Backtracking, 36–37, 47, **141**, 230
bad taste, 53
Beck, Kent, 179
Berglund, Tim, 177
best-case scenarios, 109
bibliographies, 70
big ideas, 43, 139
big picture, 39, 164
Big Why, The, **22–24**, 25, 230
blogging, 17, 18–19, 34, 136, 207, 238, 241. *See also* Social Media Advertising
"blue screen of death," 150
Bock, David, 37, 199
Bookends, 8, 33, 88, 89, 90, 107, 134, **135–37**, 137*f*, 140, 142–43, 230, 235
Borrowed Shoes, **108–9**, 230
Box, Don, 82
Brain Breaks, 40–41, **51–53**, 56–57, 61, 64, 91, 208, 217, 230

brainstorming, 35, 48, 105

Breadcrumbs, 8, 131, 132, **133–34**, 139, 230

Breathing Room, 184, 185, 194, **208**, 209, 230–31

build after previous option, 118

bullet points, 5, 8–9, 61, 72, 77–79, 82, 115, 151, 157, 216, 231, 235

Bullet-Riddled Corpse, 1, 61–62, 72, **77–79**, 83, 92, 113, 120, 121, 138, 147, 151, 227, 231

Bunker, **190**, 193, 219, 231

C

callbacks, 141

calls for papers (CFP), 19–20, 25

Carnegie Hall, 24, 27, 52, 59, 108, 148, 173, 177, 185, 190, 194, **204–6**, 209, 221, 231

case studies, 76, 77f

Cave Painting, **62–64**, 63f, 64f, 144, 231

Celery, **56–57**, 231

Chabris, Chris, 194

Charred Trail, 9, 78, 111, 113, **120–22**, 120f, 122f, 123, 123f, 124, 127, 133, 144, 226, 231

"clickers," 194, 220

clip art, 48, 51, 61, 78, 83, 89

Clojure, 79, 131

Coda, **70–71**, 96, 231

collaboration, 10, 18, 42–43, 114

competitive edge, 25

complete sentences, 73–74, 78–79

complex subjects, 43, 131, 146, 186

Composite Animation, **92–94**, 93f, 94f, 119, 226, 231

Concurrent Creation, 10, 21, **41–42**, 231

conference
    agenda, 26–27, 196
    brochure, 26, 229
    deadlines, 24, 25, 41, 146

guidelines, 20, 25, 59, 72, 78

organizers, 17, 18, 19–20, 22–23, 24–25, 55–56, 86, 89, 106, 107, 144, 152, 173, 180, 181–82, 191, 207, 211, 218

proposals for, 20, 22, 24–26, 237

websites, 17

contact information, 17, 135–36, 142, 143, 180

Context Keeper, 8, 32, 62, 64, 121, 122, **131–32**, 132f, 134, 139, 140, 141, 154, 160–61, 232, 235

continuous loops, 114

Conway, Damian, 59

Cookie Cutter, 6, 34, 35, **68–70**, 71, 72, 78, 79, 113, 116, 120, 137, 139, 159, 227, 232

copyediting, 68, 72–75

Corbis, 89

Crawling Code, 143, 144, 145, **162–63**, 232

Crawling Credits, **143–44**, 163, 232

Creative Commons licenses, 49, 90, 105, 136

Creativity Patterns, 6, 10, 11, 13, **29–64**, 115, 116

credibility, 28, 29, 52, 58, 73, 150, 155, 208, 236, 238

Crucible, 21, 24, 27, **38–41**, 52, 108, 109, 136, 186, 194, 206, 209, 218, 221, 222, 232

cruft, 87

cube transitions, 141

curse of knowledge, 210

D

data visualization, 82

Davis, Scott, 17–18

dead air, 231, 234

Dead Demo, 95, 146, 148, 150, **151–52**, 154, 156, 232. *See also* Live Demo

deadlines, 24, 25, 41, 146
default slide templates, 1, 78, 79, 107, 227
Defy Defaults, 1, 48, 51, 59, 60, 88–89, 103, **106–7**, 225, 227, 232
demonstrations, 7, 107, 150. *See also* Dead Demo; Live Demo
    Á la Carte Content and, 95
    Cave Painting and, 62–63, 63*f*
    Lipsync and, 154–56, 165, 235–36
    live coding during, 152–53, 157, 213
    Live on Tape and, 165–66
    Nikon D4 live, 149–50, 149*f*
    presentations versus, 10, 65, 145–67
design patterns, 117
Design Patterns (Gang of Four), 3
Devoxx, 26
Diemand-Yauman, Connor, 100
digressions, 40, 46, 138, 141, 156
Disowning Your Topic, 57, **186**, 189, 199, 232
Display of High Value, **177–80**, 181, 193, 211, 215, 232
Display of Low Value, 178
dissolve transitions, 68–69, 119, 134, 137–59, 160
diversions. *See* Brain Breaks
Doernenburg, Erik, 96, 131
Dr. Fox effect, 57
Dropbox, 179
DRY (Don't Repeat Yourself) principle, 141
Dual-Headed Monster, **200–201**, 233
Duarte, Nancy, 99, 143, 162, 188, 210, 241

E

Echo Chamber, **221**, 233
embedded-movie approach, 137, 142–44
Emergence, 94, 138, 145, 152, **164–65**, 233
emergent design, 140
Emergent Design talk (Ford), 50, 50*f*, 101, 117, 139–40

Emotional State, 17, **207**, 233
Encryption Boot Camp on the JVM talk (McCullough), 163
Entertainment, 53, 190, 214, **216–18**, 233
event organizers, 17, 18, 19–20, 22–23, 24–25, 55–56, 86, 89, 106, 107, 144, 152, 173, 180, 181–82, 191, 207, 211, 218
Expansion Joints, **45–46**, 181, 182, 227, 233
Exuberant Title Top, 116, 117–20, 118*f*, 119*f*, 121, 122, **123–27**, 123*f*, 125*f*, 126*f*, 144, 233

F

Facebook, 17, 18–19, 238
fade transitions, 68–70, 121, 132, 137–38, 161, 238
feast-or-famine approach, 68
feedback, 2, 17, 20–21, 38–39, 45, 135, 175, 222
    contact information and, 136
    evaluation forms, 136
    loops, 2–3
    negative, 26
FHWA Series Fonts, 84
Fields, Syd, 30, 204
first drafts, 27, 39, 72
first impressions, 25
first slide, the, 27–28, 70, 89, 131, 142–43
Flickr, 49, 89, 90, 105
Floodmarks, 48, **86–89**, 86*f*, 87*f*, 88*f*, 106–7, 132, 137, 140, 226–27, 233
Fontaholic, **83–85**, 84*f*, 89, 233
Font Book, 84
fonts
    Ant Fonts, 67, 79, **81–83**, 83*f*, 133, 229
    Arial, 84
    ChalkDuster, 101
    Fonts control panel, 84
    handwritten, 229

Helvetica, 84–85
Helvetica Neue, 85
Inconsolata, 82
Lucida Console, 82
size of, 68, 81–82, 163, 230
TrueType, 82
Verdana, 84
Ford, Neal, 3, 7–8, 27, 37–38, 40, 87, 107–
    8, 113, 146, 179, 184, 186, 209, 216,
    218, 246–48
  Á la Carte Content and, 95–99, 97*f*
  Agile Engineering Practices presentation,
      97*f*
  Analog Noise and, 103
  Ancient Philosophers & Blowhard Jamborees
      keynote (Ford), 43–44
  Backtracking and, 141
  Brain Breaks and, 51–52
  Breadcrumbs and, 134
  Breathing Room and, 208
  Carnegie Hall and, 204–5
  Cave Painting and, 63, 63*f*
  Composite Animation and, 92–93
  Context Keeper and, 131–32
  Crucible and, 38–40
  Dead Demo and, 152
  Emergent Design talk (Ford), 50, 50*f*,
      101, 117, 139–40
  Floodmarks and, 87
  Functional Thinking talk (Ford), 92,
      101–3
  Gradual Consistency and, 116–19
  Greek Chorus and, 79–81
  Hiccup Words and, 184–85
  Invisibility and, 128–29
  JavaOne Rock Star award, 107–8
  Lipsync and, 156–57
  *Neal's Master Plan for Clojure Enterprise
      Mindshare Domination* talk (Ford),
      131

  On the Lam from the Furniture Police
      keynote, 35–36, 36*f*
  Rails in the Large talk (Ford), 76–77
  Seeding the First Question and, 214
  Slideuments and, 113
  Soft Transitions and, 138–39
  Test-Driven Design talk (Ford), 32–33,
      32*f*, 76, 213
  Unifying Visual Theme and, 49–51, 50*f*
  Weatherman and, 212–13, 212*f*
Foreshadowing, 47, 51, 67, **75–77**, 77*f*, 234
Fourthought, 27, **34–37**, 39, 43, 44, 59,
    72, 78, 79, 227, 234
Fowler, Martin, 45, 46–47, 82, 89, 114–15,
    141, 179, 186–87
friendly faces, 21, 175, 176, 235. *See also*
    Posse
Functional Thinking talk (Ford), 92, 101–3

G

gaffes, 54, 185
"Gang of Four" (GoF), 3
Gates, Bill, 150
Geary, David, 165
Getting Things Done (GTD) techniques,
    113
Git, 63
GitHub, 140, 175
GitHub Git Workshop, 140
Going Meta, 46, 95, 133, 134, 149, 178,
    179, 181, 182, **193–94**, 195, 201,
    211, 234
Google, 49, 90, 114*f*
Gradual Consistency, 111, 113, **116–20**, 117*f*,
    118*f*, 119*f*, 127, 139, 234
grammar, 25, 72–75, 235. *See also* Injured
    Outlines; Leet Grammars; Peer Review
Greek Chorus, 67, **80–81**, 80*f*, 175, 214,
    215, 234
guidelines, 20, 25, 59, 72, 78

H

HalfSize Composition, 82
handouts, 61, 111, 120, 127, 136, 176, 235
hashtags, 17, 131–32, 132*f*, 196
headings, 71
heads-up display, 182, 211–13, 212*f*, 236
Hecklers, 28, 178–79, **191–93**, 234
Hiccup Words, **184–85**, 205, 208, 234
Hickey, Rich, 179
hidden elements (Keynote), 128
hidden properties (PowerPoint), 121
humor
    Alienating Artifacts and, 53
    anecdotes and, 21
    audience interactions with, 55, 81, 174, 176, 216
    backfiring, 178
    Brain Breaks and, 40, **51–53**, 230
    contextualized, 52
    Emotional State and, 207
    Entertainment and, 216–18
    inside jokes and, 52, 218
    Matthew's joke catalog, 41
    pictures and, 21, 51
    word play, 52
hyperlinks, 96, 97*f*, 98*f*

I

idiomatic patterns, 117–18, 118*f*
Ignite, 59, 136
Infodeck, 4–6, 8–9, 43, 61, 65, 71, 73, 78–79, 83, 112–13, **114–16**, 137, 144, 234
infographics, 105
information density, 52, 62, 79, 100–101, 116, 123, 127, 142, 144, 151, 157–58, 159*f*, 189
Injured Outlines, 26, 67, **71–72**, 235
instant-messaging services, 19
interludes, 2–3, 10–11, 17–18, 22, 37–38, 41, 53, 55–56, 60, 61–62, 79–80, 94–95, 105–6, 107–8, 112, 113–14, 116, 120, 144, 146–47, 150, 152–54, 156–57, 166, 175, 179–80, 184, 186–87, 190–91, 195, 198, 209, 211, 214, 216
Intermezzi, 33, 50, 76, 90, 107, 137, 138, **139–40**, 141, 234–35
Invisibility, 4, **127–30**, 129*f*, 141, 235
iPhone, 40, 52
iStockphoto, 89, 104

J

jargon, 57, 58, 74, 75, 235, 239
JavaOne conference, 26, 107–8
JavaOne Rock Star award, 108
Jazoon, 25
jokes. *See* humor

K

Keynote, 4, 6, 8, 9, 63–64, 64*f*, 71–72, 82, 93, 93*f*, 95, 96, 97*f*, 100–101, 101*f*, 105, 119, 119*f*, 121, 122, 124–26, 128–30, 129*f*, 131–32, 138, 141, 142–43, 160–61, 161*f*, 164–65, 201–13, 212*f*, 242
keynote speeches, 7, 10, 27, 36*f*, 37, 43–44, 50, 52, 54–56, 58, 60, 104, 105, 152, 153, 186–87, 190, 195
kiosk mode, 114
Know Your Audience, **16–18**, 25, 55–56, 172–73, 176–77, 179, 186, 189–90, 193, 194, 195, 199, 208, 215, 218, 235

L

Lanyrd.com, 19
laser pointers, 40, 197–98, 219–20, 235
Laser Weapons, 40, **197–98**, 220, 235. *See also* Lightsaber
Leet Grammars, 29, 52, 53, **58**, 60, 75, 235

Lessig, Lawrence, 58, 60, 61, 179, 238

Lightning Talk, **59–60**, 136, 180, 199, 235

Light on Two Sides of Every Room talk (Alexander), 7

Lightsaber, 198, **219–20**, 235. *See also* Laser Weapons

Lipstick on a Pig, **187–88**, 235

Lipsync, 62, 146–53, **154–56**, 165–67, 213, 214, 227, 235–36

Lisp, 79

Little LISPer, The, 79–80

Live Demo, 95, **147–50**, 149*f*, 150, 151–52, 155, 167, 216, 227, 236. *See also* Dead Demo

Live on Tape, **165–67**, 167*f*, 214, 236

"long-tail presenting," 200

M

M4V file format, 143

magic move transitions, 63, 131–32, 132*f*, 165

mailing lists, 18

Make It Rain, 198, 213, **215–16**, 236

Mann, Merlin, 113–14, 114*f*

master slide decks, 41

McCullough, Matthew, 7–8, 179–80, 246–48

    blog, 241

    bookmarks, 241

    Crawling Code and, 163

    Encryption Boot Camp on the JVM talk, 163

    GitHub Git Workshop, 140

    joke catalog, 41

    Lipsync and, 156–57

    Unifying Visual Theme and, 50

Meetup.com, 18–19

Mentor, 81, **210–11**, 236

metadata, 49, 236

metapresentation information. *See* Going Meta

Microsoft, 82, 96, 242

mind maps, 34–36, *36f,* 37, 105, 134, 134*f*

Morguefile.com, 49

motion sickness, 62, 198

move in transitions, 138, 144

MOV file format, 143

N

Narrative Arc, 6, 10, 27, 29, **30–33**, 30*f*, 31*f,* 32*f,* 34–35, 37, 41, 43–44, 46–47, 53, 56–57, 59, 70, 75, 76–77, 79–80, 81, 91, 108–9, 116, 131–32, 139, 172, 194, 205, 208, 211, 217, 225, 234, 236

Neal's Master Plan for Clojure Enterprise Mindshare Domination talk (Ford), 131

Negative Ignorance, 198, **199**, 236

Neward, Ted, 193

Nikon D4 live demonstration, 149–50, 149*f*

No Fluff, Just Stuff conference, 2–3, 25, 94–96, 204

O

O'Brien, Joe, 216

Oppenheimer, Daniel, 100

Oracle, 83*f*

Øredev conference, 223

O'Reilly Media, 59

orthogonal distractions, 49, 189

OSCON 2011, 59

OS X, 156, 201

outlines, 27, 34–37. *See also* Injured Outlines

    broken, 71, 72

    Bullet-Riddled Corpse and, 78–79

    Fourthought and, 34

    Infodecks and, 71, 78

    Intermezzi and, 139, 234–35

    orphaned, 71–72

    Slideuments and, 113

    Vacation Photos and, 105

P

paid events, 18
panic, 179, 181
Pattern Language, A (Alexander), 3
patterns, 3–9
    antipatterns versus, 3
    backfiring, 52
    building your own, 226–27
glossary of, 229–39
    origins of, 3, 7
    recipes versus, 7
    software, 7, 94–95
    structures, 3–6
PDFs, 9, 83, 112, 144, 166, 236, 237
Pecha Kucha, 59, 136
Peer Review, 25, 26, **72–75**, 236
Performance Antipatterns, 10, 169, 183–201
Performance Patterns, 10, 169, 203–23
Perry, Rick, 185
personality, 17, 24, 26, 172
personas, 10–11, 17, 79–80
photo credits, 49
Photomaniac, 21, 51, 85, **89–92**, 90*f*, 91*f*, 105, 188, 236
Plug and Play capabilities, 150
Pop! Tech, 194, 241
Posse, 21, 81, **174–75**, 197, 236–37
PowerPoint, 4–6, 8–9, 63, 68, 71–72, 79, 82, 89, 93–94, 94*f*, 96, 98*f*, 100, 103, 113, 121–22, 121*f*, 126–28, 126*f*, 130, 132, 138, 142–43, 161–62, 162*f*, 164, 201, 211, 242
practicing, 59, 149, 175, 194, 204–6
pre*appearance* moves, 119
Prelude Patterns, **13–28**
preparation, 5, 16, 22, 37, 157
    all-nighters, 209
    Ant Fonts and, 81
    Borrowed Shoes and, 108
    Bullet-Riddled Corpse and, 77, 79
    Carnegie Hall and, 231
    Coda and, 70
    environmental, 171
    Fourthought and, 34
    hecklers and, 234
    insufficient, 51, 178, 187
    Lightning Talk and, 59
    Lipstick on a Pig, 187
    Lipsync and, 154
    Make It Rain and, 215
    relaxing, 16
    Social Media Advertising and, 18
    sufficient, 18, 81, 108
Preparation, **172–73**, 182, 237
Preroll, 28, 137, **142–43**, 144, 214–15, 237
presentations. *See also* slides: slide decks
    advertising, 18
    agendas, 26–27, 45, 76, 95, 133–34, 138, 146, 149, 192, 230
    allotted time for, 45
    architecture, 39
    building tension in, 30, 47, 77, 94, 119, 124
    collaborating on, 10, 41–42, 114
    demonstrations versus, 10, 65, 145–67
    ends of, 70. *See also* Bookends
    four stages of building, 34
    giving. *See* Performance Antipatterns; Performance Patterns
    information channels of, 48
    lifecycle of, 10
    mode, 120
    printed versions of, 114, 119–21, 124, 201
    promoting, 18
    purposes of, 43
    recipes and, 7, 124, 225–27, 227*f*
    recording your own, 40, 165–67, 205
    resources about, 241–42
    tools. *See* Keynote; PowerPoint
Presentation Zen (Reynolds), 8, 112, 188, 241

Proposed, 19–20, 21, **22–24**, 237
props, 178, 215, 236

Q

QCon, 223
questions, 70, 79–80, 135–36, 139–40, 149, 163, 169, 176, 178, 180–82, 191–92, 194, 196, 199, 214–15, 218, 221, 227, 237

R

RailsConf, 37, 186
Rails in the Large talk (Ford), 76–77
recipes, 7, 124, 225–27, 227*f*
Red, Yellow, Green, **222–23**, 237
Remember the Team pattern, 226
Required, 19–20, **20–21**, 26, 34, 56, 237
Reynolds, Garr, 8, 112, 188, 241
Richards, Mark, 94–95
Rock, Paper, Scissors (RPS) method, 76–77
Ruby on Rails, 37, 186

S

safety nets, 45
Schutta, Nathaniel, 7–8, 61–62, 156–57, 180, 196, 211, 214, 247–48
screen-capture tools, 142, 154, 156, 158
screen shots, 157–59
search engines, 17, 24
Seeding Satisfaction, 10, 17, 19, **175–77**, 181, 190–97, 218, 219, 223, 225, 237
Seeding the First Question, **214–15**, 237
Shoeless, 146, 172, **209**, 238
Shortchanged, **181–82**, 238
ShutterStock, 89
silence, 53, 140, 184, 185, 186, 192, 194, 208
skipping slides, 46
slide advancer. *See* "clickers"
Slide Construction Patterns, 10, 65, **67–109**
Slide:ology (Duarte), 188, 241

slides
    agenda, 133–34
    bullet points in. *See* Bullet-Riddled Corpse
    default templates, 1, 78, 79, 107, 227
    duplicate, 141
    first slides, 27–28, 70, 89, 131, 142–43
    headings in, 71
    shows, 1, 111, 114
    sidebars on, 70
    slide decks, 41, 61–62, 70–72, 104–5, 107–9, 112–13, 147, 179, 231
    Slide Wrangler, 41–42
    subheadings in, 71
    templates, 9, 48, 71, 86, 107, 157, 226–27
    Title Top Slide, 125*f*
    word-heavy, 115
SlideShare, 17, 242
Slideuments, 5–6, 82, 111, **112–13**, 115–17, 119–20, 121, 124–28, 130, 144, 158, 164, 201, 233, 234, 235, 238
"smiling lady" pictures, 104
Social Media Advertising, **18–20**, 207, 238
Soft Transitions, 63, 68, 70, 113, **137–39**, 213, 238
sound checks, 205
source code, 2, 32, 37, 82, 148, 155, 157–58, 158*f*, 165, 216, 233
Spam, 18
SpeakerRate, 137
spell-checking, 74
split sites, 200
sprout pictures, 140, 140*f*
stage lighting, 186, 190, 205
Stage Prep patterns, 171–82
Stakeout, The, **218–19**, 238
stock photos, 38, 49–50, 50*f*, 76, 89–92, 90*f*, 91*f*, 104–5, 140, 143, 203, 205, 236
story arcs. *See* Narrative Arc

storytelling, 30, 63, 75, 104, 236
Strange Loop conference, 58
stroke property, 101, 101*f*
styles, 2–3, 108, 209
    "Build Your Own Adventure," 96
    Cave Painting style, 63
distinctive, 106–7
    evangelical, 105
    learning, 208
    Lightning Talk style, 59
Socratic, 79–80
    Takahashi style, 60–62
    transition, 138*f*
    tutorial, 139
    Vacation Photos style, 104, 224
    writing style, 72
submission packets, 24
Subramaniam, Venkat, 22, 55, 96–99, 146
supplementary materials, 24
syntax highlighting, 158

T

Takahashi, 58, **60–62**, 64, 116, 197–98, 238
Takahashi, Masayoshi, 60
Talklet, 42, 43, **46–47**, 60, 91, 96, 99, 199,
    225, 229, 239
Tate, Bruce, 215
technical bullies, 190–92
TelePresence, 200
tempo, 211
Temporal Patterns, 9, 10, 65, **111–44**
Test-Driven Design talk (Ford), 32–33, 32*f*,
    76, 213
test-driven development (TDD), 32–33
text boxes, 79, 93–94, 96, 117–19, 119*f*,
    121–22, 158
ThoughtWorks, 46, 76–77, 114, 141
Time and Attention talk (Mann), 113–14,
    114*f*
title boxes, 124–26
Title Top Slide, 125*f*

Tower of Babble, 75, **188–89**, 239
transitions, 6, 9, 33, 38, 60, 92, 106, 213,
    226, 233, 238, 239
    after, 160
    dissolve, 68–69, 119, 134, 137–59, 160
    Cave Painting and, 62–64
    Charred Trail and, 125–26
    cube, 141
    hiding, 68–70
    Infodecks and, 115–16
    lack of, 59
    magic move, 63, 131–32, 132*f*, 165
    narrative flow and, 138*f*
    Soft Transitions, 63, 68, 70, 113, **137–
        39**, 213, 238
Traveling Highlights, 40, 145, 151–52, **157–
    62**, 158*f*, 159*f*, 160*f*, 162*f*, 165, 198,
    219–20, 235, 239
Triad, 27, 31–33, **43–44**, 139, 234, 239
Tufte, Edward, 82
Twitter, 17, 18–19, 26, 131, 135–36, 195–
    96, 207, 238, 241. *See also* Social
    Media Advertising
two-file approach, 142

U

Unifying Visual Theme, 16, 33–34, 36–37,
    42, 46, **48–51**, 88–89, 90–92, 105,
    139–40, 140*f*, 225, 239

V

Vacation Photos, 70–71, 92, **104–5**, 227, 239
Vaughan, Erikka, 100
version-control tools, 155
video
    embedded-movie approach, 144, 156,
        237
    file formats, 143
    files, 166–67
    Lipsync and, 154–57
    Live on Tape and, 165–67, 167*f*

Preroll and, 142–43, 237
   problems with, 154, 156
video-conferences, 200
visual elements, 91, 99, 219
   common repeating, 48
   embedded, 48
   layering, 63
   repetitive, 88
visual interest, 48, 62
visual layout, 62
visual metaphors, 62
visual themes, 48, 50–51, 53, 100
voice
   active, 25
   passive, 72–74
   speaking, 8, 17–18, 196, 205

Voltaire, 39
Vonnegut, Kurt, 54

W

Weatherman, 9, 182, **211–13**, 239
When Intuition Fails talk (Chabris), 194
whiteboards, 108
whitespace, 48, 68
Wi-Fi, 147, 155
wikis, 18–19
Windows, 82, 84, 133, 150, 156, 201
WMV file format, 143
worst-case scenarios, 94–95

Z

zoom, 62, 130, 160*f*, 182, 231

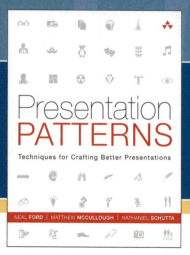

FREE
Online Edition

Your purchase of **Presentation Patterns** includes access to a free online edition for 45 days through the **Safari Books Online** subscription service. Nearly every Addison-Wesley Professional book is available online through **Safari Books Online**, along with thousands of books and videos from publishers such as Cisco Press, Exam Cram, IBM Press, O'Reilly Media, Prentice Hall, Que, Sams, and VMware Press.

Safari Books Online is a digital library providing searchable, on-demand access to thousands of technology, digital media, and professional development books and videos from leading publishers. With one monthly or yearly subscription price, you get unlimited access to learning tools and information on topics including mobile app and software development, tips and tricks on using your favorite gadgets, networking, project management, graphic design, and much more.

Activate your FREE Online Edition at
informit.com/safarifree

STEP 1: Enter the coupon code: JTAMPEH.

STEP 2: New Safari users, complete the brief registration form.
Safari subscribers, just log in.

If you have difficulty registering on Safari or accessing the online edition,
please e-mail customer-service@safaribooksonline.com